ART AND ESKIMO POWER
The Life and Times of Alaskan Howard Rock

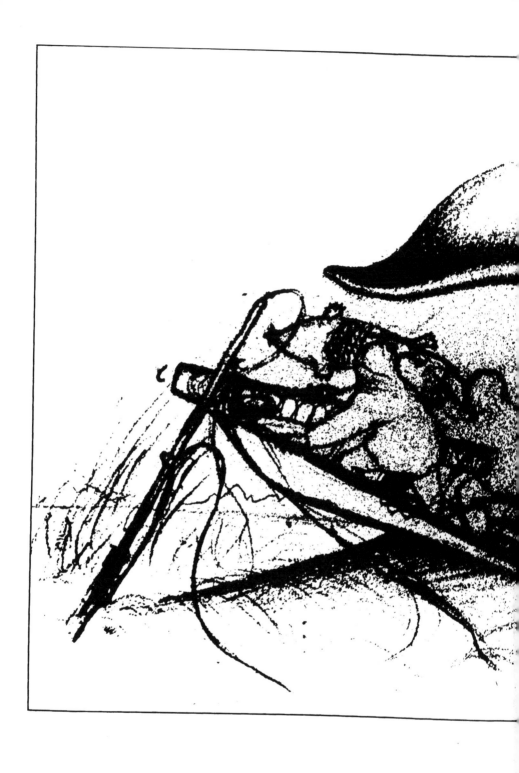

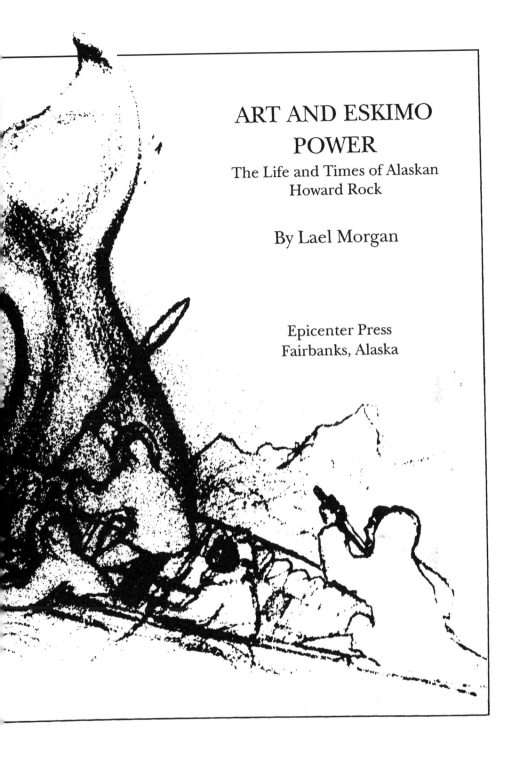

ART AND ESKIMO
POWER

The Life and Times of Alaskan
Howard Rock

By Lael Morgan

Epicenter Press
Fairbanks, Alaska

University of Alaska Press
PO Box 756240
Fairbanks, AK 99775-6240
Published by arrangement with Epicenter Press, Inc.

ISBN: 978-1-60223-021-7

This publication was printed on paper that meets the minimum requirements for
ANSI/NISO Z39.48-1992 (permanence of paper).

The Library of Congress has cataloged the earlier edition of this book as follows:
Morgan, Lael
        Art and Eskimo Power

        Bibliography: p.
        Includes index.
1. Rock, Howard. 2. Eskimos—Alaska—Biography. 3. Eskimos—Alaska— Art.
4. Eskimos—Alaska—Government relations. 5. Indians of North America—
Alaska—Biography. 6. Indians of North America—Alaska—Art. 7. Indians of North
America—Alaska—Government relations. I. Title.
E99.E7R5976   1988   979.8'00497   88-24408
ISBN: 0-945397-02-X
ISBN: 0-945391-03-8 (pbk.)

Cover Design: Dixon Jones, UAF Rasmuson Library Graphics
Interior Design: Lael Morgan & Stephen Herold
Interior Typesetting: Lasergraphics
Editor: Virginia Sims
Index: Marti Summer

Dedicated to the coming generations of Alaska Native People.

Table of Contents

All other doubts, by time let them be clear'd;
Fortune brings in some boats that are not steer'd.

Shakespeare, Cymbeline, Act IV, Scene III. Quoted in a letter to Howard Rock from his patron, Dr. Henry Forbes, October 22, 1965, in respect to the launching of a newspaper to champion the cause of Alaska's aboriginal people.

Introduction

FEW, IF ANY, aboriginal people have managed to span as wide a cultural gap as did Eskimo Howard Rock. Born in the high arctic, raised in a harshly primitive hunting society, he turned his back on his homeland for nearly half a century to enjoy a highly cosmopolitan lifestyle. Yet his efforts as a commercial artist brought him more money than satisfaction. His travels in the States, Europe and North Africa served only to make him better appreciate what he had left behind. And when, in 1961, he returned to find his native Alaska village in jeopardy of becoming a target for a bizarre experiment by the Atomic Energy Commission, he moved to defend his people and their heritage with extraordinary decisiveness and skill.

Howard Rock's story is not just a biography but the chronicle of a nation of tough survivors—Eskimo, Indian and Aleut—and their fight to retain the raw, wild lands on which they had managed to subsist for many centuries. It offers a hard look at the gains and losses involved in the transition from living off the land to the complexities of the 20th century; a transition requiring difficult decisions that must still be made today by Native* Alaskans and those of many Third World countries.

This book was first undertaken by Rock at the urging of advocates for Native American rights after he had helped his people win the largest land settlement ever voted by the United States Congress. Pressures of running an under-financed newspaper and illness prevented him from making a real start and, shortly before his death in 1976, he turned the project over to this writer, whose goals he felt compatible with his own.

---

* The word "Native," written with a capital "N," is used by Alaskans to designate their indigenous people, while whites born there are referred to as "native" with a small "n."

Initially, I had no intention of investing much time in Rock's book. He'd always been successful at luring me from lucrative jobs to write for him in times of crisis at less than subsistence wages, but I found him utterly frustrating to deal with. Although he was quick to defend me when others were unnerved by my Caucasian presence within the Native ranks, he seldom came through with a direct word of praise or thanks, and I never quite knew where I stood. His personal efforts on behalf of the Native cause were so intense they left me feeling inadequate. And I'd already put in my time.

Yet, in his final days, Rock won me back.

"It will be wonderful!" he lied, that old, enthusiastic smile lighting up a face now painfully drawn by cancer. "We've got a Ford Foundation grant for you to travel around the country and research bilingual education."

"You know I hate to cover bilingual education, Howard."

"You'll spend two months in Alaska and then two months studying Indian reservations outside the state," he continued, blithely.

"But I've got a job I love!"

"You will take a leave of absence," he announced. "I'll match your salary. The Ford Foundation will pay half."

"But Howard, you can't afford to pay half my salary ..."

"I know," he said, matter-of-factly. "You'll take a cut."

When he died, right on schedule at the beginning of the week he had planned that I leave Alaska on the second half of the Ford assignment, I was surprised to find myself devastated. Although I had long admired him and prized his vision, it had never occurred to me that I might also love him. Love him enough so that his influence over me would go well beyond the grave and skew the following decade of my life which was dominated by this research.

Rock left no correspondence beyond nine love letters, and no diary. He had written a charming series of early childhood recollections but seldom alluded to his family's cruelty. He discussed his disastrous marriage only in brief terms which did not include the name of his ex-wife. And never did he speak of the hard-drinking days in Seattle that drove him to the edge.

Yet as I came to understand the depth of Rock's early dissipation and despair, my admiration for him grew. To have failed so hopelessly after such promising beginnings; to have engineered his own redemption against such heavy odds.... It explained Rock's remarkable patience with our young leaders when wine, women, song and greed occasionally overcame them. And it also explained his firm conviction that the course of man's destiny and that of his Native nation could be altered for the better, no matter how black the past.

Thanks are due the Ford Foundation, the Alicia Patterson Foundation, the Alaska Historical Commission and the Rockefeller Foundation's Bellagio Study and Conference Center for supporting this endeavor. To Hildegarde Forbes for the wonderful job she did in organizing her husband's papers, and to Princeton University for allowing me to study them there. Thanks, also, to Bill Byler and the Association of American Indian Affairs for their help and careful record keeping, and to the University of Alaska, Fairbanks, for marvelous help.

And I am deeply indebted to some two hundred people who took time to give me interviews and sorted through old photos, to Kathleen "Mike" Dalton who helped me set my course and John Shively who steadied it, to Jane Sutherland Niebergall for the loan (twice) of her *Tundra Times* collection and to Jean Ward who waded through a first draft. Virginia Sims, who undertook the editing of the original manuscript when objectivity failed me and saw it through to the end, deserves a Purple Heart. Thanks to anthropologist Jacq Bachmann Siracusa for her eagle eyes, to Jimmy Bedford for his help.

I'm indebted to my publisher, Kent Sturgis, for his enthusiasm and his patience. Thanks, also, to Jack Silbaugh for his encouragement during the dark days and to Steve Kline for his guidance and enthusiasm.

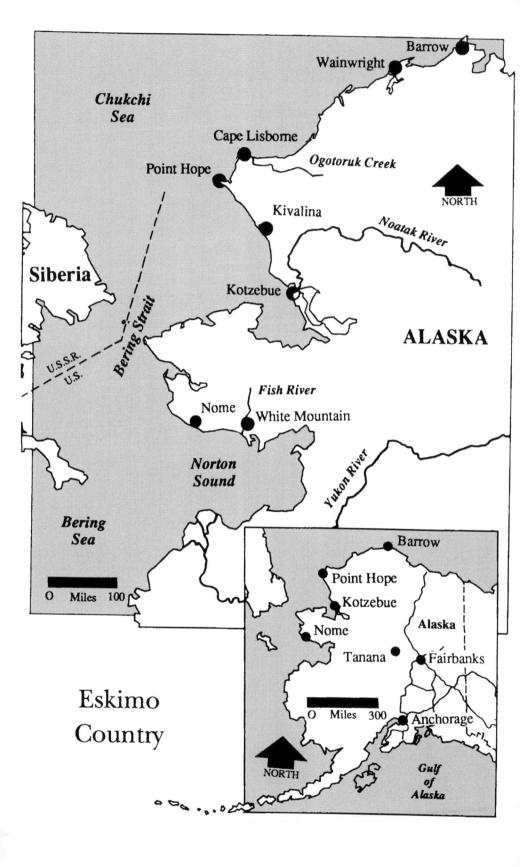

Chukchi
Sea

Siberia

Bering
Sea

O Miles 100

Eskimo
Country

Barrow
Wainwright

Cape Lisborne

Point Hope

Ogotoruk Creek

NORTH

Kivalina

Noatak River

Kotzebue

ALASKA

Bering Strait

U.S.S.R.
U.S.

Fish River

Nome   White Mountain

Norton
Sound

Yukon River

Barrow

Point Hope

Kotzebue

Nome

Alaska

Tanana

Fairbanks

O Miles 300

Anchorage

NORTH

Gulf
of
Alaska

1

A Puzzling Prophecy

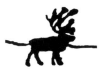

THE FALL OF 1911 was a strangely gentle one in the Alaskan arctic, with scarcely a hint of the deep, numbing winter to follow. Eskimo children played barefoot and shirtless, even as the days softened in the absence of summer's midnight sun. Berries and delicate tundra flowers defied the frost. Ponds and puddles remained unencumbered with ice well beyond its due, and the great Chukchi Sea stayed open almost two months after the usual time of freeze-up.[1]

Hunters and gatherers took full advantage of the warm reprieve from the Eskimo weather spirit, Silam Inua, (or perhaps from the Christian god newly in fashion) to fill their ice cellars with a wealth of dried fish, caribou meat, ducks, geese and many seal pokes of tundra berries, greens and roots. And despite the awkwardness of her pregnancy, Keshorna labored with the most ambitious, for she was anxious to ensure the comfort of her husband and three children. At 34, she was taller and stronger than the average Eskimo woman, had survived famine, numerous epidemics of white man's diseases and at least five pregnancies. So she continued to work until the pains of her labor came in quick succession before dispatching her oldest daughter, Kaipuk, to summon the village midwife.

Keshorna's family lived a mile from the Eskimo village of Tigara near the recently established Episcopal mission where her husband, Weyahok, served as interpreter and general handyman for their close friend, the Rev. Augustus Hoare. Hoare was visiting his wife and children in the States, but his relief man, the Rev. Frederick W. Goodman, had volunteered the mission house as a place for Keshorna's delivery. Not that the mission was much better than her own sod house. It was also an earthen structure shored up with whalebone in the usual Eskimo fashion. But it was considerably larger than the Weyahok igloo, boasting two rooms and a real door and window in place of the usual crawl space and skylight covered with seal gut. Then, too, Goodman was a trained medical missionary, although it soon became apparent that the local midwife was so skillful she would have no need of his aid.

Keshorna knelt, as was the custom, on a rolled-up caribou skin which placed her a foot above the earthen floor. Her older sister, Mumangeena, stood at her side to assist, while the midwife delivered the child from behind, deftly cutting its umbilical cord with her half-moon bladed "ulu" or woman's knife.

Some months earlier, the midwife had selected several hairs of extraordinary thickness from the head of a neighbor, had washed them in strong soap and stored them in a special packet sewn from the gut of a giant bearded seal. Now she chose the strongest to tie the cord, making certain the child would not have a downcast navel which was believed to be an omen of misfortune. Although well-endowed with manhood, this baby was not a large one, the midwife observed. Nor did he appear to be very strong. But at least he did not have any teeth—another definite sign of bad luck—nor was he marked or deformed in any way. Satisfied that she had done her work well, she swaddled the infant in soft, clean fawn skins and without further ceremony, presented him to his mother.[2]

Keshorna inspected the boy anxiously, for not two years earlier she had borne another undersized son who had died eight days after delivery.[3] This one hardly seemed more robust. He was frail in comparison to his husky older brother, Eebrulik, but he howled lustily and she held out hope for him beyond appearances. Although it was August, the old men of Tigara forecast a late winter which would increase the baby's chances of survival. And, if one dared to trust ancient magic, his future was assured anyhow, for a shaman had predicted that this boy would become a great man.

Of course not everyone, even those who favored Eskimo witchcraft, put stock in the prophecies of Sikvoan. Shamans, or "unutkoots," as the Eskimos called them, had varying degrees of power. The most gifted were men whose vision and knowledge extended to the world beyond so that they were immortal and could not be wounded or killed. Although women unutkoots could also walk in spirit realms, they were thought to be inferior and it was generally believed that Sikvoan valued her abilities beyond their worth.[4] Even Keshorna, who was Sikvoan's daughter, had never been much impressed with the old lady as a medicine woman, but she loved her mother deeply and was proud of her fierce independence.

Blind in her last years, Sikvoan nevertheless pegged about with her walking stick, finding her own way without help, visiting among her children and grandchildren and trying to be of service. Before the Christian influence, a useless old person would be cast out of the village, and

Sikvoan might well have suspected the possibility could still exist if times grew lean and the missionary unobservant.[5] It was to make herself more valuable, perhaps, that she touted her magical powers, real or imagined. Yet she knew of Keshorna's pregnancy even before Keshorna suspected, and had predicted the child's future with extraordinary self-assurance.

Keshorna's husband had been among the first of Tigara to convert to the new Christian faith. Keshorna and Weyahok had been married in an Episcopal service and baptized in the church eight years earlier, and none among the converts was more devout. Yet Sikvoan's certainty in the future of her grandson caused the expectant parents to pay more than casual attention to her spirit talk.

"One boy born in the village about the same time will be a great hunter, but this son of yours will be a great man," she assured them and all else who would listen.

"What sort of great man?" they asked her, puzzled, for she predicted no future for him as a hunter. The greatest men in any village had always been hunters, but, alas, Sikvoan could not explain that. This child would excel in some manner heretofore unknown. She knew only that he would be in some way remarkable. And at the time of her death less than two weeks before his birth, she seemed well-pleased, and certain that she had seen an enviable future for one of her own line.[6]

So Keshorna and the Bible-reading Weyahok, too, looked on this frail boy and dared to hope. Rev. Goodman was a reasonable man who did not feel that speculation on the old shaman's prediction compromised newfound Christian ethics. Indeed, he wrote the prophecy into the church record so it comes to us today as more than simply legend. Still, mindful of his church, the missionary suggested they baptize the infant with the Christian name "Howard"—after Howard Caldwell, 16, who had just arrived to work at the mission[7]. This they did in the prescribed Episcopal service on August 14, 1911, just three days after the child's birth.

Goodman also Anglicized Weyahok to "Rock," a direct translation from the father's Eskimo name by which the family was henceforth to be known. Keshorna would be Emma. Weyahok formally adopted the name of Sam Rock. Yet the missionary was neither surprised nor displeased to learn that the couple privately called their new son "Sikvoan" in Eskimo fashion, honoring a recently departed spirit who merited respect.

2

Aristocrats of the Arctic

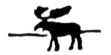

The whisperings of the Eskimo past mold the people of the arctic as surely as does the cold starkness of their environment. And it is to this past we must look to begin to understand them.

—Howard Rock in conversation May 1967

THE FROZEN, SNOW-SCOURED DOMAIN of the Eskimo is the most inhospitable environment known to man and yet Howard Rock's ancestors not only managed to survive here, they survived in style. His village is thought to be the longest continually inhabited site in North America,[1] and at their peak his Inupiaq-speaking forefathers controlled enough wealth to consider themselves aristocrats.

While many arctic tribes were forced to wander in search of food, Rock's people settled comfortably on an amazing piece of real estate. They called it Tigara, a word that translates as "index finger" and is an apt description of their peninsula thrust like a slender digit into the Chukchi Sea, directly in the migration route of sea mammals and a myriad of game.

"It seems as if nature carefully planned Tigara and worked out a system of spacing a succession of animals to be hunted," Rock marveled after seeing the rest of the world and returning with new appreciation for his native village.

In winter—February and March—giant polar bears are taken. In spring the small white whales migrate north past our coast preceding the big bowhead whales which our people start hunting in mid-April. Whale meat and muktuk (skin and fat of the whale) are traditionally the favorite Eskimo foods and a big, 40-ton bowhead is an awesome catch.

Then a few oogruks (large bearded seals) start showing up. About the time whaling season is over, they come more and more until, in late spring, there will be quite a few of them. In that time, too, the eider ducks fly north in flocks.

When the ice begins to break up, the walrus start coming, migrating towards Barrow. They like to get up on large cakes of ice and sun themselves and sleep. That's when the people get them. And once in a while in summer there will be stragglers traveling leisurely by the village. And there are seal year-round and caribou, too, and the fishing is good. Sometimes in March great schools of tomcod come by. There are also whitefish, salmon, arctic char, herring and smelt in the lakes and tiny crabs by the hundreds.

Blessed with such bounty, Tigara is and was a successful and prosperous village.[2]

Howard's people traveled, of course, sometimes going as far afield as Siberia, Canada or the Aleutian Islands to trade. When nature failed, they hunted elsewhere, but their peninsula usually served them well and its bounty afforded them more comfort and leisure than was enjoyed by their migrant cousins.

The Tigara tribe (Tigaramiut) apparently reached the height of its power about 1775, expanding in numbers and capturing territory until it controlled the entire 600-mile coastline from Kotzebue to Barrow. However, leaders made the mistake of challenging their coastal neighbors, the Kivalinamiut to the south, and the inland Noataqmiut who were also expanding and anxious to gain access to the sea.

Oral history accounts vary, but apparently the advance of Tigara's enemies was climaxed by a pitched battle about the turn of the 19th century. The outcome was a draw; 400 left of 4,000 original combatants with the best hunters on all sides lost and survivors faced with famine as their ultimate enemy. The boundaries of the Tigara were again reduced to the immediate area around their small peninsula,[3] and the first American census of 1880 reckons their population at a mere 276.

The era into which Howard Rock was born was one of extraordinary change. His people had learned of the existence of Europeans through trade with the Siberian Natives before the beginning of the 18th century. Explorer Otto von Kotzebue sailed past Tigara shores in 1816 but made no contact, leaving actual discovery to Capt. Frederick Beechey of the HMS Blossom in 1826. Beechey named their spit Point Hope[4] but based about 200 miles south and had little contact with the Tigaramiut. The following year a barge from the Blossom, under the command of Lt. Edward Belcher, was forced ashore in bad weather near Tigara and plundered by locals. Both Eskimos and whites were killed in the confrontation, and the truce that followed was uneasy.

Alexander Kashevarov led a Russian expedition of five skin boats with 10 Aleut paddlers to the farthest-north Eskimo settlement of Point Barrow in 1838 and put into the lagoon behind Point Hope on the return trip to find the population "more dangerous and threatening" than had been reported by those before him.[5]

In 1845 the expedition of Sir John Franklin disappeared in search of the Northwest Passage and ships attempting to find him occasionally sailed the Chukchi and stopped to trade. But it wasn't until the Yankee whaling fleet began plying these waters in the early 1850s that Tigara had any real contact with outsiders.

Initially whalers feared the Eskimos and, although the Siberians soon ceased to be a threat, American Natives remained hostile well into the 1880s. Among the most feared were Tigara men who, under the iron-fisted leadership of Attungowruk, appeared to be regaining some vestige of their former glory. This chief, who was Howard Rock's great uncle, was reputed to be the strongest of all Eskimos. He had become head of Tigara after beating his predecessor in a vicious fight and his feats of physical prowess were known throughout the arctic. Much admired for his hunting skills, Attungowruk proved at first a good leader, a man of considerable generosity and wisdom. But as time went on, he drew increasingly bad reviews, especially from outsiders who were forced to deal with him.[6]

"In his efforts to become absolute master of his people, he passed from tyranny to assassination," Ensign Roger Wells, USN, reported in the introduction of a government publication.

"For trivial causes, such as losing something or failing to be prompt in paying tribute, he would sally forth on a shotgun expedition and either hold the victim while one of his fellows did the shooting or shoot while someone else held the man; but usually he did the holding himself as he was the most powerful man of his tribe."[7]

It was Attungowruk's custom to take strangers to the outskirts of the village where dead bodies were laid Eskimo-fashion above the ground and point out the men he had killed, a tour that most visitors found impressive. However, one of his would-be victims is said to have gained revenge by winning the chief over and introducing him to whiskey.

In October of 1880 the bark *Small Ohio* wrecked off Point Hope spit and its few survivors were the first outsiders to winter with the Tigara.[8] Then, in 1887, a San Francisco-based whaling company built a shore station at Point Hope. Attungowruk objected vehemently to the competition, noting the superior weaponry of these strange pale men and, also, the way they eyed his women. His power was such that he forced the whites to build five miles down the spit and kept them from whaling in Eskimo waters.

But later Attungowruk began indulging in monumental drinking sprees during which he became totally unreasonable with his own people, taking anything he wanted, beating his wives, violating the wives of others and leaving a general wake of terror. Several families fled Tigara for fear of him and when, in March of 1889, he killed a woman while other men were hunting, three Eskimos took revenge by murdering him as he slept off a hangover.[9]

The man that succeeded Attungowruk was well-liked but lacked the muscle to hold outsiders in check. While Attungowruk had encouraged his men to harass the newcomers, villagers now made overtures of peace. Fraternization and trade were encouraged with devastating results.

The whaling station had become known as "Jabbertown" because of the diversity of nationalities and languages of the sailors camped there. They were, however, pretty much of one type:

"They came from the lowest class of San Francisco slums; hijacked from the waterfront saloons," one observer wrote home. "They mistreated the Natives and taught them how to make moonshine liquor. When I asked them what they used to make the liquor, they said molasses and tobacco, an awful mixture but somehow fermented and cooked and cooled in a gun barrel. It made them both sick and drunk. They would go on wild sprees and fight and kill as they would not do when they were sober."[10]

By the summer of 1897, things had gotten out of hand. "Although under the flag of the United States, there is nothing but chaos and paganism," Lt. Cmdr. Charles Stockton of the Revenue Cutter *Thetis* wrote the Episcopal Board of Missions in an appeal for help. He had seen fur bundles lying on the beach, dying Eskimos banished from their sod igloos because of tribal taboos. Drunkenness prevailed, he reported. The women were being prostituted. Venereal disease was rampant. Deaths outnumbered births two to one.

In response, the church sent a medical man who had yet to be ordained. Dr. John B. Driggs, born on a Cuban sugar plantation and raised on a Delaware farm, had studied in New Haven and gone on to graduate from New York University Medical School in 1889. He had practiced in the tenement district of New York, toured as staff physician with the New York Opera Company and had a yen for adventure.[11]

Equipped with a stock of firearms, medical supplies and a dictionary in an Eskimo dialect that proved unintelligible to the Tigaramiut, Driggs made the 6,000-mile trip to Point Hope by boat, only to be refused permission to land. After considerable argument, the Eskimos allowed the physician to winter several miles down the beach from their settlement. If the white man survived, they said, then they would decide whether to kill him or let him live among them. And amazingly, this was a pact to which

Driggs readily agreed. At 38 the missionary was in the prime of health, stood six feet tall and weighed 200 pounds. He was sure of his ability as a physician and he had all the instincts of a survivor. He believed strongly in God, and he could afford to wait.

3

A Change of Heart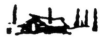

In 1898, the year the missionary began camping on Tigara Spit, Sam Weyahok turned 16. He was taller than most of his race and built solidly, as "Rock," the English translation of his Eskimo name, implied. He was already emerging as a leader, concerned about his people's welfare, and he observed that John Driggs was different from Jabbertown white men.

The children who spied on the newcomer reported he spent his first night sleeping under a tarp. Next day he dug himself a shelter and, although a high tide carried away most of his supplies, he lived off the land and survived. He also managed to capture Kineeveeuk, one of the youngsters who had taken to watching him, conveyed good will by offering the lad some cake, and taught him something called "alphabet," by which Kineeveeuk began to learn the white man's language.

Except for occasional visits from his pupil and other children curious to try his strange food, Driggs remained alone in his isolated camp well into the winter when the son of the chief was felled by a sickness that Eskimo shamans could not cure. Then, in desperation, the chief brought the white man into the village, telling him if he could save the boy, he would be allowed to live among them. If not, Driggs, too, would die.

Somehow the missionary managed to revive this patient, much to the surprise of everyone, for his prayers seemed subdued and his medicine lackluster compared to the magic of the unutkoots. So Driggs moved into the village, built himself a sod house, and before the year was out he mastered Inupiaq.

The Eskimos were pleased to learn that Driggs found merit in their legends, setting them down in a little book so other white men might admire the accuracy with which the Tigaramiut had recorded the ice ages and the great flood without a written language.[1] He also seemed to enjoy their food, even frozen raw meat and fish which outsiders usually shunned. So the women sewed him fur clothing in which he could move freely in the harshness of the winter and the men taught him to hunt.

In return, John Driggs doctored them and, because his medicine usually worked, the Eskimos began to seek his advice on other matters. Driggs was firm in damning the lascivious ways of foreign whalers and traders and he also condemned harsh Eskimo customs and taboos. Tigaramiut must not abandon old people and unwanted babies to the frozen tundra. Clever hunters like the Tigaramiut should be able to provide for the weak if they did not drown themselves in a sea of whisky, he maintained. It was also wrong for a man to have many wives, to beat them or to loan them to another.

For a missionary, Driggs did little Bible preaching in his first years among the Eskimos. But he did try to explain the Christian doctrine of love, and Sam Rock was among the first to become interested, for he had long chafed at the cruelties of Inupiat custom.

The circumstances of Sam's birth had not been happy. Ahknora, his mother, came from the Upicksonamiut, a powerful Tigara clan, and had been married off for political reasons at age 11 to Kakairnook, one of the finest hunters in their village.[2]

Ahknora, herself, was not consulted on the marriage and when she raised courage to object, she was laughed at. Women had no say in such matters. When Kuna, a childhood friend of Ahknora, had haughtily refused to marry, six young men had kidnapped her and used her brutally to strip her of such foolish pride. Ahknora should consider herself lucky to be married early to a good provider, her family insisted. He might, if he was pleased with her, occasionally exchange her for the wife of a friend in the time-honored practice of their sparsely populated land. But that would be an honor and the family was certain a man of Kakairnook's stature would never let their daughter be used casually, as happened to girls who had no strong protector.

So Ahknora moved to Kakairnook's igloo and he quickly gave her Sam, a sturdy son for whom she was most grateful, but any love she might have borne her husband vanished as he grew rich and took three additional wives.

In Inupiat law it was custom for a wife to place her belt, or "tapsik," as it was called, on the pillow beside her head while she slept, and if her husband wished to divorce her, he simply sliced the topsik into pieces with his hunting knife, giving notice that she must be gone in the morning.[3] Women had no such recourse, but Ahknora grew determined to leave Kakairnook and she was strong-willed. Luckily she had the backing of her older brother, Chief Attungowruk, and the rest of her family, seeing her great unhappiness, came to agree she should be free. Divorce was unthinkable, but she was allowed to return to the igloo of her father, Naynkuk, taking young Sam with her.[4]

"Three wives is three too many!" she told the boy firmly in a statement her descendents would recall verbatim.

Life improved under Naynkuk's patronage, for Sam's grandfather was soft-hearted beyond the bounds of Eskimo convention. A renowned hunter, wealthy enough to afford two wives and many children, Naynkuk also provided for destitute families others chose to ignore. His igloo was always filled with a good-natured throng of uncles, cousins, aunts and rescued orphans, whom the old man often entertained with marvelous stories of ancient Tigara.[5]

Naynkuk could recall how his people had once hunted the fearsome polar bear using only a spear, counting on the forward lunge of the great carnivore to impale it before the animal managed to crush a hunter's skull. Or how those less brave would coil a long spring of baleen whalebone, freeze it into a tempting ball of seal fat and follow the bear that consumed it until he fell with the havoc it caused inside his stomach.

He told them, too, of the cleverness of Tigara warriors who once defeated the habitually barefoot Kivalinamiut by strewing sharp bones of caribou legs in their path, and how—battle by battle—the Tigaramiut conquered the coast.

It was Naynkuk who taught Sam the basics of hunting; how to ensnare ducks with an ivory bolo, how to stalk the seal in a way that the animal would think man one of his own kind, how to drive the dimwitted caribou. Naynkuk taught him well but, despite his skill, the old grandfather sometimes showed puzzling weakness.

Once Sam had seen him weep shamelessly at the site of a small, stoned-up house where a friend had been abandoned to die of injuries sustained from a brown bear attack. The hunter had been strangled in a prescribed ritual to prevent long suffering, the old man explained. But the compassion with which Naynkuk spoke seemed a dangerous liability in the harsh environment of the arctic.[6]

When Sam was about ten, Kakairnook began to take interest in his training and during spring whale hunts the boy found himself at his father's side. During this period hunters camped for weeks on the dangerous, shifting ice of the Chukchi, waiting for bowheads migrating northward through slim leads of open water, pursuing animals up to 60 feet long in frail skin boats scarcely one third that size. Sam was deemed a "boy" in this society of experienced whale men and served a traditional apprenticeship, performing chores usually delegated to women, speaking only when spoken to, but observing everything. And he was proud when, in his 13th year, Kakairnook made him a crewman worthy of a man's share of the catch.

Ahknora, too, was delighted at this honor. But she also worried that whaling could be a risky business, and she occupied herself in sewing her son a parka and trousers of heavy winter caribou skin, chosen for warmth and because the hollow-haired fur is remarkably buoyant in water.

Spring whaling was the single most important event in Tigara, for the well-being of the entire village depended on it. With tons of whale meat stored in its ice cellars, the village could weather a failed caribou migration or the temporary disappearance of seals and walrus from its shores. But if no bowhead were caught, the margin for survival would be slim. So each man, woman and child prepared for this event with ritualistic ceremony. Women sewed oogruk skins together in a network of complex waterproof seams for boat coverings. Men laced these covers to driftwood umiak frames. Floats were fashioned out of headless seal carcasses from which flesh and bone had been removed. Hunting equipment—long harpoons with detachable ivory heads and slate points—were inspected and overhauled. Children fetched and carried. Wives of whaling captains carefully obeyed the many taboos laid out by shamans and prayed nightly to Allingnuk, the whaling god who lived in the moon. Each hunter donned his special talisman. And, at last, 20 crews loaded their umiaks on sleds, hitched up their dog teams and set off to search for open water.

It was with nervous excitement that young Sam took his place in his father's boat, for he had much to learn. The balance of this Eskimo craft is tender and handling requires cooperation and a skillful team. Paddlers must be swift—and silent, too, because the fast-swimming bowhead is keen of hearing. No oar must touch the gunwale of the umiak; blades must bite the water firmly without bubbling, or the skill of the helmsman with his steering paddle will be for naught.

Kakairnook's crew that year was unseasoned, for he'd taken on two more novices, Koonook, who was even younger than Sam and Akniachak, who had only three years experience. They learned quickly under the tutorage of three apt hunters, but by mid-season they'd seen few whales on which to test their skill and Kakairnook decided to try another hunting site.

It was mid-morning when they broke camp, loaded their tent, supplies and the woman who was their cook into the umiak and paddled leisurely a mile north where the ice jutted seaward. Then, as they rounded the bend, a larger than average whale surfaced some 75 feet directly ahead. Kakairnook, who was in the bow, signaled silently with his paddle for pursuit and readied his harpoon. The boat was heavy with the unaccustomed weight of camping gear and the cook, but the men pulled for all they were worth. Sam, striving for silence, listened to his own fast-beating heart and worried that the whale might hear it, but their quarry was unaware as it surfaced for the third time.

Without hesitation, Kakairnook raised his harpoon and plunged it deep into the kidney of the bowhead, counting on the momentum of the umiak to further the thrust. It was a sure shot and immediately the helmsman turned the boat more than 45 degrees from the wounded animal, a move calculated to ensure the safety of their fragile craft. But they were not clear. The whale's tail shifted beneath them—a move quite unprecedented—and its huge flukes hit the umiak just forward of midbeam, propelling it skyward and breaking it like a toy.

Sam heard the sound of splintering wood mingled with the screams of the woman cook. There was the sickening feeling of being lifted aloft, of sailing into space and then the hard impact of icy water. He went under, engulfed helplessly in blackness, swallowing the bitter sea. Then, finally, he felt air around his head and gasped for breath, blinking the salt from his eyes. Their umiak was nearby, a shapeless, deflated thing. To the left of it was Kakairnook bleeding badly about the head.

"Eeqneeng (son), try to make it to the ice!" he shouted. "Try hard, eeqneeng. I cannot make it ... my bones are broken. Hurry, eeqneeng! Try to make it to the ice."

Sam stared at him. His father's left hand clung to a floating paddle, the right appeared injured beyond use.

"I cannot swim, father," Sam said helplessly.

"Use your arms and hands and paddle them," his father commanded.

Sam's right knee hurt terribly. His movements were awkward, but the hollow-hair fur of his hunting outfit buoyed him and slowly he began to crawl in the direction of the shore ice some 125 feet away. Ahead, to the right, he saw Akniachak making good progress with Koonook floundering behind, whimpering. The screaming of the woman had stopped. Kakairnook encouraged the boy for a while but then he, too, fell silent. Sam concentrated on swimming.

"Not much farther," called Akniachak who had reached the ice and pulled himself up. "You can make it."

Sam had passed the struggling Koonook and neared the frozen rim where Akniachak lay on his stomach, his arm extended. Blindly Sam groped for his friend's hand and found himself being pulled to safety. Koonook was still 20 feet away, crying hopelessly. Now it was Sam's turn to yell encouragement, but as he did so he found himself crying, too, because beyond Koonook he saw no sign of life. All the rest were gone.

Most women of Tigara wept openly, for the death of able hunters was a severe economic loss to the village as well as a personal tragedy. Proud Ahknora stepped forward dry-eyed to embrace her returning son, but she, too, grieved for she knew Sam had come to love his father and the loss of Kakairnook's support was a deadening blow. Her own father was too old to shoulder their burden and Sam was too young to be a fully effective hunter. Soon, however, her brother, Attungowruk, invited Sam to finish out the season on his crew, promising him a share of the whale they had killed earlier. And just two days after Sam joined them, they caught a second whale, so the young hunter was able to provide for his mother for the coming year.[7]

Sam's unexpected apprenticeship under Attungowruk proved valuable, for the legendary chief was at the height of his prowess, the best hunter of his day and also the leading politician. He gave generously to the poor and adopted many orphans. The village caches were well-filled by the hunts he planned. And it was not without pride that Sam watched his burly uncle face down the white whalers, forcing them out of Eskimo waters and allowing them to settle only on Eskimo terms. Nor did Sam, his mother or their descendents ever find it in their hearts to condemn their famous kinsman when his mind clouded with alcohol and he became unreasonable beyond all bounds. They buried him with honor and they avenged his murder. But there was no one to replace him and their shamans could not defend the Tigaramiut from the vices of the whale men that threatened to take their village down.

For this reason, Sam listened with interest to the missionary, John Driggs. And he saw that under Driggs' influence, life in the village improved. The white medicine man soon bettered health conditions to a point where births outnumbered deaths. The religion he introduced provided comfort in the confusing new era and it especially appealed to Sam because it allowed for the compassion he had come to admire in his grandfather.

John Driggs also pioneered a school, despite the fact that schools were not roundly popular. At Cape Prince of Wales, just south of Tigara, Eskimos had murdered a white teacher. However, Driggs' effort was so successful that hunters neglected their hunting to attend, and the missionary finally had to insist they make "better" use of daylight hours and established a special night class for them.[8]

Sam Rock was one of Driggs' best pupils, slow to speak English but quick to understand it. Driggs presented the Eskimo with a Bible and a dictionary which Sam would study faithfully until his death some 60 years later. He became Driggs' interpreter and his faith in Christianity grew so firm that Driggs decided to send him to school in the States to become a preacher. Sam prepared for the trip, but just before the arrival of the annual boat he fell in love with Keshorna who was tall and beautiful and not unlike his mother. He could not bring himself to leave her for the required training and with regret he declined Driggs' generous offer of sponsorship.

Howard Rock's Family Tree

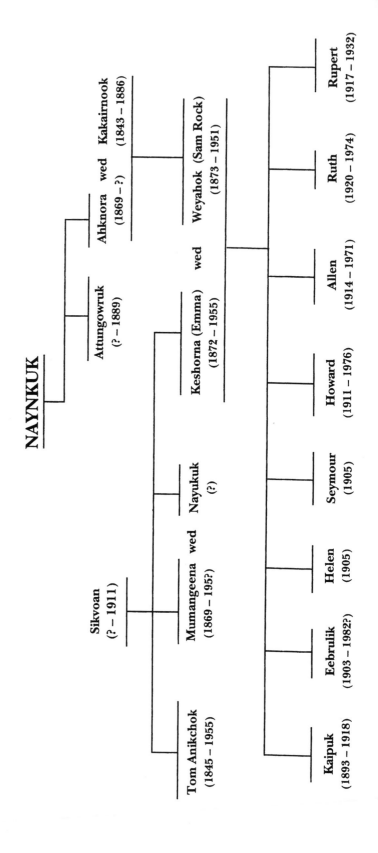

NAYNKUK

Tom Anikchok
(1845 – 1955)

Sikvoan
(? – 1911)

Mumangeena wed
(1869 – 1952?)

Nayukuk
(?)

Attungowruk
(? – 1889)

Ahknora wed Kakairnook
(1869 –?)   (1843 – 1886)

Keshorna (Emma)   wed
(1872 – 1955)

Weyahok (Sam Rock)
(1873 – 1951)

Kaipuk
(1893 – 1918)

Eebrulik
(1903 – 1982?)

Helen
(1905)

Seymour
(1905)

Howard
(1911 – 1976)

Allen
(1914 – 1971)

Ruth
(1920 – 1974)

Rupert
(1917 – 1932)

4

A Child At Odds

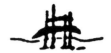

By 1911, Sam was literate enough to address a birth announcement for his second son to the Rev. Augustus Hoare.

"Dear A.R. Hoare: I will try to write a very little letter to you," the Eskimo began. "If I don't spell the words not right then you will come back and teach me again I hope.

"I have a new son now, and after you gone was born in August 10 about Bering Straight. My wife Emma was well at the time when the child was born. Mr. Goodman (Hoare's stand-in) give him a name called Howard. This year the Arctic Ocean is too late come the ice. It is roughing now the sea at November 16. I am wonderful like this, and never see before. After you gone about one month the walrus come up here from the North moved South all days and night until the November medle. I forget how many killed by Natives, I think 25 more they killed walrus …"[1]

Howard's first memory was the vivid one of being cold. In ancient times his people would have immersed him in the frigid water of a little lagoon about a mile east of the village, a baptism designed to winnow out the weak and acclimatize the strong. But even without this cruel test, the fate of Eskimo children was still governed by survival of the fittest and the long arctic winter with its frequent temperatures of -50°F left a marked impression on early Inupiat childhood.

The Rock family lived in a typical igloo built of sod, shored up by whalebone, planked with rough-hewn driftwood. Its one room was about the size of the average American living room, snug when heated with seal oil lamps. But fuel was precious and lamps often went unlit. Young Eskimos were usually left naked in the crawling and early walking stages to toughen them, so it is no wonder that Rock's first memory of the arctic was so basic.

At the time, his family was better off than most. According to an explanation published in *The Alaska Churchman Quarterly* along with Sam Rock's 1911 letter to the Rev. Hoare, the missionary had recently built a house for the Rocks between his own and the church and had arranged for an annual salary of $200 to compensate for Sam's services as interpreter and mission handyman. Sam also supported his family by hunting and, in a successful year, could expect a few hundred dollars more from the sale of whalebone and furs. They occasionally purchased flour, sugar, salt, beans, rice, cotton cloth for parka covers and ammunition from Peter Kuniak, the local trader. They owned an innovative wood cookstove fashioned from scrap metal and also a few cooking pots, soup plates and metal spoons. Otherwise the Rocks possessed few commercially manufactured items and almost no furniture. They slept on caribou skins on the floor with additional skins for blankets, and sat on the floor—feet straight out—for meals and tasks such as sewing and carving.

Howard's infancy in this Spartan environment was touch and go, especially during mandatory Episcopal services in the crowded, poorly vented sod church.

"When I took you to church you used to start crying and wouldn't breathe anymore," his mother told him in later years. "I used to have to take you out into the fresh air, turn you upside down and into the wind to start you breathing again."

From a sickly baby, Howard grew to an undersized toddler, making unsatisfactory adjustment from breast-feeding to a diet of meat pre-chewed by his mother and a mixture of flour and water served up in a two-foot-long baby bottle of dried oogruk intestine. He was small in comparison to older siblings and also dwarfed by brother Allen, three years his junior. Fortunately his mother had two older daughters, Helen and Kaipuk, to help. But Howard was far more of a trial than any previous baby and, despite his grandmother's intriguing prediction of a bright future, Emma found raising him a tedious struggle.

In the early walking stage he proved more amusing. Emma recalled later, not without fondness, that he looked like a "round little porcupine" in the first parka she sewed for him because its reindeer fur was so thick for his small build it would not allow his arms to hang naturally, but propped them out at 45-degree angles from his sides.

He was walking and talking sooner than most children, quick and eager to learn. Adoringly he trotted along behind Emma on his short legs, willing to try any task she set for him. But she was pregnant again and with a new baby she would have even less time to give her "little porcupine."

By default, Howard's care fell to his oldest sister, Kaipuk, who assumed it cheerfully. At 21, she was already beyond the age when most Tigara girls started families of their own and, perhaps because she had not done so, she gave more love and attention to her neglected little brother then he would ever know from any other family member. She was a blithe spirit, always laughing and joking, quick to use her disarming smile. And he credited her with nothing less than saving his life.

"Being aware of my sickly nature, she took to me and took care of me," he recalled. "When I ached she sympathized and cooed me into feeling better. She made my clothes and carried me around with her, and her sisterly love was intense. This, along with her help in caring for me, gave me the will to go on and I became stronger."

He also continued to trail his mother and she packed him along with the rest of the children when opportunity arose. One of their first excursions was berry-picking, which Rock would recall in later years not only for the delights of the fruit they picked but because it afforded a chance to study the tundra. Early in August they sought the black crowberries and large pink salmonberries and also sourdock, a leafy green not unlike rhubarb in flavor. Then, in late fall, they went out again, this time in search of tasty roots which had been gathered and stored for the winter in underground caches by tundra mice. This was, of necessity, a cooperative venture in which Howard, his siblings and his mother would fan out for a careful ground-search.

"If you step on something soft under your feet, be sure and tell me," his mother would explain and, small though he was, Howard sometimes discovered such a spot. Then his mother would take her ulu, slit the top about six inches and draw out a handful of roots to put in her sealskin pack. The mouse's storeroom was a surprisingly large chamber, usually round in shape and about a foot in diameter and depth. Some mice were more industrious than others, for sometimes the chamber would be full to the top and sometimes not.

"If you ever get these when I'm not around, don't take all the roots," his mother would remind them. "If you do, this little mouse is going to starve and then he will not be around next year to work for us."

His father spent time with him, too, and proved less stern than Emma, pointing out faults gently by teasing instead of sharp reprimand.

"Son, there was a little boy's tracks leaving the house. I wonder whose tracks they could be?" he would muse aloud, concerned because his child walked pigeon-toed. And when the youngster corrected his mistakes, Sam would lift him up bodily and say with enthusiasm, "But that's the way you do, my son."[2]

Then there was Nikka, the big, black-and-white malamute dog, so powerful no other dog in the village dared mix with him, who had been Howard's self-appointed guardian since birth. Together they romped for hours, Nikka occasionally knocking the child down, then swiping him with his enormous tongue as if to say he was sorry. Sam built a small sled with walrus-ivory runners and Howard soon learned to harness Nikka to it, driving him when the dog felt like being driven, tugging at his collar when the animal balked. And when, in frustration, Howard pummeled the husky with his fists, Nikka simply closed his eyes and endured, unruffled.[3]

Still, it was the laughing Kaipuk who was the center of Howard's universe. Whatever she did, he wanted to do, too, and he listened spellbound to her talk of the mission school which she attended with the younger children.

One afternoon Kaipuk came home to report that a boy had let wind audibly during class and that the teacher had become so angry with him, the child cried. Although only three, Howard had been pestering Kaipuk to take him to classes but now she said it was impossible.

"The teacher won't let you go because you're too little and too young," she insisted. Yet shortly thereafter, miraculously, she arranged for his attendance. His mother apparently had second thoughts as she watched the tiny boy trot off behind his sisters, and she was waiting anxiously outside their igloo when class let out to see the child running ahead shouting excitedly.

"Ahkahng! Ahkahng! Nillingitchoonga schooluknd!" Emma was amused and relieved to hear. "Mother! I didn't break wind in school!"[4]

Impressed by such decorum, the teacher allowed Howard to stay on, and classes became the high point of his existence. His most unforgettable experience during this period was a visit paid the school by the rugged Archdeacon Hudson Stuck who had just made a name for himself by climbing Alaska's Mt. McKinley, the highest mountain in North America. With him came the Native who had been his climbing partner, a fine-looking youth named Walter Harper. Born of an Athabascan woman and an Irish gold miner, Harper had been raised in Indian tradition, then educated in the States. Despite his strange looks and a penchant for reading Shakespeare and Tennyson, he was definitely a man of the country and quickly put the Eskimos at ease.[5] But Archdeacon Stuck, with his fearsome mustache and beard, was something else. Howard had never encountered anyone with thick facial hair. And when Sam Rock picked up his son for an introduction, Howard broke into terrified sobs.

Next day during school recess this bearded apparition appeared again and, frightened though he was, Howard was determined to be brave, even when the strange man plucked him from the crowd of youngsters by his parka shoulder and dangled him in his strong grip as he walked toward a mound of snow. Here Stuck ordered the boy to sit, then disappeared behind a black cloth draped over a large black box on a tripod. To his credit, Howard, who had never seen a camera, managed to keep his composure. After some time the glass eye of the box blinked— quite painlessly, it turned out—and Stuck emerged, gave him an affectionate pat that nearly bowled him over and departed. This display of bravery earned the respect of Howard's classmates who seemed to think he'd done something special and he enjoyed a glimmering of pride.

An even greater triumph followed when Howard was given a part in the school Christmas program despite the fact that he was far younger than other students. This holiday event ranked second only to the annual whaling festival. Rev. Hoare went 40 miles inland to secure a Christmas tree—actually four scraggly willows tied together but nonetheless impressive in a barren tundra village. Sam and the reverend spent the day before cooking 900 doughnuts of flour, sugar and seal oil. The school was festively decorated. Everyone came dressed in their best and the program was launched with high excitement.

There was much carol singing. The Bible was read. Then at last it was announced that Howard would recite "Little Jack Horner" *in English.* Someone ushered him to a spot in front of the audience which numbered about 250, and the four-year-old began bravely.

"Little Jack Horner

"Sat in a cor ... "

"Qinilaitkikput imna Howardnguraq!" ("We can't see little Howard,") someone complained loudly from the back of the room.

"Tavra kee," ("So it is,") someone else agreed.

The child hesitated ... unsure of what to do next. There was a flurry of activity, the murmur of conversation. Someone came forward with a wooden box in which two five-gallon kerosene cans had been shipped. It was placed as a podium and a man lifted Howard atop it. Now the crowd hushed, so quiet you could hear a caribou hair drop, he later recalled, and he was told to go on with his recitation.

"Little Jack Horner

"Sat in a corner

"Eating his Christmas pie.

"He put in his thumb

"And pulled out a plum ... " Howard demonstrated as he went, making a motion with his arm and thumb although he had no idea what a plum might be ...

"And said, 'What a good boy am I!'" he concluded with a flourish, putting his right hand on his chest, extending the left and bowing gravely to the audience. The crowd broke into wild applause. Some shouted approval; others were laughing too hard. Young though he was, Howard knew beyond doubt that most of his audience had no inkling of what the poem was all about. Their sudden outburst startled him and he wasn't sure whether to laugh with the audience or cry. He was more inclined to cry when, to his enormous relief, his mother rushed to him, lifted him off the box and carried him to safety, hugging him all the way.

"I'm very proud of you, my son," she murmured, and Howard was ecstatic. Emma rarely gave any demonstration of her love and this reward he never forgot.[6]

At school Howard made just one close friend. Like himself, Roger Bolt was undersized and at loose ends. His parents had given him to grandparents who did their best to make him happy, but Roger had no brother or sister in whom to confide and he and Howard became almost inseparable.[7]

After the fierce storms of fall, the two youngsters would comb the beach for clams or still-wiggling tomcod that littered their coastline by the thousands. Later, in September when the sun disappeared in early afternoon, they returned to study the great, ice-laden swells of the Chukchi by moonlight, jumping clear as breakers crashed, marveling as freezing slush layered on pebbles and grew into fat icy knobs a foot high.

Often they craned their necks to stare at the shimmering, multi-hued aurora borealis, trying to muster enough nerve to whistle which, old-timers warned, would cause the magic lights to pursue them. Ultimately they survived this dare, although they were never sure whether it was due to the speed at which they galloped home or because the legend was untrue.

In early winter they would sneak out on dangerously thin, newly formed "rubber" ice, trying to make it bounce under their weight, scampering away from anyone who approached to scold them for their lack of caution. In spring they chased snow buntings made conspicuous in their white feathers against newly bared tundra. And when daylight refused to leave night skies in summer, they begged for and were granted permission to stay up and play under the midnight sun, only to be defeated by heavy eyelids and fall asleep wherever they happened to be chasing ptarmigan or pestering ground squirrels.[8]

It was an idyllic time, for the arctic was such an exciting place to explore. But it was also disquieting because Howard began to suspect that he somehow didn't fit. With the exception of his friend, Roger, the children with whom he grew up tended to ignore him and his family did likewise. This puzzled him although, by his own admission, he was an "oddball," quiet and intense, who had little in common with his Eskimo peers.[9]

His first confirmation of this came when his father made a small bow and arrow and taught him to use it. Howard's eye was good and soon he shot a song bird as he had seen other boys do. The problem was that it broke his heart to kill the melodic creature and, worse yet, he could not bring himself to shoot another which came as a disagreeable shock to his family. True, the shaman had predicted this boy would not be a great hunter, but to be incapable of killing was unheard of in a society that depended on hunting. How would he live, they worried? And they were embarrassed because of him.[10]

The awkwardness of Howard's position was not lost on Allen who took great pleasure in announcing, "Look, I'm stronger than my older brother," and flattening his peace-loving sibling whenever he could gather a crowd. Noting with disgust that the undersized youth cried at slight provocation, his family assigned him woman's work—gathering driftwood, emptying slop, tending the moss wicks of seal oil lamps—or simply left him to his own weird devices.[11]

While other boys snared arctic hare, Howard studied the layers of ice crystals built up on streams or admired frost patterns on window panes. He became fascinated with the unique symmetry of snowflakes and, in summer, with the vibrant colors of the tundra—moss flowers, anemones, forget-me-nots and fireweed— that his peers trampled in their haste to shoot ducks. He wasted considerable time drawing pictures and even more puzzling was his affinity for the tattered school library. His father labored over the Bible, dictionary in hand, to better understand the word of the Lord but how, Sam Rock wondered, could anyone find pleasure in so difficult a task as reading? His son's efforts would better be spent learning the ways of a hunter, he knew, but he comforted himself with the fact that Howard was still young. At the time, Sam could afford to be indulgent but he prayed fervently that this strange boy would come to his senses before it was too late.[12]

5

The Cold World

POINT HOPE, in Howard's earliest years, was an unusually prosperous village because of the whaling industry. The bone from a single bowhead could be sold for $1,000 or more for corset stays and there was a market for whale oil for lighting. In addition, the village reindeer herd, established by the government, provided meat and profits from the sale of hides. Fur prices were on the rise. Subsistence hunting and fishing were lucrative.

Ill health had forced missionary Driggs to retire but men sent by the Episcopal Board of Missions to fill his job were, for the most part, well-educated, progressive and dedicated to the well-being of their Eskimo charges. Rev. Hoare, longest tenured among them, was the most practical, having come to the priesthood from engineering, and he was determined to make Point Hope a model village.

Hoare first organized the congregation to clean up the human bones that littered the landscape as a result of the Eskimo practice of above-ground burial. These they interred in a Christian cemetery ringed with an impressive fence of whale ribs. Hoare encouraged replacement of seal oil lamps with coal stoves as a heat source, purchasing a boat with which to haul the fuel from a deposit at Cape Lisburne a few miles to the north. He also built a modern parish house and church of imported lumber.[1] A government post office was established in 1905. Several stores were in operation. Health care improved to the point that births outnumbered deaths two to one.

But in 1914 the price of whalebone began a decline from which it would not recover and Fred Sickles, the government teacher, became uneasy about the future.

"The financial condition of Point Hope is not encouraging," he reported to the Northwest District Superintendent Walter Shields.

The Natives, having enjoyed 20 years of prosperity owing to the high price of whalebone, are having a hard time to make their present expenditures correspond to the drop in the price of whalebone from $8 per pound to $.50 per pound. The fur catch last winter was a rather poor one, and this season's whale catch furnished no bone of considerable value. Fish are more plentiful than usual and there are a large number of seals taken. A number of families made their living by making Native boots or 'mukluks' for the white trade. There is practically no work for wages except for a few days longshoring, coaling, gathering eggs and sometimes helping on building. Most of the Natives owe from $20 to $750 to the stores and unless they happen to have extraordinary success in some direction, they will not be able to pay their debts for a number of years.[2]

Seal hunting proved disastrous the following winter due to unusual ice conditions and Eskimos felt the real pinch of hunger. At one point, Sickles established a soup kitchen and, although Howard was only four at the time, he would never forget the hardship his family had endured. Again and again his father would risk hunting in bad weather, and worrying about him, waiting for him long after dark knowing he might well return empty-handed or not at all was agonizing. His mother would reboil the same blubber to offer the barest pretense of broth. Sometimes they went without and when Sam was fortunate enough to shoot two seals after one long fast, Emma gave away so much of the meat Howard voiced fear that they, themselves, might go hungry.

"Keep your opinions to yourself," Emma told him sharply. Then, a day or so later, someone knocked at their door with a generous piece of caribou meat and Howard began to understand the value of sharing in a community such as theirs. People took care of one another in times of need and the giver might often receive more than he gave. It was the way the Tigaramiut had weathered many a bad season.[3]

The following year, 1916, Rev. Hoare reported to superiors that seal hunting had never been better but fur prices had dropped to a discouraging low.

"Traders were going to jack up the price (of flour) but the mission offered Natives flour at cost which brought them in line," he added, pleased with himself. "The price dropped from $10 per 100 pounds to $5.50 and the price offered for fox skins rose from $3-$4 to $12-$15 when the mission offered to pay the Outside price."[4]

But the hard times that descended on the Rock family were due to more than poor hunting and fluctuating prices. Sam had resigned his job as mission interpreter in deference to younger men whom he had once taught and who now spoke English more fluently than he.[5] The collapse of the whaling industry further reduced his income and, although Sam was among the best hunters, there was growing need for cash. His family pulled in their belts and bought less at the store, but when it was discovered Emma was again pregnant their future became precarious.

Howard knew little about his parents' financial straits and the summer of 1918 began as a happy one for him. This was his favorite season when the mania for hunting was relaxed and the whole village camped on the beach to fish. Sun shone around the clock. Children were allowed to play all night. The weather was wonderful.

Then, one morning, a joyous cry of "Ahy! Ahy!" woke the village. A ship was making its way to the lee of the spit beyond the north beach. The children went wild with excitement and adults hastily prepared for trading. Emma was asking her husband to get some towels and soap when she noticed Howard bobbing anxiously at her side.

"I have just thought of something, Sam," she said speculatively. "Our little son here can talk the language of these white people and I think he would be good at trading artifacts for soap and things."

The idea amused Sam.

"It's true," he answered. "But I doubt whether his knowledge of the language is enough."

"Why don't you take him with you when you go aboard ship?" she persisted. "You can do it, can't you, son?"

Howard was thrilled at the prospect. The only English he knew at the time was "Hello," "How are you," "Yes, sir," "No, sir," "Thank you, sir," and a few single words like "soap," but he wasn't about to pass up a chance to see the big ship. He assured them he would be useful and when his father agreed to take him, he rushed to the beach to tell his schoolmates.

"You're too small to go. Besides, our parents don't allow little children around," they scoffed.

"You watch and see. My father is going to take me," he insisted. "I'm going to talk to the people on ship in their language."

"You can't talk in their language."

"I can, too. Listen. 'I don't know.' You see, I can talk like a white man."

"What does that mean?" someone asked, incredulous.

"It means, 'amuy' (I don't know)," he translated smugly.

A moderate wind was blowing and the vessel had its sails set. Black smoke issued from its black stack which meant an auxiliary engine was also in use.

"Umiakpuk munna Cutter Bearngumaruq! (The ship is the Cutter

Bear)," someone shouted and Howard was beside himself for this was the Coast Guard's great square-rigger, the most famous vessel on their coast.

Most of the villagers had gathered on the north beach and Howard stuck close to his father for fear he might be left behind. Their skin boat was launched into gentle swells, people boarded and at length Sam lifted him into the stern.

They steered directly for the ship. In awe, Howard studied its massive sides and watched the green water lap up and down beneath it. How could anything so enormous stay afloat, he wondered, staring up at the masts. Their height was truly unbelievable. When they moved with the roll of the ship, it looked as if they would tip the whole boat over, but naturally he knew better. He gave his attention to the crew lined up at the rail. Some of them looked like Hudson Stuck, but he was not afraid. He worried only about his fluency in English which he had certainly overstated.

A rope ladder was lowered but its rungs were too far apart for Howard to climb and he wondered how he would get aboard. A fine-looking man wearing a different type of hat than the rest anticipated the problem. Down came a rope which Sam tied about the boy's chest.

"Thank you, sir. How are you?" Howard asked brightly of the man who hauled him aboard. The sailor, completely taken by surprise, broke into laughter.

"Hey, men, this little boy can speak English," he announced and a crowd gathered.

"What is your name, little boy?"

"I don't know."

More laughter.

"How do you like this ship?"

"I don't know."

"Do you like oranges, little boy?"

"No, sir."

"Bring some oranges for this boy," said the man in the distinctive hat. "I don't think he understands what they are."

"Yes, sir," Howard said, struggling to maintain his poise.

Soon the man came back with a bag and handed the youngster a large orange. It was beautiful but he had no idea what to do with it so the crewman peeled it, pulled it in halves and put a section in his own mouth. Then he offered the child a piece.

"Here little boy, eat it," he said. Howard understood.

It was a taste unlike any he'd ever experienced: juicy, succulent, wonderful, and his face lit with a smile.

"You liked it, didn't you, little boy?" the man queried.

"*Thank you*, sir," he answered, still beaming. And Sam, who had come aboard, chuckled at the child's delight.

"My son," he told the sailors proudly.

Later, armed with a bag of Eskimo artifacts, Howard was taken below decks to the galley.

"Hey, Cookie, I want you to meet Howard and give him something to eat," his guide called ahead in a loud voice.

"Yes, sir. Who is Howard and where is he?" a low, resonant voice responded.

"You have to look pretty far down here before you can see him, Cookie."

There emerged the strangest-looking person Howard had ever seen; huge in stature, skin of black, dressed in a gleaming white mess coat. He was the first black man Howard had ever encountered and he stared in amazement.

"So that's where you are, Howard. You're sticking right close to the deck, aren't you," Cookie observed good-naturedly. "You're really a tiny little fellow."

"Hello, sir. How are you?" Howard ventured, taking full courage, and the day was won. The cook, delighted with this bold display of English, offered bread and jam and he and his young guest soon got down to trading.

"Soap—towel," Howard began hesitantly. He wanted to ask for under-clothing but didn't know a word for it. Finally he got the cook to bend down, tugged at his undershirt and the man understood, swapping him a full set of underwear, three cakes of soap, a towel and a pair of trousers for assorted artifacts and a harpoon head.

Having completed his mission, Howard went topside where he was allowed to explore while his father finished negotiations. It was a fascinating world of ropes, canvas and tar and he felt great pangs of regret on leaving it. Everything about the ship, its mast, spars, bowsprit and the lines of the hull seemed to belong exactly where they were. To a small boy it was a wonderful vision in the late day sun, a soft gray hull with amber masts.

Then, on the beach, he spotted Emma with a look of expectancy on her face and he could not wait to tell her the news.

"Mother! Mother! I got some soap for you. I got some towels, too. And I got underwear. I got trousers and I got oerr—oranges—they are real good."

"I've never seen this boy so excited before," his father marveled. Emma, as usual, made no comment but she smiled when she looked at him and Howard thought surely she must be pleased.[6] Later, all too soon, he would recall the wistful quality of her smile and understand the sadness of his father's mission aboard the *Bear* that day, for Sam had gone to arrange passage to the States for their beloved Kaipuk. As the brightest of Rev. Hoare's students, she had been selected to attend nursing school in Seattle, Washington. She left when the boat returned on its southern run in the fall.

The loss of Kaipuk ended any illusion of security Howard might have cherished, for without her there was no one to take care of him and apparently no one who cared much about him. His mother was busy with their new baby, Rupert, and the precocious Allen. His sister, Helen, 18, was planning a family of her own. Eebrulik, 15, had become a hunter and, like their father, was preoccupied in the newly formidable job of supporting the family.

For a time Howard dared hope that Kaipuk might return, but when word came that she had died in a flu epidemic that winter he was inconsolable. Poorly dressed for want of someone to sew for him, wearing mission-donated, hand-me-down white man's shoes that did not begin to keep out the cold, he wandered about the village doing odd jobs for neighbors who occasionally took pity on him.

Howard's neglect became the topic of gossip and speculation.[7] Nanny Ooyahtuonah, a girlhood friend of Kaipuk, married now but without a family, watched the child sadly, knowing it was not her place to intercede. Dina and David Frankson made work for him at their small store in exchange for an occasional meal, careful lest their charity become too obvious. Rev. Hoare kept an uneasy silence, embarrassed to broach the subject of child neglect with such a good friend and staunch parishioner as Sam Rock.

At last Mumangeena, Emma's older sister, took courage and spoke in Howard's behalf. She had long fancied her tiny nephew for she had no children of her own, she said. Her husband, Nayukuk, was not the most successful of hunters but they could certainly support the boy more comfortably than was his present lot. Howard would be of much help to them and brighten their lonesome home and they would be grateful if they might be allowed to adopt him.

Swapping children was a well-established custom among the Tigaramiut who believed childlessness was poverty no woman should have to endure. However, adoption was usually accomplished when a child was small.

Howard was seven at the time his family consigned him to Mumangeena and Nayukuk's igloo and their abandonment came as a brutal shock. Repeatedly he walked the long mile from the village back to their home near the mission, only to be rebuffed by all save his faithful dog, Nikka. And never would he understand why the parents he loved so deeply had given him away.[8]

6

Adopted

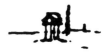

THE CHOICE OF MUMANGEENA AND NAYUKUK as foster parents must have pained Howard almost as much as the fact that his own family did not want him, for the community standing of his relatives was tenuous. Mumangeena was nearly 50 when she adopted her nephew and, in marked contrast to Howard's mother who was tall, beautiful and eight years younger, this aunt was a comic figure. Her face was long by Eskimo standards with prominent cheekbones, a definite Roman nose and a traditional tattoo half an inch wide that ran down her chin flanked by a narrow stripe on either side. She stood only four feet, nine inches tall and her legs were so bowed they often pained her and caused her to waddle when she walked.

Even more unfortunate in the eyes of her family was her choice of a husband, for Nayukuk was considered a lazy dullard. He was a well-built, handsome man with an unusual black mustache. A dozen or so years Mumangeena's junior, five feet, seven inches in height, he was apparently in his prime. But he complained of a chronic back ailment and would hunt only when driven to it by his wife's persistent nagging. Too often Mumangeena was forced to beg meat from family and neighbors. Seldom did she have anything to give in return.[1]

Like the Rocks, Howard's adopted parents lived in a sod house, but it was a decidedly poorer camp. Since Nayukuk seldom worked for wages, the only store-bought items they could obtain were from the proceeds of his spasmodic attempts at trapping. Nor did they own a boat or dog team, so they were forced to accept the charity of others to travel to out-of-the-way hunting areas or the annual spring encampment on Kotzebue Sound to visit friends and trade.

Despite her sorry lot, or perhaps because of it, Mumangeena displayed extraordinary sympathy for unfortunates. She adored her tiny nephew, as she did all babies and puppies, and because she believed her mother's prediction of a special future for Howard, she secretly hoped the boy might improve her family's lot. True, he was one more mouth to feed when they could scarcely feed themselves, and he was still too small to be of any real help with the many chores Nayukuk left unattended. But Mumangeena had been devoted to her mother after whom Howard had been named. She took comfort in having him close to her. And, to the youngster's great consternation, she completely ignored his Anglicized name and called him "Mother."

Being addressed in the feminine was so humiliating that Howard studiously avoided his aunt in crowds where others might overhear, but he realized her good intentions and tried his best to please her. She was, after all, the only person in the village who did not seem to regard him as hopeless.

Mumangeena was determined to turn the boy into a hunter, cheerfully overlooking his bothersome compassion towards birds and animals along with the fact that she was a woman, ill-equipped to instruct. For starters, she required him to muster naked each morning to relieve himself out-of-doors, regardless of the weather. Howard cried and protested, for temperatures on their coast averaged 40 below or more in winter. But his aunt stood firm, refusing him breakfast when he failed the test.

"Mother, a great hunter never cries. He has to be tough to be able to meet all kinds of hardships," she would explain, not without sympathy. And when the day came when he could brave the elements without whimpering, she was elated.

"You will be a great hunter, I'm sure of it," she declared, taking him in her arms. "You will live a good life with many good things to eat. Your village will look up to you. I'm very proud of you and I will do something nice for you. I'll make you a nice new parka with a pair of mukluks." And Howard, who was certain at last that he had done something of major importance, was so proud he almost wept on her shoulder.[2]

Mumangeena also trained the child to read weather, dispatching him on dark winter mornings to evaluate cloud formations, estimate wind direction and velocity and report to his uncle on the off chance Nayukuk might undertake a hunt. In addition, he was required to fetch and carry, empty slop and, as he grew stronger, undertake the never-ending task of hauling coal or collecting driftwood for the stove.[3] It was difficult work for an undersized boy but he did not resent it. In fact, the bond between nephew and aunt grew to the point that Mumangeena even managed to interest him in religion, something his zealously Christian father had failed to do.

Each evening, just before his bedtime, she would take his hand and make him kneel in prayer beside her and when she felt unwell, she earnestly asked him to speak to the Lord on her behalf. She was so sincere about it that Howard would concentrate as mightily as he could. And when she felt better, she would credit him, telling everyone that the child was responsible for her improving health.[4]

Health was a major concern during this period for an influenza epidemic raged along the coast, taking so many lives in 1918 that schools were closed as part of a quarantine effort for most of the next two years.[5] In the 1800s a similar plague had wiped out more than half the Point Hope population, killing many of Mumangeena's ancestors, so family fears were not unfounded. But this time the village was left generally unscathed.[6]

A sad exception was the death of Roger Bolt, age eight, who had been Howard's major solace since adoption. One of the few good things about the move to Nayukuk's igloo was that Roger lived next door with his grandparents. Samaroona, the grandfather, lavished attention on Roger, carving toys for him, entertaining him with exciting stories from the past. Howard was often invited to share this good fortune, so he missed not only his companion but the exposure to a happy home that their friendship had afforded.

Attempts to fill this gap by visiting his own parents proved futile, for his brother, Allen, showed potential as a hunter and demanded most of their father's attention, while Emma was busy with Rupert, 3, and Ruth who had been born that fall. Howard's misery was soon noted by the grieving Samaroona and his wife who invited him to supper.

"Since your little friend died, I have not told a story," the old-timer said after the meal had been enjoyed. "I know little boys like to listen to them. I did when I was younger and I wanted to listen to more and more of them. You're no different than any other little boy. How would you like it if I told you a legend tonight?"

Rock was delighted to become a surrogate grandson and he began spending every spare hour he could with the elder. Unlike Sam Rock, whose church training caused him to condemn ancient beliefs, Samaroona clung to Inupiat custom. He was the only man in the village who still wore his hair, Eskimo fashion, with shorn crown surrounded by a fringed halo. He fought successfully to preserve ancient Eskimo dances despite stout opposition from the missionaries.[7] And, although he had no quarrel with the newly adopted Episcopal faith, he was genuinely proud of Tigara's past.

Samaroona proved a master storyteller, acting out each part, carefully prolonging the suspense through long dark winter evenings. And his repertoire, gleaned from one-thousand years or more of oral history, was astonishing.

Howard's favorite was the legend of the eldest son of a great Tigara chief sent by kayak on a dangerous mission to the Aleutian Islands more than a thousand miles distant in search of a treasure of beads. It was a saga like "Jason and the Golden Fleece" and took many winter evenings in telling, for Samaroona covered the subject island-by-island in detail.[8]

Another story began with a young hunter's disappearance at sea. Throughout the winter his devoted father prowled the beaches in search of his son's body until by eerie moonlight he spotted the boy paddling over heavy, slush-laden swells. The son was seen again on subsequent evenings but refused to heed his father's calls. Then the parents woke one night to hear the soft brush of fur as a parka-clad apparition entered their igloo in search of food. Night after night it eluded them and when they finally did capture it they discovered to their horror it was the rotting corpse of their son covered with gnawing sea animals.[9]

Howard was nine when Samaroona entertained him with this ghost story and visions of monsters and ogres danced before him when he bid his host good night and started down the long, dark hallway that led from the old man's living room to the outer door of his dwelling. There were little storage rooms on both sides, perfect hiding places for heaven-only-knew what. The boy's skin crawled with goose bumps and hair rose on the back of his neck but he couldn't very well return and admit to Samaroona that he was afraid to go home. Shaking, he stumbled on, reached the outer door and escaped. The sky was bright with moon and stars. He could see a glow from the gut-skin skylight of his own igloo. Then he realized with panic that he had it all to do over again for there was an equally long, dark tunnel that led from the outer door to the sanctity of his own home.

Plucking up full courage, he dashed through Nayukuk's entrance at breakneck speed, triumphantly pushed open the door to the inner chamber, caught his toe on the crosspiece of the sill and fell flat on his face at his aunt's feet.

Mumangeena screamed, her eyes wide with fright.

"Why Mother, has someone been chasing you?" she asked. "I've never seen anyone enter with such suddenness."[10]

Ironically, the most engrossing horror story that year actually occurred in front of the Point Hope Episcopal Mission where the Rev. Augustus

Hoare was gunned down in cold blood. His murder came as a shock, for the missionary was generally well thought of and, after 12 years' residence, his ambitious dream of molding Tigara into a model village was nearing fruition. With Hoare's encouragement, many Eskimos had moved to modern clapboard houses. The brightest of his Native students, Tony Joule, was well on his way to a teaching degree in the States. Young David Frankson excelled as a teacher's aide and planned to attend college as soon as Hoare could afford to send him. Village mining of a nearby coal deposit had proved encouraging enough to consider commercial development which would provide jobs for Eskimos no longer able to support themselves through whaling. An electric light plant had just been ordered for the village—the first in the arctic.[11]

However, Hoare was concerned by rumors that strange, primitive religious doctrines were springing up among Natives in outlying areas, and even more worried about intrusion by missionaries of other faiths.[12] To counter, he hired James MacGuire to teach at the Point Hope school in his stead and began to spend his time traveling to far-flung villages by dog team, spreading the Episcopal word.

MacGuire was white, the son of the district school superintendent. Hoare spoke well of him but during one of the missionary's long absences, MacGuire took up with a Native girl. At her prompting, for reasons never clear, he awaited Hoare's return with a shotgun, shot him twice, point blank, then finished the job with three more shells from a rifle.

The crime provided villagers with a puzzling introduction to the American system of justice. The murderer's accomplice was freed and later married a local man (despite her father's insistence that she should be put to death) and MacGuire was released after serving a stint in a mental institution.[13] Yet, inadvertently, the tragedy benefited Howard Rock and fellow students.

The Episcopal bishop had often spoken against the federal Bureau of Education but shortly after the shooting he decided that his church could no longer support a teacher at Point Hope and requested the government to send in a well-qualified instructor.[14]

Mission teachers, who concentrated more on religion than academics, kept few records and Howard had served three years in the second grade without realizing there was a problem. Happily he whiled away his time blowing spitballs through the hollow femur bone of an Arctic owl. His aim was well perfected by the time the government teacher noted he was rather an exceptional second grader and advanced him to third. Three months later he was promoted again and began to catch up somewhat with his schooling.[15]

Howard also grew stronger and Mumangeena decided, come freeze-up, to take him fishing up the Kukpuk River. The traditional grayling grounds were about five miles from the village and about 30 people were camped there in ancient igloos built for the same purpose by their ancestors.

Uncle Nayukuk declined to budge.

"That sharp pain in my back has returned again. I can't move," he pleaded, gingerly touching his left ribs. Howard voiced concern. He'd grown to like his shy, inarticulate uncle and always tried to be helpful to him, delighting in the rare smile that sometimes rewarded his efforts. Perhaps Nayukuk really was sick.

"Nonsense, your uncle never had a sick day in his life," Mumangeena maintained. But without further nagging she set off alone with Howard, armed with three stout gunny sacks.

"We will probably need only one, but I'm known to be a good fisherman when it comes to hooking grayling," she confided with an air of satisfaction. "And what pleasure I'll get out of teaching you to fish, Mother. You must pay strict attention to everything I do. This is going to be part of your training as a hunter."

Mumangeena chose a location across from the bluff near their igloo and carefully chipped away the thin river ice with a sounding rod. Then she produced two five-foot willow rods equipped with lines of polished whale baleen, leaders of sea gull quill and metal hooks set in ivory bases. Bait was a piece of yellow cloth or yarn, although some preferred red, Mumangeena said.

"Now, Mother, watch carefully," she instructed, casting her line in the water and undulating it by flexing the pole. "When the fish bites, you simply haul it out and land it on the ice far enough so it won't jump back in."

Demonstrating with a sweeping motion, she neatly landed a grayling.

"Why, Mother, this is the finest lesson I've ever given to anyone in all my life!" she exclaimed. Results were immediate for no sooner had Howard cast his hook than he, too, produced a fat fish.

"I knew it all the time, Mother. You are going to be one of the finest hunters alive," she declared, even more excited than he. "This should convince your parents that you are going to be one. We'll save the fish and give it to them when we get back."

As the day wore on, Howard outfished her and she wasted no time in bragging about his prowess to passers-by.

"Take a good look at Mother's pile of fish," she chattered. "I'm as good or better than anyone when it comes to fishing but you'd never know it from the way he kept hooking grayling today. It's unbelievable. This is the first time he ever fished in his life. And Mother is such a *little* boy, too."

By mid-afternoon their catch filled two and a quarter sacks which was more than they could manage and Mumangeena dispatched Howard to fetch his uncle. Unfortunately, Nayukuk declined to help on the grounds that he was busy carving hooks for them. Howard saw no evidence of industry but he'd been taught not to question his elders. Determined to do the job himself, he returned pulling a sled.

All went well until they reached a sharp incline near the igloo where, hard as they tugged, the heavy-laden sled would not budge. Furious, Mumangeena went herself to fetch the reluctant Nayukuk, still berating him loudly as he mustered with a long rope. In an amazing display of strength, he pulled the sled in, tossed all their catch on a high meat rack and stamped off without a word, leaving them nothing to cook for supper. Howard was elected to climb up to retrieve some fish and, in the process, slipped off, flattening his aunt in his fall. Only their dignity was injured. The ludicrousness of the situation struck Mumangeena and she began to smile.

"Mother, since I married that lazy walrus my life has been one abnormal happening after another. I wanted to live like any woman in our village, but it's impossible the way that man is. He forces some comical events without meaning to. I have to laugh because he makes them happen without a smile on his face or without saying a word.

"This need not have happened if he had been like other men," she added not without fondness. "Sometimes I wonder what will happen tomorrow."

When they returned to the igloo they found Nayukuk cleaning his 30-30 rifle, a sure sign he planned to go hunting next morning. This usually heartened Mumangeena but it was plain she had said something to her husband during her earlier tirade that weighed heavily on her conscience. She was so quiet Howard wished she would go back to her annoying chatter.

After a good meal of boiled grayling, Uncle Nayukuk began rummaging in a little box where he kept his carving tools and picked out pieces of ivory. The atmosphere of the small household became lighter as he worked throughout the evening. He was an excellent carver and all was forgiven when, with the faintest of smiles, he presented his wife and nephew with fine new fishhooks.[16]

7

Better Luck

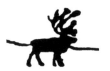

Howard's tenth summer began with the loss of his last good friend. The malamute, Nikka, had grown grizzled, his springy gait slowed to the point that he no longer was of service as a leader.

He was 15 which was ancient by arctic standards, but Emma indulged him. She had traveled with him often and once, when she misjudged the weather and got lost in a storm, Nikka saved her life by leading her through heavy snows. Now that he had outlived his usefulness, she reciprocated. Since the concept of a house pet was unacceptable in their Spartan society, Nikka was dubbed a watchdog, but on cold nights he slept among warm reindeer skins that served as bedding for the family.

Nikka still followed Howard at every opportunity, and the family allowed the boy to drop by to play with the dog, even though it was painfully clear he was otherwise unwelcome. Howard looked forward to these romps but en route one Sunday evening in June he was suddenly overcome with foreboding. Emma and Sam were working over the animal outside their igloo. He was covered with blood and apparently unable to move except for a faint wag of his tail in greeting.

Earlier that day, the family had been watching a game of Eskimo football on the beach. As usual, Nikka trailed off after Howard who was playing on the sidelines, but some time during the event the dog returned to Rock's igloo where he was attacked by two of their team.

It was obvious that Emma had been crying because she did not trust her voice. Angrily Howard turned to his father.

"Which one did this to Nikka?" he demanded.

"That one over there, and that one," Sam answered, pointing out two young malamutes who had always hated the favored pet. "They got loose while we were gone."

Sobbing bitterly, Howard began collecting rocks and hurling them at the attackers. Briefly his father let him vent his rage, then quietly interceded.

"Stop that now, son. Those dogs will not eat or drink for three days!" he promised. Without a word, Howard went to Nikka who looked at him sorrowfully. The animal's breathing was labored; his right ear almost completely chewed off. His throat and flanks were gashed with fatal wounds. Howard realized the dog would never recover but with his parents he busied himself trying to make Nikka comfortable on a reindeer skin in a nook near the door.

"We can't do much more for him now. It's getting late," Sam finally said. "We better go in and go to bed."

Howard protested. He wanted to stay with the dog but obviously there was nothing to be done. Reluctantly he stumbled off to the home of his adopted parents. Sleep failed him and he was up early, only to find Nikka gone.

All day he searched without success. It was his sister, Ruth, who discovered a deep hole about a quarter of a mile away, where the dog had crawled to die. Together the children lifted Nikka's body onto the toy sled with ivory runners that he'd pulled so often to amuse them, and dragged it to a favored spot near the beach where their father dug a grave. Choked with his own grief, Sam offered a prayer on behalf of their faithful leader but Howard found scant comfort in his words.[1]

That same summer, Mumangeena's husky bitch gave birth to nine puppies but Howard took little interest until his aunt made the astonishing announcement that she was going to raise a dog team.

"Their father is one of the best dogs in the village," she reasoned. "Everyone knows that a team of huskies from the same litter is considered the best."

Although Uncle Nayukuk was not convinced, Mumangeena took remarkable care of the pups, talking to them as if they were children, babying the weakest, and they became a frisky lot.

"It's about time we had a good team. We'll need them this winter, so you'd better train them right away," she nagged until Nayukuk bestirred himself and hitched seven of the neophytes into a harness behind two seasoned sled dogs. As Howard watched anxiously, the untrained pups became a tangled, barking mass of snarled traces. Aunt Mumangeena helped straighten them out. Uncle Nayukuk commanded, "Mush!" The two experienced dogs lunged forward but the greenhorns just rolled in the snow, played with neighbors or attempted to escape their collars. Despite Nayukuk's commands, they had proceeded no farther than 300 feet in a quarter of an hour. Then, in an attempt to chase a neighbor's dog team, they upset the driver, dragging him 500 feet over hard ground.

Nayukuk extricated himself wearily. A crowd gathered. Howard's heart sank as they snickered and laughed. Unheeding, Nayukuk continued to work the animals. They began moving in spurts and stops. The farther they got, the better they performed and after another hour, Howard could barely make them out on the horizon. They returned traveling slowly but behaving almost like a team. Nayukuk was sweating and the leader looked tired, but the pups were exhausted and wiser for their wear.

Nayukuk continued to train the dogs and Mumangeena was elated. Howard was allowed to ride on the sled while his uncle manned the runners so the boy could learn with the pups and, as a result, the Nayukuks ended up with one of the best teams in the village.[2]

Even more amazing, Nayukuk began to hunt more frequently and, to his nephew's astonishment, he was good at it. The weather had turned unusually cold with high winds and blizzards and most men had difficulty bringing in game. Sam Rock was only mildly successful but Nayukuk seemed to take the lean period as a personal challenge. Determined and silent, apparently without fear, he went out daily, climbing the highest ice ridges, returning with his eyebrows, lashes and mustache covered with hoarfrost, lugging a seal or sometimes two. Neighbors no longer made jokes at his expense. Many were forced to swallow their pride and take meat from him. Mumangeena was in her glory as she cut up the seals her husband brought home and directed dispersal.

"All right, Mother, bring this to Samaroona. This one is for the Koorook family. I'll bring this to my sister, myself," she'd say, savoring the thought. Although Howard's mother had never refused her in times of need, Emma often berated her as a common beggar and cast terrible aspersions on Nayukuk. Now Mumangeena chatted endlessly, never mentioning the slights but subtly evening the score.

"We are having unusually bad weather this year, sister. I feel sorry for our poor men who have to hunt in it," she'd begin casually. "That man, Nayukuk, never ceases to amaze me. Isn't he something? As much as I nagged him when he wasn't hunting, there is something exciting about Nayukuk. He may be quiet and lazy at times but he is my man. He's good looking too, don't you think?"

Nor did she miss a chance to put in a good word for Howard.

"I noticed a hole in my Mother's right mukluk today. I must patch it right away. I have to make him a new parka, too. Children certainly wear their clothes out fast. He has been so helpful. I don't know what I'd do without him.

"Did you know the teacher hired him to make kindling and bring coal into the school? He is really among the very best of students."

It would be a long time, Mumangeena guessed, before her sister would attempt to malign the Nayukuk family again.[3] Especially after Nayukuk killed a record-sized polar bear.

It was a Saturday and Howard was chopping driftwood when he saw his uncle coming from the north pulling an enormous hide. Scrambling atop their igloo, he called the good news down through the skylight to his aunt, then rushed to help the hunter. Three layers of the man's parka were torn and claw marks were clearly visible, but Nayukuk fended off the youngster's eager questions and was reluctant to talk, even when a large group of villagers gathered to view the huge bearskin. Realizing, at length, that his audience would stay until satisfied, he began to tell his story.

Skirting an ice ridge, it had been his ill luck to startle the big bear no more than 20 feet away, causing it to rear up and roar at him, then hump its back, kick powerfully with its massive hind legs and charge.

"There was no time to pull my rifle out of the scabbard," he told them. "I knew I had no chance if I tried to dodge either to the right or to the left. A polar bear is extremely fast in striking with either of its forelegs. There was not a chance to run back from him.... It amazes me how clearly I was thinking during that short instant.... There was only one thing to do that might save my life and I did it."

Bracing his legs, Nayukuk dived headlong, aiming at the gap between the legs of the oncoming bear, landing on his face in the snow. As he did so he felt sharp pressure on his right ribs. Glancing over the crook of his left elbow he saw the animal snarling wickedly, readying for another charge. Luckily the bear was turning to the right. For some reason this is a much slower maneuver for bears than a left turn, Nayukuk explained, and in the brief reprieve, he pulled his .30-.30 and felled the animal.

The hunter's story was told with such reticence that many, including Howard's father, were skeptical until they investigated the scene and discovered that tracks bore out Nayukuk's account. The bear hide skinned out at 12$\frac{1}{2}$ feet. It sold for the unheard-of sum of $62.50. And even when Nayukuk slipped back into his lazy ways a few weeks later, he remained a village hero.[4]

During this period, Howard also came into his own, not only through Nayukuk's reflected glory but because his new job at school suddenly provided him with some valuable assets.

His teacher was the Rev. Frederick Goodman who had officiated at Howard's birth. Recently widowed, he had returned following a long stay in his native England to assume a government teaching assignment in addition to the work of the Point Hope church. Although a man of personal wealth, with a fine education, the missionary had committed his life to the Eskimos and become engrossed in translating Episcopal services into their language.

Goodman hired Rock ostensibly because he spoke better English than his peers. Actually he was concerned over the sorry state of this child he had helped bring into the world, and Howard responded gratefully. Although still undersized, he worked hard to please his benefactor and the family began looking forward to his Friday paydays which Goodman made an education in themselves.

Howard's stipend was selected from school stores, apparently at random. Sometimes it was canned peaches, a delicacy that utterly delighted Mumangeena. Stewed tomatoes proved a fair success but Nayukuk turned down the offering of canned cabbage without comment; Mumangeena compared it unfavorably to oogruk gut peelings and even their ravenous dogs refused to eat it.

Then came a box—two inches thick, four inches wide and six inches long—that Howard couldn't figure out. Goodman spent an hour trying to explain it.

"Pie. P-I-E!" he repeated carefully, but Howard's English was still too limited to comprehend. At length, the exasperated educator thrust the package into the boy's hands and told him to go home. Obediently clutching his prize, Howard hurried to his parent's house where his brothers and sisters gathered around curiously.

"What have you got in the box?" they asked, almost in unison.

"I don't know," he admitted.

"Let's see what's in it," Ruth demanded. Obligingly, Howard opened the cardboard, unwrapped the waxed paper-covered contents and sniffed it. They all sniffed.

"It smells something like prunes yet it's not," Emma decided. "What does it say on the box?"

"The teacher told me it was 'mincemeat', but I don't know what a 'mince' is."

Everyone took a taste.

"If that is meat, it's the strangest kind of meat I have ever tasted," his mother declared. "You better take it to your aunt. That woman can eat anything and she'll probably like it."

Mumangeena was busy cooking seal when Howard arrived, but she remembered it was payday.

"What is it this time?" she asked eagerly.

"I don't know. Here, you taste it," he suggested.

"This stuff doesn't taste like anything I've ever tasted," she said chewing gingerly. "I don't think I like It. I wish the teacher had paid you a can of peaches. My, how good those peaches are."

The next week's reward was even more of a mystery.

"Little grains in a bag? They look like willow seeds to me. What are they?" Mumangeena demanded.

This time Howard knew, for he had seen Goodman pop corn. His aunt didn't have a frying pan but he made do with a coffee tin rigged with a kindling stick handle.

"That's ridiculous," his aunt insisted. "A coffee can is so small. How can you cook anything in it? You're not very rational today, Mother. If you're going to cook those things, why don't you put water on them?"

"They don't need any water," he maintained. "Come over here and watch while I do this."

Mumangeena sidled over and Uncle Nayukuk interrupted his meditation to stare as Howard shook the can from side to side over hot coals. All of a sudden there was a distinct "pop" followed by a tiny "ping."

"What's that?" Mumangeena cried, watching the can intently. Other pops followed in rapid succession.

"You'd better stop that, Mother. You might hurt yourself," she warned, backing off in haste. But when he took the can from the fire and coaxed her to look at the clean white fluffs with their savory aroma, she was wide-eyed with delight.

"I know them! I know what they are," exclaimed Uncle Nayukuk who had been keeping a discreet distance. "So that's the way they do them!" [5]

Everyone enjoyed the popcorn so much that Uncle Nayukuk decided to experiment further, trading seal skins with Goodman in return for some strange white pellets along with the usual tea and coffee.

"What are they?" his wife asked.

"I don't know," he said.

"I don't know, either," Howard echoed.

Nayukuk broke one between his teeth and grimaced at the disgusting taste. The strong odor was so unpleasant that Howard and his aunt lost interest, but Nayukuk took a few of the pellets trapping and returned in triumph with a fine white arctic fox pelt worth $35. He was probably the only man in the world, Howard later speculated, who successfully baited a trap with mothballs.[6]

Misadventures with the white man's labeling system ceased abruptly when Howard learned to read at age 11. Understanding books proved even more exhilarating, and when he discovered fairy tales he was so excited he just had to share the experience. Welcome or not, he had gotten into the habit of dropping by his parents' house after work, and late one November afternoon he arrived, book in hand. Emma was cooking meat, an aroma Howard found tantalizing for in recent months his appetite had doubled and he was always hungry.

"Mother, can … can I tell you a story tonight?" he asked hesitantly. She scarcely acknowledged his presence. "A story from this book. See?"

Emma stared at *McGuffey's Reader* which he proffered over her stewpot.

"You mean there is a story in that thing?" she asked disbelieving. "I think what you're really after is an excuse to eat with us tonight. You should be going home to do chores for your uncle and aunt."

Howard prevailed, but before he could ingratiate himself by volunteering, she set him to sawing wood, then dispatched him to help his father who arrived dragging two seals. Ultimately he was allowed to eat, but his sister, Ruth, protested indignantly. "Mother, you know what Howard does? He eats here and eats again when he goes home," she charged. "Look, he's taking the biggest piece!"

"Never mind, Ruth. He's going to tell us a story tonight," Emma replied. She sounded dubious, but Sam smiled encouragement when Howard produced his primer after the meal.

"I have often wished that I had good ability to read books, but I never had the opportunity," Sam confessed. "Perhaps I was too old when I tried to learn. I hope our son has learned enough so he can help me read my Bible."

For this occasion, Howard had chosen "Jack and the Beanstalk," the tale of a brave lad and his widowed mother who were so desperately poor they were forced to sell their cow for a few beans. At first the audience was restless but when the beans grew into a giant beanstalk—Howard likened it to a huge willow shrub—and Jack climbed to a fabulous castle in the sky which was owned by the wicked giant who had killed his father, everyone became attentive.

There was some confusion about castles in general and about the red hen that laid the golden eggs which Howard described as a ptarmigan with red feathers, but when Jack stole the ogre's magic harp and the giant yelled, "Fee Fie Fo Fum! I smell the blood of an Englishman!" the audience tensed. Then Jack chopped down the beanstalk just in the nick of time, causing the giant to fall headlong to earth, and Jack and his mother got back his father's riches, and the company was wide-eyed.

"I never would have believed such a thing could happen," Emma marveled. "Son, will you have another story to tell us tomorrow night?"[7]

Welcomed home at last, Howard regaled his family with the sufferings of "Hansel and Gretel," "The Ugly Duckling," Dick Whittington who sold his cat to the king, and all the Grimm's classics. Mumangeena grew suspicious because he was coming in so late and came to investigate one night, only to become intrigued with the story of the poor miller's daughter who was indentured to the king with the promise she could spin straw into gold.

"How can a flour-maker be poor when we have to pay so much for flour?" she interrupted. "And how can anyone make money out of grass?"

She was further boggled by Rumpelstiltskin, the wicked little man who helped the girl spin gold but demanded her first-born in return. And the usually reticent Nayukuk dissolved into fits of laughter, not over the story, but at his wife's hopeless attempts to pronounce the name of the villain.[8]

During this heady period, Howard managed to charm both sets of parents into feeding him and suddenly he began to grow. Within a year he had reached his adult height of five feet, six inches and developed his strength to a point where he could face down his brother, Allen, hold his own at Eskimo football and box effectively.[9]

That winter, for the first time, he joined his peers competing in the traditional Eskimo games that were staged over the Christmas holidays. These were harsh competitions requiring agility and endurance—foot races, wrestling, high jumps, and gruesome tests of pain such as ear-pulling matches in which the unwary might be maimed for life.

Practicing by himself well away from the village, Howard discovered his greatest strength lay in jumping. Marking his progress on an old whale rib he planted upright behind a secluded tundra hummock, he quickly reached the five-foot level and then began to exceed his own height, moving smoothly from the required flat-footed position, kicking straight up with both feet well over his head.

There were giggles from the crowd when he appeared at the village meet, but his final jump of six feet, two inches won him second place and the grudging respect of those who had laughed. Changes in the youth were so impressive, that the following spring Sam Rock offered him the job of "boy" on his whaling crew.

Howard was ecstatic. He would have walked to hell for a chance to serve at his father's side, and the world in which he found himself was awesomely beautiful. They camped in a white cotton tent at the edge of a deep blue lead of open water about seven miles out on the frozen Chukchi Sea. Mountainous blocks of ice surrounded them, giant crystals fractured with prisms and shadow that subtly changed color with the constant shifting of ice and light. It was dangerous, for a reversal of wind would cause the ice pack to move and break, freeing their campsite from the shore, sending them floating towards Siberia. On more than one occasion they were forced to decamp and dash for land, leaping cracks and crevasses, but Howard was so intrigued with the skills by which experienced hunters managed to survive, he was not afraid.

Equally fascinating to him was the wildlife: comically fat seals, schools of white beluga whales that played like puppies, great skeins of eider ducks honking happily overhead. Then came gigantic bowheads which often measured more than 50 feet in length and weighed a ton per foot. Slow moving but remarkably graceful, they swam northward through narrow leads, traveling alone or in pairs, sometimes trailed by a young one. And when his crew launched their skin-covered umiak to paddle silently in pursuit, Howard was torn. It seemed an unequal contest—giant leviathan against the small, fragile boat—and he was concerned for the safety of his loved ones. Yet his father's whaling gun (antiquated though it was) evened the odds, and the killing of the majestic bowhead troubled Howard in ways he could not explain.

His job as "boy" was demanding. Not only was he expected to cook and run errands, but he must also pay strict attention to every action of the crew. He watched intently as Sam readied their weapons and organized the hunt, but, to his surprise, his Uncle Nayukuk was to be his best teacher. Much as he had come to love Nayukuk, Howard had wondered why his father entrusted such a lethargic individual with the key job of helmsman. Now he observed that the danger of the chase brought out the best in his adopted parent. With the safety of the entire crew at stake, his uncle proved the most skilled boat-handler among them.

Nayukuk's most remarkable performance occurred during Howard's first hunt. A whale was spotted about 4:30 a.m. and Howard, who was sleeping soundly in the cook tent, was awakened about an hour later by triumphant shouts and hearty laughter. The crew had launched swiftly, Sam in his accustomed position as harpooner in the bow, Nayukuk in the stern with his steering oar backing six paddlers. Swiftly he maneuvered their craft to the right side of the whale at a perfect angle. Sam hit the mark but the black powder bomb lodged neatly in the bowhead's temple failed to explode.

Angrily the wounded whale sounded, kicking up its massive flukes as it dove. The heavy hemp harpoon line played out at dizzying speed, then snagged on the bowsprit, pulling the umiak forward and down. Sam grappled for his hunting knife to sever the tow and, glancing over his shoulder in the process, saw a sight that made him smile in spite of their dangerous plight.

"The stern of the umiak was clear off the water, quite high," he recounted to Howard. "We were speeding forward by our bow and yawing and there was Nayukuk frantically trying to reach the water with his paddle, still doing his job. The spectacle was one of the most comical I have ever seen. I would have laughed out loud but at the moment we were being taken under by the whale."

He managed to cut the tow and they could afford to laugh because ultimately they captured the whale with the help of other crews. The broken bow of their umiak was quickly mended and later they made another successful strike, this time with Howard manning a paddle behind his father, acquitting himself well.

It was, by most counts, a successful season.[10] Howard learned quickly and showed no fear. Yet it became painfully obvious that he had no real appetite for hunting. Sam was reminded of the soft-heartedness of his grandfather and worried that the boy had inherited this weakness in the extreme. Older brother, Eebrulik, tried to take him in hand but he soon gave up, too.

"Howard just doesn't care to go," he told their father, bewildered. "I try to teach him but he doesn't want to hunt."[11]

Instead, Howard concentrated his efforts on formal education, for which he showed increasing aptitude. His teacher at the time was 26-year-old Tony Joule, the Point Hope Eskimo whose college education had been sponsored by Rev. Hoare. Joule was a respected hunter and a fine athlete, but he placed a high premium on book learning.

Like Howard, Joule had been adopted out. Some speculated he was actually Howard's brother, for Joule and Sam Rock were much alike in many ways and, although Joule claimed only a distant kinship, he took special interest in the precocious Rock boy.

The conditions under which Joule was forced to teach were dismal. His schoolroom measured only 20 by 24 feet and often housed more than 60 youngsters. Many were barely conversant in English (the language of instruction required by the Bureau of Education) and misbehaved to stave off boredom. To counter, Joule became a strict disciplinarian, beating the palms of malcontents with a heavy ruler to keep peace for those who wished to learn.

Eager students slogged a mile through heavy snows in the coldest weather to attend Joule's classes. Patiently they endured a shortage of desks, textbooks and other teaching materials.[12] In winter, the building was so cold that inkwells froze solid. When students attempted to thaw them near the pot-bellied stove, the glass sometimes exploded, spraying great splotches of ink on the whitewashed ceiling.[13] Yet Joule somehow managed to teach the basics and provoked in his brighter students a healthy curiosity about the world that lay beyond their isolated village.

Joule's personal experience with this new realm had been something of a horror story. As a young man with little grounding, he had been sent alone, all the way to Massachusetts by train in summer, dressed in winter clothing, complete with a felt hat. He had persevered, nonetheless; made his way through the foreign school system and returned to become the first Eskimo teacher hired by the Bureau of Indian Affairs. And it was apparent to him that his young charges would soon have to cope with many of the problems he had encountered, even if they never left home.[14]

In 1924 Congress had granted citizenship to all Native Americans and politicians began to argue over whether Eskimos should pay taxes if, indeed, they were allowed to vote. The next year, William Paul Sr., a Tlingit Indian from Southeastern Alaska, won a seat in the Territorial Legislature and when a bill was introduced to exclude Natives from public schools, Paul successfully organized to defeated it. Point Hope men, including Sam Rock and the elder, Samaroona, formed a village council to gain better leverage in the white man's political system. The village built a small, modern hospital. A reindeer-raising cooperative was formed. And then, on August 3, 1927, Peter Trimble Rowe, Episcopal Bishop of Alaska, pioneered the first airplane expedition to Point Hope, opening the remote area to anyone who could afford the price of a charter.

Increasing contact with the outsiders gave Howard tantalizing glimpses of the outside world. His mother's older brother, Tom Anikchok, had traveled the Canadian arctic with explorer Vilhjalmur Stefansson, and later, when Stefansson came to visit Anikchok in Point Hope, he selected Howard as his favorite companion. Adventurer Knud Rasmussen, Smithsonian-based anthropologist Ales Hrdlicka and a steady stream of well-traveled churchmen also singled the lad out. Howard made it his mission to absorb all he could from them, and Joule noted his progress.

In 1926 Point Hope school closed early for want of coal to heat it. The Bureau of Education was recruiting bright Eskimo youths for the industrial boarding school it had just opened at White Mountain about 400 miles south, and Joule suggested his advanced students attend. The training would equip them to enter the white man's society, he explained. White Mountain would provide a much finer education than he could give them at home.

Howard's schooling made him feel vaguely ashamed that he was not living in a frame house. He wondered what the white man's life was like. And he hoped he might adapt.[15] He was 15 years old—an adult by Eskimo standards. Because he would not hunt it was apparent even to his over-enthusiastic aunt that he faced a dismal future in the village. The Rev. Goodman recommended White Mountain. And with little or no hesitation, Sam consented to Howard's enrollment.

Emma displayed no emotion as her son set out in their umiak to meet the Indian Service boat *Boxer* which would provide transport. Would she miss him at all, Howard wondered? Was she relieved that he was leaving? One day, when he had mastered the white man's ways, he must return to make her proud.

Sam was smiling. Uncle Nayukuk seemed even more withdrawn than usual. Mumangeena stifled a sob, but she was heartened by the look of anticipation on the boy's face. This was something like the fairy tale he had told them, she decided, Jack going off to the giant's palace in the sky. No one, least of all Howard, could guess what lay in store for him beyond the confines of Point Hope. But Mumangeena trusted the shaman's prediction of a fine future for her nephew and Howard, himself, had come to believe it.

8

A Place In The World

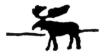

By DEFAULT, the task of educating Alaska's Native people fell to missionaries. In 1886, Presbyterian Sheldon Jackson beseeched the U.S. government to build schools and when refused, ten church groups divvied up the territory.[1] Later, tax monies helped fund missionary teachers and when this subsidy was discontinued, the government established dayschools only through fourth grade. Boarding institutions for higher levels remained church-sponsored until the influenza epidemic of 1917-1919 wiped out roughly one-tenth of the Native population and the government was forced to aid several hundred homeless youngsters. In the process, it was discovered that the arctic had no facility for higher learning, church-sponsored or otherwise, and the Department of Interior decided to build an industrial school there, along with orphanages at Bristol Bay and Cook Inlet to the south.

Policy of the new facilities was to select as students "potential native leaders of superior intelligence and capacity, to be subjected to intensified training to fit them for places of influence and power among their people." This lofty goal was undercut by a requirement that charity be offered government wards who did not respond well to intensified classes. There were 258 parentless children in the Bristol Bay area and many more in Cook Inlet. However, few potential students from the north were orphans and it was hoped the Eskimo industrial school would prove a showcase for leadership training.[2]

Thurman P. McCollester, a dayschool teacher at White Mountain, surveyed the site which was ultimately chosen for this experiment and, despite the fact it was the last stop on a desolate mail run, he gave it high marks. White Mountain was a new village, founded by wage-seeking Eskimos around a supply depot for the Council Mining District on the meandering Fish River about 22 miles from the shallow port of Golovin.

"The native population at present numbers about 200.... They are law-abiding, industrious and moral," McCollester wrote Jonathan Wagner, chief of the U.S. Bureau of Education, Alaska Division. "They have an elected council of five members who act as a governing board in all matters that concern village welfare, adjudicate any disputes or wrangles; and while it has no legal sanction, nevertheless all abide by what it rules."

The settlement could easily expand to double or triple its present size to accommodate Native families attracted by the educational facility, he wrote. And he suggested the site be made into a reservation to keep out "undesirable whites" who might corrupt the Native students.

McCollester took it upon himself to outline a course of study which would focus on Native industries such as fishing, hunting, reindeer husbandry, carving and fur-sewing. Carpentry, mechanics, household management, homemaking, nursing and sanitation would also be taught.

"I believe it would be a good plan to try to attract those who have skill together with sufficient general knowledge to assist the regular teachers," he concluded practically. "If we are to help the native, we must help him to help himself."[3]

Seattle-based Jonathan Wagner, newly appointed head of the U. S. Bureau of Education, Alaska Division, read the report with interest. According to McCollester's projections, the Eskimo students would be well-equipped to earn their keep while they studied, certainly an important consideration with the bureau's chronically-short budget. And McCollester, who had been a carpenter before he embarked on his teaching career, seemed ideally suited to oversee building of the new school.

William T. Lopp, Wagner's immediate superior who was familiar with the arctic by virtue of having taught there, failed to comment on the plan, perhaps because Wagner was busy edging the old-timer out of his job. Calling attention to Lopp's apparent disinterest, Wagner recommended all McCollester's suggestions to his supervisors in Washington, D.C. and they, in turn, appointed McCollester to head the facility.[4]

Less than a year later, in the fall of 1926, the "very best of the native youth of Northwest Alaska" were delivered to White Mountain[5] and in June of 1927 four of them were hailed as "the First Eskimo Graduating Class" in a flurry of press releases. Their commencement address was prepared by no less than John T. Tigert, the U.S. Commissioner of Education in Washington, D.C., and read over the radio from Seattle by Jonathan Wagner, whose static-laden words of encouragement were heard throughout the arctic.

One graduate, Roger Menadelook, had received a scholarship to Alaska

College in Fairbanks, Wagner reported. Two others, Isaac Newlin and his wife, Jennie, would stay to assist regular White Mountain staff, while Josephine Kalarak returned to better the lot of her village.[6]

Having no access to a radio, Howard Rock heard about the remarkable broadcast after the fact, as he was packing his meager belongings in an old sealskin bag. Curiously he looked up the word "scholarship" in Sam Rock's dictionary and that night when he previewed his future before falling asleep, he set his sights even higher than usual. There was no way for him to know that Roger Menadelook would soon drop out of college and attend Fairbanks High School to fill the appalling gaps in his White Mountain education[7] or that McCollester's hastily trained Eskimo teachers had been given such scanty grounding in English, their instruction would handicap their even less fortunate students.[8]

In September, 1927, Howard Rock embarked with the highest of hopes on the Indian Service supply ship, *Boxer.* His heart quickened as he heard the anchor chains rattle and watched the triangular sails belly out smartly with the afternoon winds. A hundred sea birds screamed in the ship's wake, vying for galley scraps, diving and soaring, and Howard became so absorbed in watching them, he scarcely noticed when Point Hope disappeared from view.

The *Boxer* was not as grand as her square-rigged predecessor *Bear,* which had thrilled Howard as a child, but she was a neatly designed schooner with one mast ingeniously serving as an exhaust for a 300 hp. diesel engine. She could do 9.6 knots which made up somewhat for the loss of aesthetics. She had been built by the Navy as a training ship for Annapolis and now served in the same capacity for Native youths in another of the government's ambitious "earn while you learn" programs.

Captain S.T.L. Whitlam noted approvingly that young Rock was quick to lend a hand where needed and allowed him to remain topside with the crew while other students were required to travel in the hold for warmth and safety. Whitlam was a short, jolly Britisher who spoke with much the same accent as the Rev. Goodman and Howard felt at home immediately. He knew most of the crew from Point Hope stopovers. Several of the trainees enjoyed showing him the ropes and he also spent time with Jimmy Kalerak, the personable Native cook from Golovin. Captain Whitlam prided himself on serving fresh apples, oranges or frozen strawberries with every meal and visits to Kalerak's galley quite literally proved fruitful.

At Nome, Howard debarked with the other students to await transport to Golovin Bay. Here government teachers greeted them gingerly. Each child had brought a bundle of untanned reindeer skins, required "tuition" which the school planned to use in sewing classes to provide them with warm outer clothing. Unfortunately, those who had traveled in the hold with the furs emerged with body lice and, although Howard was not infected, he suffered the humiliation of being "deloused" with the rank and file.

They were lodged in a boarding house under supervision of a buxom woman who had a big green bird that talked and small gold fish in a big glass bowl of water. The beds had real sheets and woolen blankets, all things that Howard had read about but never seen before.[9]

He shared a room with Edward Kanguk, 14, from Wales and Ernest Asuk, 11, and Paul Agayak, 15, from the reindeer camp at Sinuk. Martha Stein, Polly Solomon and Edna Driggs, who had traveled with him from Point Hope, occupied a room across the hall and were allowed to join them for meals at a restaurant called The Bakery.

Nome was a mining town, established in the rush of '98 when gold was discovered on its beaches. The population, which peaked at 30,000, had since dwindled to about 1,300. But it was the biggest city any of them had ever seen, with modern buildings, several automobiles, five miles of road, horses and a movie house.

The trouble was, the youngsters were not allowed to go anywhere on their own or associate with any of the local children.

They were growing increasingly restless when, after two weeks, they were joined by Robert Wagner. The jovial bureau chief arrived from the Seattle Office of Education for an inspection tour of White Mountain and embarked with them on the evening of September 28 aboard the big, gas-powered boat, *Donaldson*.

Again students were consigned to the hold with their reindeer skins, but they made the best of it. One boy played a tiny box organ and the rest sang songs that had been popularized in the arctic by missionaries and teachers—"Onward Christian Soldiers," "Home on the Range," "Amazing Grace," "My Old Kentucky Home," and "It Ain't Goin' to Rain No Mo." They sang with spirit, and Wagner, who was drawn below decks by their music, marveled that there were no sad faces among them.

Next morning they woke to the sight of a hilly shoreline with scatterings of spruce. Few, including Howard, had ever seen real trees and they crowded along the rail to stare. Two whales took up escort and, cold though it was, everyone stayed on deck to watch.

In early afternoon they anchored in Golovin Bay where they were met by a pert river boat named the *Sampan*. McCollester, their school principal, was at the helm. He was a tall, gray, tight-lipped man whom Howard found painfully formal. But he spoke with such earnest excitement about the progress of the school, the weary students became eager to see it.

McCollester planned to take them upriver that afternoon, but a strong wind came up, blowing water from the upper reaches of the bay, making it too shallow for the school boat. Instead, they overnighted at Dexter's Roadhouse, a gold rush relic which was the largest building in Golovin. Mr. Dexter, the owner, was a good-natured Boston Irishman with an Eskimo wife and four pretty daughters who made the stop enjoyable.

Next morning was clear and calm and they set off again, only to discover, five miles out, that the bay was beginning to freeze. Planks were fastened to the bow of the flat-bottomed scow to save it from being ground to pieces and men and boys stood forward to break ice ahead of the vessel.

By noon they'd worked their way up to the open water of Fish River Flats which afforded a view of well-forested country ahead. Howard had no idea there were so many trees in the world ... and how wonderful they smelled! Then, some 15 miles distant on the snaking river course, he saw the school, a mammoth complex of 11 well-ordered buildings set on a neatly cleared mountainside.

"A most inspiring view," Jonathan Wagner declared. Howard silently agreed, for the dormitory alone could house 65 and even in Nome he had seen nothing so impressive. No wonder the worn old man who was their principal seemed so proud. He had built the whole school in just two years, he told them, producing lumber from local trees with a portable sawmill and Eskimo labor.[10]

A large crowd of young people was at the riverbank to greet them when they arrived in mid-afternoon. Howard spotted Andrew Frankson and Maude Killingbuk from Point Hope but there was no time to talk. Incoming students were immediately delivered to the laundry room where once again they were checked for lice, given a scrubdown, haircuts and a change of clothing. Then they were hustled to the big dormitory; girls to the south wing, boys to the north.[11]

The setting was Spartan. Some 20 boys were to share one cold, close, foul-smelling room stocked with narrow bunks three tiers high. There was only one washbasin, no plumbing, and the drafty outhouses had no seats.

A bell announced supper. The dorm matron, Mrs. Burlingame, marshalled new recruits into line and lectured them roundly on etiquette. Then they were marched, single file, into the cavernous dining room where teachers were already seated at a corner table. Utter silence prevailed and Howard was wondering if they were to remain mute throughout the meal when Mr. McCollester rang a bell and the buzz of natural conversation followed.

"Where from?" the burly boy next to him asked in Eskimo, shoving a sad-looking mound of canned spinach aside with his fork and digging into his corned beef.

"Howard Rock from Point Hope. And you?"

"Ray Barster. Barrow. Never did care too much for Point Hopers but it pays to stick together here. Us against them."

"Them?" Howard asked, perplexed.

"McCollester and his crowd over there with all their fancy manners. Especially Neeley. See the younger one on the end with the good-looking wife. One of these days I'm going to take him on. Can you fight?"

"If necessary," Howard replied, trying to sound sure of himself. To his relief, a pretty girl across the table broke in boldly.

"Ray's the school bully," she said in excellent English, giving the Barrow boy a winning smile. "He's also the biggest, strongest boy we've got and he's mad because Mr. Neeley works him so hard."

Ray didn't seem offended and Howard was happy to turn his attention to the girl who introduced herself as Esther Apodruk from White Mountain.

"Where did you learn such good English?" he asked.

"I got sent to the orphanage near Anchorage after my mother died in the flu epidemic," she told him matter-of-factly, as if hard luck warranted no sympathy here.[12]

Supper was lackluster—white man's canned goods with nothing fresh. Food had been much better on the *Boxer*, Howard realized. But later, when he discovered two pianos, a Victrola with stacks of records and a library of books he had not read, he began to feel incredibly pleased with his luck. So much so, he was surprised when he heard someone sobbing after lights out. Little Ernest Asuk from Sinuk, he guessed. The boy was only 11. Probably came from a big, happy family.

His thoughts turned to Uncle Nayukuk and dear, silly Aunt Mumangeena, to Sam and Emma and his sister, Kiapuk, whom he loved so deeply. But the wave of homesickness that engulfed him was countered by the realization that he had no real place in Point Hope. His only hope lay in excelling at White Mountain.

Since Howard had enjoyed little social success with people he'd known all his life, he concentrated on his books. He was enrolled in the sixth-grade class of Flora Dexter, a daughter of the roadhouse-keeper he had met at Golovin. To his chagrin she was a year younger than he, but she'd just graduated from Chemawa Indian School in the States and proved to be a good teacher. Besides, age had little to do with grade level, for most

Eskimos had little chance at formal education. There were older students even in Jennie Newlin's kindergarten. One reindeer herder had presented himself at the school and asked to be placed in her beginners' class because she came from his village and he did not feel self-conscious with her.

"We big boys in reindeer camp, we never had a chance to go to school except one spring from February to May," he explained to Howard. "I'm glad to be able to learn the alphabet and numbers at last."[13]

Still, Howard felt oddly out of place. Few students shared his interest in literature and art, so he kept to himself, spending free time alone with his books or outdoors drawing. Then, late one afternoon, seeking a site from which to sketch the broad sweep of White Mountain, he happened on Mrs. Rolyn Ball, an upper-grade teacher. She appeared to be sketching a picture but from time to time she would look out at the mountain and hold up her pencil as if taking measurements.

Howard was intrigued. "Excuse me, ma'am, but I'm wondering what you are doing?" he interrupted. Mrs. Ball jumped a good foot, then blushed.

"Oblivious. Never saw you at all," she apologized, glancing at his sketchpad. "Are you an artist, too?"

"I try, ma'am, but I've had no real training. I wondered what you are doing when you … when you measure the air with your pencil?"

"Measure the air … " she repeated with smile, as if the thought amused her. "What's your name young man?"

"Howard Rock, ma'am," he answered uncomfortably. "I'm new."

"So am I, Mr. Rock. That's one reason I'm out here. Not easy to meet new people, is it?" she observed. "Here, have a seat and I'll teach you how to measure the air."

With one eye closed, using her pencil as a gauge, she showed him how to judge the proportions of a scene from afar.

"One of the basics," she said. "Perhaps next Saturday, if you're interested, I could explain perspective to you. You see drawing has rules just like everything else. That doesn't mean you have to stick with them, but you should understand a theory before you depart from it."

She was charming and direct; younger than her husband who also taught, but surprisingly well grounded in art.[14] She gladly schooled Howard in the fundamentals, praising his work and—even more important—becoming his first real friend. He marveled at the experience. Then, surer of himself because of her, he found courage to reach out to others.

Most of his classmates had been selected because they showed scholastic promise, but a fair number also came from troubled homes. With them Howard found a bond. Polly Solomon, who traveled from Point Hope with him, had begged Tony Joule to send her away to school because her family seemed determined to marry her off at 14 to a man she didn't love, and she looked to Howard for support. Ethel Smith of Kivalina escaped parental abuse by moving in with grandparents. Their death forced her back into a household where fighting grew so bitter she had pleaded to attend White Mountain despite the fact that she didn't have high grades.

"My teacher, Mr. Morelander, said he would send me reluctantly because he'd never seen me help anyone else. But I promised him I would learn as much as I could; that I would go home and help my people," she told Howard, earnestly. "Mr. Morelander put it in my mind."[15]

Ethel, in turn, planted the idea in Howard's mind. Hers was an idealistic goal much to his liking. It formed the basis of their firm friendship and he seriously considered committing himself to the same course.

At age 12, Sophie Amaruk was the youngest girl. Her brilliant father, Samuel Amaruk, had roomed with Jim Thorpe at Carlisle Indian School, then returned to Alaska to teach. The Indian Bureau transferred him every two years and, although motherless Sophie loved him and spoke all the languages from Barrow to Bethel because of their travels, she longed for a family. White Mountain served well and she quickly adopted Howard as her big brother.

"The snow is so crusty today, Howard … just right for sliding if only someone would do my arithmetic problems for me … " she would hint.

"Sophie, little one, you're better at math than I will ever be … "

"Exactly. I don't really need to do those little problems and I do so want to go out and play, Howard.… " and, laughing, he would give in and do the homework for her, knowing she was bright enough so that his indulgence would do her no harm.[16]

The boys in his class were much like himself, for any Eskimo family that allowed a good hunter to attend boarding school faced economic hardship. Most who enrolled lacked hunting skills, displayed a bookish bent and, with it, a keen curiosity to learn the ways of the whites.

Among the first friends Howard made were bespectacled Eugene Sours, a fun-loving youngster close to his own age from Shishmaref, and Mickey Downey of Kivalina who was two years their senior. Ray Barster continued to bait him, especially when he noticed Howard "shining up to that fancy Mrs. Ball," but Downey, who had entered school with Ray a year earlier, predicted the Barrow youth would not be with them long.

Scholastically, Howard found himself ahead of most students but, although he had qualified for fifth grade at Point Hope, it would take him four years of hard work to complete White Mountain grammar school because the curriculum was much broader. In addition to academics which filled each morning, boys were required to take 20 hours of manual training a week while the girls learned skin-sewing. Bill Burlingame taught the shop course so successfully that McCollester was able to contract his class out to the Territorial Road Commission to build an airport at Golovin. Howard proved adept as a mechanic and after he had completely dismantled and overhauled their woefully overworked Fordson tractor, Burlingame assigned him permanently to the job of repair which meant even longer hours.[17]

School operation also depended on student labor. Kitchen duty, which was shared by both boys and girls in three-week shifts, required rising at 5 a.m. and working late after supper. The cook, Billy Trigg, was easygoing and well-liked, but assisting him—baking bread, butchering meat, cleaning up and doing dishes for more than 40 people—was a formidable assignment. Girls did all the cleaning and laundry. Each was assigned a boy to sew for and was expected to make her own clothes. Water for cooking, cleaning and baths was laboriously hauled from the river by boys wearing wooden yokes that would support two buckets. Boys also chopped wood, ported coal, emptied slop, maintained the outhouses, looked after building repairs and ran the school boat.

Weekday evenings, with chores behind them, the youngsters were expected to reassemble in the dining room to do their homework under the vigilant eye of a teacher.[18]

"I'll be damned if I will!" Big Ray exploded one night after a particularly wearing afternoon of road repair under Neeley's direction. "I'm 21 and I'll do what I please, Everett Neeley. And if you don't like it you can fight me like a man."

No one dared breathe. It was strictly forbidden to call a teacher by his first name and, with his challenge, Ray had gone beyond all bounds. Neeley looked distressed. He and his recent bride, Gladys, were the youngest of the teachers. He was a hard taskmaster but generally well-liked. He enjoyed the Eskimo way of life, sometimes hunting and camping with the boys. Few bore him ill will.

"Look, Ray, I know it's been a hard week and you've got problems of your own," the teacher reasoned. "I'll overlook … "

"Like hell you will," Ray threatened. "I'm going to pound you to a pulp."

"All right!" Neeley said, slamming down his book with such force the small Asuk boy began to cry. "I've had enough of you to last a millennium, Ray Barster, and, God help me, I'll really enjoy taking you on. OUTSIDE!"

"What's a millennium?" Ernest Asuk asked anxiously.

"It means a long time," Howard told him, nearly trampling the boy in his haste to follow Neeley and Ray to the door.

"Do you think we should watch?" a small girl wondered.

"Best show of the year," Mickey Downey assured her, and it was. Neeley whipped Barster soundly and fair, and as Mickey had predicted, the Barrow bully departed shortly thereafter. Unfortunately, the work load of which he had complained remained unchanged, but most expected to work for a chance at higher education. Besides, there was plenty of fun to counter the drudgery.

Hiking, winter sports and basketball were encouraged. Movies were shown on Saturday nights and youngsters were invited to listen to a teacher's radio if the air waves were right to receive a popular program like the "Iceworms" from KFQD in Anchorage or something exotic from Samoa or Fiji.[19] There were special treats of homemade ice cream and fudge. And occasionally—to the utter delight of students and the distress of local missionaries—there was a dance.

Howard attended the first one with reservations, amused by preliminaries—the frantic pressing of pants and ties, skirts and ribbons—worried because he hadn't mastered the two-step. It was the heyday of the flapper. With the help of Gladys Neeley, who had been a beautician, most of the dorm girls bobbed their hair and shortened their skirts to appear dazzlingly daring in contrast to the long-haired, modestly clad village girls.

Participants ranged in age from three to 70. Lively music rattled nonstop out of the small Victrola—waltzes and fox trots, even square dances which everybody tried to call and everybody tried to dance—and it didn't matter if you could do the two-step or not.

A new round of excitement came with the Christmas holidays when White Mountain levied a poll tax on residents to host a banquet for the students. The school reciprocated with a lavish stage production. Blankets were tailored into curtains; banana crates hammered into appropriate scenery. The evening was made perfect by a fresh coat of powdery snow and a break in the winter storm that brought it.

Just about every man, woman and child from White Mountain and neighboring Council gathered in the school gym, dressed in their best. The program of music, punctuated by well-rehearsed poetry recitations, proved entertaining.

Santa and his helpers distributed a collection of gifts ranging from reindeer skins to wooden baskets full of frozen salmonberries. An older girl presented her gingham parka cover to a friend who had none. One small boy gave away all his neckties, forgetting to save any for himself. Carefully sewn items of clothing, figurines representing many hours of carving, drawings, verses and even, from Lord-knows-where at 40° below, a potted plant.

Harry Apodruk, age seven, recited "Just Before Christmas I'm As Good As I Can Be," provoking howls of laughter even from those who didn't know how devilish he could be. A husky, dusky Madonna rocked an Eskimo baby Jesus with tender authority. And when Howard lent his fine tenor to "Joy to the World" which ended the show, he sang from the heart.[20]

Earlier, when the girls were making popcorn balls, he had recounted with amusement how his father and the Rev. Hoare fried 900 doughnuts for a similar celebration so many years ago, but he'd been too busy to be homesick. He worked on a picture of White Mountain as a gift for Flora Dexter, labored over his first oil painting—depicting a rose and a book— for Mrs. Ball. He wrote some amusing poems for friends and a special one for Esther Apodruk. He carved toys for several of the younger children. They were his family, he realized. White Mountain had become home.

A few weeks later, Ambrose Kozevnikoff rattled Rock's bunk in the middle of the night yelling that he smelled smoke. The matron routinely locked their dormitory from the outside and no one could wake her. Nimbly Kozevnikoff legged it out the second- floor window, made it safely to the ground and alerted the staff. Howard and the older boys tied blankets together in preparation for lowering the children. Burlingame and Neeley arrived to free them, and a bucket brigade—uphill all the way from the riverbank—quelled the blaze.

The speed with which the youngsters worked was responsible for saving the dorm, for the fire had already broken though to the kitchen and was raging fiercely when discovered.

"I've been to war and seen soldiers work under pressure," Burlingame marveled, "but I've never seen people move this fast in all my life."[21]

"We just didn't want to miss Mrs. Burlingame's math test, tomorrow, sir," Howard said modestly. But, in truth, he had come to love the school and the following summer he elected to stay on when the majority of students returned to their villages.

9

The Beginnings of Eskimo Power

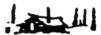

It was miserably hot. Sweat ran down Howard's brow, dripped off his chin and made rivulets on his bare back. He ached all over and citronella repellent couldn't begin to hold its own against the mosquitos and no-see-ums. Still, he'd never been happier.

Up on the riverbank he could hear Eugene Sours humming. The tune was "I'm in the Money" and Howard chuckled to himself. Mickey Downey appeared lugging another load of freight from the scow.

"Weighs a ton. Mining equipment, I guess," Mickey puffed. "Looks like another four hours work at least!"

"Could end up making as much as five dollars this week," Howard grinned.

Early that summer, old man McCollester contracted some of the White Mountain students to longshore for barges that came upriver to deliver to the mining camps and, because he had more heart than folks generally gave him credit for, he let them keep half their earnings. It was their first chance to make money and suddenly long hours delighted them.

When river traffic slackened, they ran their own lightering operation, piloting the *Sampan*, around the Fish River sand bars to ferry in supplies. They also worked for their keep in the school garden, helped the girls with canning and tended to school maintenance. But there was still time for swimming parties and camping and in late summer there were berry-picking expeditions and trips to fish camp where everyone turned out to catch and smoke salmon for the winter ahead. Only a dozen or so boarding students had stayed on but Howard's close friends were among them and it was the best summer ever.[1]

The following fall, raw-boned Mark Kineeveauk and his girl, Kitty John, enrolled from Point Hope along with the outgoing Lorena Lincoln of Kotzebue, Arthur "Big Boy" Upicksoun of Wainwright and Mickey

Downey's cousin George from Kivalina. Like Howard, they were all in their late teens—optimistic and ambitious—and they made a good team.

George Downey had lived briefly in Point Hope and, although he never spoke of his home life, Howard suspected it had been as painful as his own. George was a year older than Howard but they were much alike, introspective and self-contained, and almost from the beginning the two were inseparable.

To Howard's regret, Rolyn Ball and his wife had resigned under a cloud. She was rumored to have fallen in love with an older student and, whether or not it was true, Howard missed her company and the direction she had given his art. He had used up the oil paints she left before he really got the hand of mixing them but he continued to draw, knowing she would want him to keep trying.

"Mind if I come along?' George asked one evening as the would-be artist pulled on his rubber boots to hike the soggy tundra.

"O.K. If you don't mind stopping while I sketch,' Howard said. "I'm working on a panorama of the village.'

They struck off across the hills in silence, keeping well to the ridges. George stopped to collect some wildflower seeds and an old bird's nest. Then under a low tree, slightly off the beaten path, he noticed a small box covered with blue oil cloth.

"Should I open it?" he wondered.

"Go ahead." Howard said. "Probably just an old…"

"Oh my Lord…" Downey whispered.

The content was a skeleton, a child of about two. It's clothes were well preserved and flesh remained on the bones. Carefully, George replaced the cover and set the homemade coffin back exactly where he had found it.

Probably died in the winter when they couldn't dig the ground., Howard speculated. Or maybe they were traditional. Farther down the trail he saw a pair of tiny mukluks hanging from a tree and wished they'd taken another route.[2]

"Do you think that's the end of it?" George wanted to know. "Or do you think the soul lives on like they tell us in church?"

"I'm a good Christian," Howard answered. Then, embarrassed at his own smugness, he added that he hoped they did not have test the preacher's theory too soon.

"The old-timers say that you can come back," George persisted. "Maybe as a bird or animal or another person…"

Howard nodded. Samaroona had once told him that the spirit was a tiny spark that would never die. "What would you come back as?" he asked.

"A polar bear," George decided. "They are the strongest."

"But Eskimos hunt them," Howard reminded him. "I'd rather come back as an owl. They're smart, they can fly and nobody wants to eat one."

Through some miracle, Mr. McCollester had managed to acquire a battered pool table from the dwindling mining town of Council. "Big Boy" Upicksoun boasted he was a champ and Howard accepted the challenge, helping him sand down the pitted slate and rehabilitate the relic. Other boys soon joined in the competition, but try as they would, it was hard to beat Big Boy's edge.[3]

"We'll just have to content ourselves with being better looking than he is," Eugene suggested. "We never should have let him work at sanding that table himself."

Howard tried his hand at boxing with Mickey and Mark, suffered the girls' attempts to teach him the latest dance steps and went out of his way to help younger students who seemed homesick or blue. He became well-accepted in the village where he attended church each Sunday and was welcomed at the home of a local student, Frances Walker, and by Grandma Blatchford, a lively old lady who'd raised 17 children (including two sets of twins) and had countless grandchildren who were attached to the school. He sometimes visited Harry and John Apodruk, Esther's motherless young cousins, and he usually dropped by to see storekeeper "Pop" Hansen because the gregarious old pioneer was genuinely entertaining.

Yet, although he was accepted, Howard still felt awkwardly different. Instead of skating or participating in team sports that were popular, he preferred reading about the lives of great and famous painters. Others idolized baseball players and movie stars, but Howard's heroes were Michelangelo, Raphael, Leonardo da Vinci, Whistler, Sargent and Monet. And stranger yet was his taste in music, for he persisted in playing the classics— Beethoven, Mozart, Rachmaninoff—when Western music was the rage.[4]

"There is something special about the classics. Don't you hear it?" he asked George Downey who was most like himself. "It's the same thing I used to feel when I watched the best Eskimo dances in our village... . You know, something special ... "

But George didn't hear it. Such talk made him uncomfortable and there were no teachers with whom Howard felt free to discuss his "oddball" tastes. Flora Dexter was in Oregon attending teachers' college. The likable Neeley couple had transferred to Unalakleet. McCollester remained aloof and the rest of the staff seemed to prefer Western music themselves.

With the departure of Ray Barster, Howard became one of the longest-tenured students. He was, in addition, the top ranking student in his class, conscientious and dependable, and he soon found himself with special privileges.

"Howard, I don't want you to go if you don't want to, but you and George may go to reindeer roundup, if you wish," McCollester announced one night after supper. It was a generous offer. Although his brother, Eebrulik, sometimes worked as a reindeer herder, Howard had never been to a roundup and neither had Downey. It would be work, they realized, but they jumped at a chance to escape the class routine and go camping.[5]

The sky was a delicate pink the morning they set off in a party of joking herders. Frost sparkled on the grass and Howard became so engrossed with the scenery that about three miles out he carelessly fell into water past his knees. Their leader, Abraham Lincoln, let him slog on for a while, heavy-footed and shivering, then stopped to build a fire for lunch where the boy was allowed to change into dry boots. After that, Howard was decidedly more watchful, but neither he nor George had any real experience with the country. It was hard walking—lumpy tundra tussocks surrounded by spongy bog. Traveling from sunup to sundown toting 35-pound packs proved a real trial, and when they reached a shelter cabin, they could barely stay awake for supper.

"A good day's walk," Lincoln said encouragingly as they tumbled into their sleeping bags. He was one of the best herders in the country and without a doubt the finest speaker of their Eskimo language. But he'd also put in time at Chemawa School in Oregon where he'd mastered accounting, and he knew how tough the transition in lifestyles could be.

At sunup, stiff and sore, they were off again, stopping in early afternoon at another shelter cabin. Here they killed a reindeer for food and the boys were sent out for firewood which was scarce. They returned with just enough to cook supper and briefly warm the cabin. Congratulating themselves on having overcome their exhaustion they stayed up to listen to the stories of the herders, but the night was windy and when the fire went out neither could sleep for shivering.

Next day men were dispatched in all directions to search for the main body of the herd, but Lincoln kept Howard and George with him. It was still miserably cold. The boys were tired before they started and it wasn't until late afternoon that they located the animals. Then, rather than sleep in the open, they picked their way back over rugged tundra to the cabin as darkness fell.

"George, are you all right?"

"Darned icy," George muttered. "I'm down more than I'm up. How far do you think it is?"

"Probably another hundred miles," Howard predicted glumly. He could just barely see Lincoln up ahead.

"We'd better hurry or we're going to lose him" George said.

"I'd love to lose him," Howard grumbled. "You hurry if you want to. I think I'll just stay in this hole and sleep. Maybe the water will warm up after a while."

"Mind over matter," Downey insisted—then slipped and landed next to Howard who laughed in spite of himself.

"Behold, the mighty reindeer herders. I just don't know how an old guy like Lincoln manages."

"Well, he sure out-manages us," George conceded. And then with relief he spotted the distant glow of a kerosene lantern. Lincoln, who was probably in his 30s at the time, had reached the cabin and provided them with a beacon.

Two days later it all seemed worth the struggle as they watched 2,000 deer massing before them; big bucks in full velvet, buff-colored fawns trotting behind their svelte mothers. The herder's job was to keep the deer within bounds, driving them steadily in the direction of the big Golovin corral. At first the boys feared they might be stampeded by the nervous animals but they quickly discovered they could divert them by yelling, jumping and waving their arms. It was superb excitement.

"Two thousand animals, eight-thousand thundering hoofs," Howard calculated dramatically after they stood off a harrowing breakthrough and rerouted the animals to their appointed course.

"Thirty-thousand reindeer steaks and an ocean of reindeer stew," George enthused and Howard groaned at the thought. The man who was supposed to supply their group had failed to arrive from Golovin and they'd worked 36 hours without food.

"I'd even settle for canned spinach," Howard said wistfully.

"Fasting builds character," his friend maintained, but George was first in line when supplies finally arrived.

Toughened at last, the boys returned to the school quite proud of themselves. But the acquisition of a good education was their goal and they were glad to be back.

"Mark's talking about getting married," George reported one night as they put away their books. "I think he's going back to Point Hope."

"He could do better," Howard said.

"Well Kitty's an awfully nice girl... . "

"I didn't mean Kitty. Any man would be lucky to have her," Howard hastened to assure him. "But marriage so soon ... and going back to the village. It's the last thing I'd do."

"I'm with you," George considered. "Let the women eat their hearts out. Old George is in love with his books."

During the winter of 1929 nothing seemed to go right. Two girls contracted typhoid. An Eskimo from Council came in to the school nurse and wanted her to cure his chest cold. He had expected to get well in a week or so but it was obvious, even to the youngsters, that the man had tuberculosis in the advanced stages. McCollester had boasted to superiors a year earlier that there were no deaths on White Mountain's record but he had good reason to fear this luck would not hold.[6]

The appropriation McCollester sought to upgrade the light plant and heating system was turned down, as was his request for a large building to house the shop. Manual training and home economics classes for the rapidly expanding student body were relegated to a cramped, two-room log cabin set up on a "temporary basis" in 1926, a building so difficult to heat that the phonograph often froze.

Worse yet was the loss of cook Billy Trigg who took a better job in Nome. Meals suddenly diminished in quality and size. Complaints fell on deaf ears and when some older boys broke into the pantry to steal food for themselves and younger students, McCollester caught them and beat them.[7]

Nor was that the end of it. Records for the Bureau of Education for this period have been purged, but a Stanford University study made shortly thereafter states that responsible personnel at White Mountain were accused of "illicit relationships with Natives within the school" and were subsequently fired.[8]

Intimacy between men and women was no mystery to White Mountain students who came from homes where the only privacy was a reindeer skin blanket and darkness. Most were at the age when Eskimos married, and premarital sex was traditionally considered a natural thing. Since they had enrolled, however, they had been carefully chaperoned and the school's moral instruction left them with an ambivalence towards sex which could only have grown more clouded when advances came from faculty. There was no way a student could say "no" to a teacher and, in desperation, the older boys decided to take the problem to the village which McCollester had placed off-limits.

White Mountain had doubled in size since the building of the industrial school. Although McCollester had succeeded in having it declared a reservation where white men were not allowed, several were excepted because they had Eskimo families. Howard's first thought was to approach one of them on behalf of the students.

Foremost was Fred Walker, part Eskimo, part white Russian, fluent in both Eskimo and English, who served as preacher and judge. George Ashenfelter also qualified and any reservations Howard had about the gruff, outspoken German engineer were countered by his accomplished Eskimo wife. Both men had several children in school and should protests fail, teachers might be tempted to retaliate. Abraham Lincoln, who served as village mayor, sometimes worked for McCollester and students feared he would be compromised by their complaints.

Instead, they turned to Edward Hansen who had long been a thorn in the side of school authorities. As a young man Hansen had clerked at a store in Council but he'd moved to White Mountain with the earliest Eskimo settlers, opening a store to support himself. Caucasian and a bachelor, he was technically not allowed to stay on when the village gained reservation status. Area Superintendent E. L. Range had done his best to evict Hansen but residents successfully rose to his defense. Even the teachers liked him, especially after sampling his Faluman Backleseed, a Danish pastry involving 12 egg whites, which was his specialty as a cook. Boarding school students, who universally called the aging storekeeper "Pop," were in the habit of taking their problems to him and one afternoon, by pre-arrangement, a delegation of older boys quietly slipped off campus to call the area superintendent in Nome from Hansen's phone.

Although he emerged as leader of the group, Howard was ambivalent. McCollester had been better than fair with him, but had allowed others to be taken advantage of and taken advantage of them himself. McCollester led them to hope they might someday earn the rights of American citizens, he had also indentured them, allowing them no recourse. Even Eskimos were entitled to human dignity, Howard decided.

The protest took courage. If McCollester found out that they had complained against him, they would be at his mercy, and should higher authorities fail to believe them, they would certainly be expelled. Fortunately, the Nome office dispatched a team to investigate and the entire

White Mountain staff, with the exception of the Eskimo skin-sewing teacher, Jenny Richardson, resigned.[9]

Students who testified at the hearing remained anonymous and Howard and his friends never discussed the incident with those outside the school. However their coup was one of the first effective displays of Eskimo power—short of massacre—on record. And its potential was not lost on those who participated.

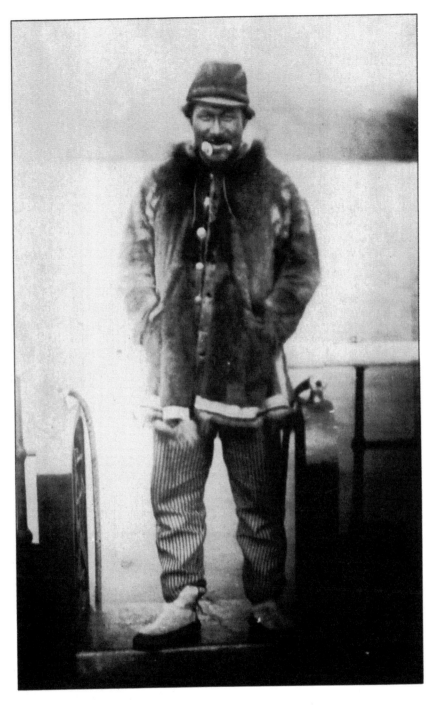

ATTUNGOWRUK Howard Rock's great uncle was a powerful Tigara chief who was reputed to be the strongest man in the arctic and ruled with an iron hand. This photo of him, taken about 1885, is in the scrapbook of Michael Healy, a captain for the U.S. Revenue Service which was forerunner for the Coast Guard in Alaskan waters. *Courtesy of the Huntington Library.*

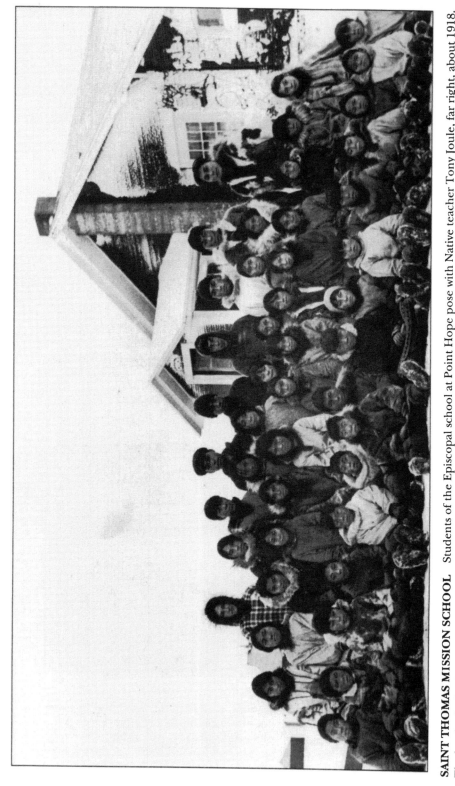

SAINT THOMAS MISSION SCHOOL Students of the Episcopal school at Point Hope pose with Native teacher Tony Joule, far right, about 1918. The boy in the back row, third from the left, appears to be Howard Rock. *Photo from Archives, Historical Collections, Episcopal Church.*

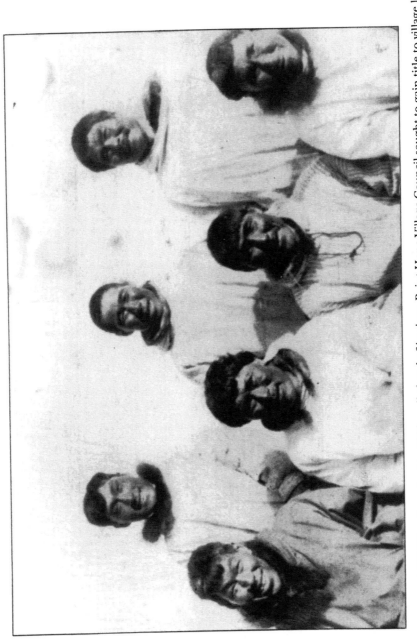

POINT HOPE VILLAGE COUNCIL Organized in 1928, well ahead of its time, Point Hope Village Council sought to gain title to village lands. Members are from back row left: Henry Nash, Boon Omiloruk and Howard's father, Sam Rock. In the front, from the left: Peter Keniak, Samaroona, Chu Kunnak and Amituk Puk. *Photo courtesy of Mr. and Mrs. David Frankson, Point Hope.*

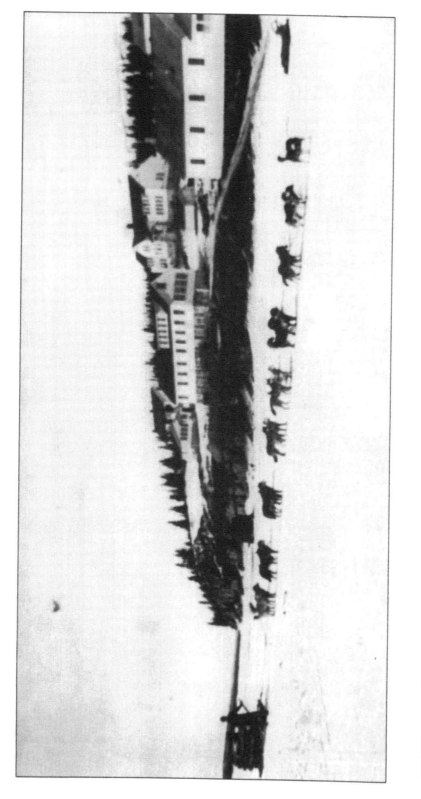

INDUSTRIAL SCHOOL Teacher Frank Pickett poses with his dog team on the frozen river below the government school at White Mountain village, about 60 miles northeast of Nome. The 11-building boarding facility was built with local labor by Thurman McCollester, the first principal, in 1925. *Photo courtesy of Frank and Mamie Pickett.*

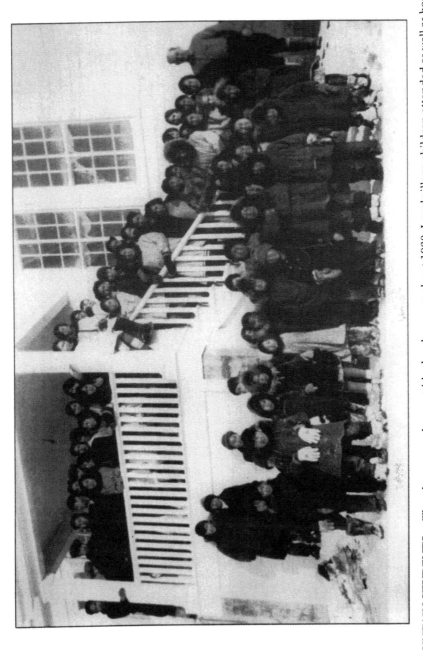

WHITE MOUNTAIN STUDENTS   The photo was taken outside the classroom about 1930. Local village children attended as well as boarding students from throughout the Alaskan arctic. *Courtesy of Frank and Mamie Pickett.*

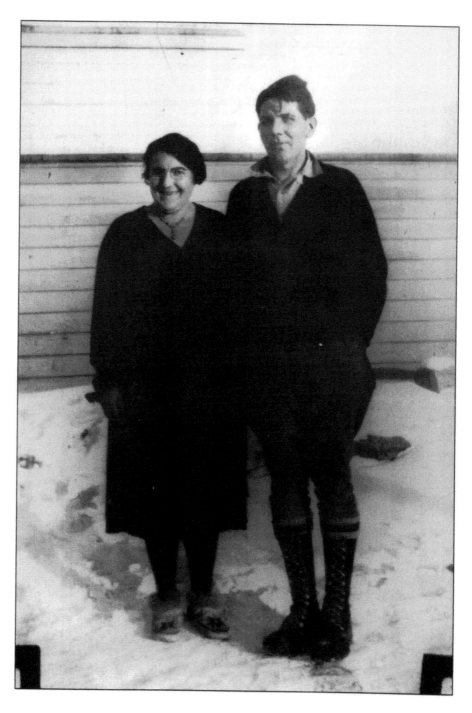

RUBY AND COLA DINGEE IN 1931   Mrs. Dingee, housemother at White Mountain and also an excellent artist, encouraged Howard Rock with his painting and finally arranged for him to apprentice with a well-known artist near her home in Oregon. Her husband, Cola, taught shop at the school. *Photo courtesy of Ruby Dingee.*

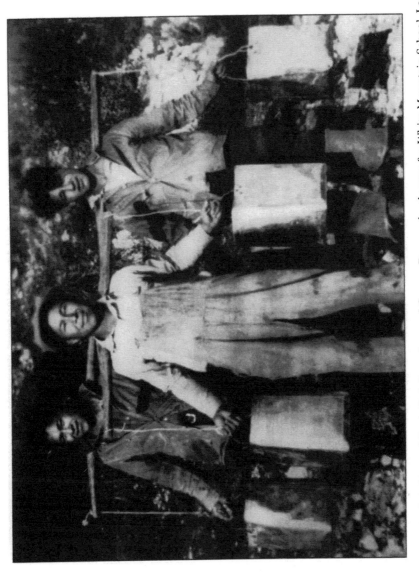

RUNNING WATER From the left, Howard Rock, Bob Sunnyboy and George Downey haul water for White Mountain School. Later plumbing was installed. *Photo courtesy of Frank and Mamie Pickett.*

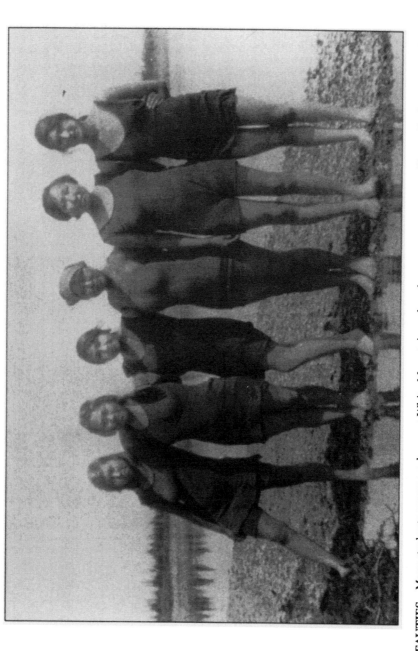

BATHING BEAUTIES Many students summered over at White Mountain rather than return to remote villages. Posing at a nearby lake are Mary Cole, (unidentified), Kitty John, Evelyn Weber, Pauline Curtis and Lorena Lincoln. *Photo courtesy of Grace Downie Ekvall.*

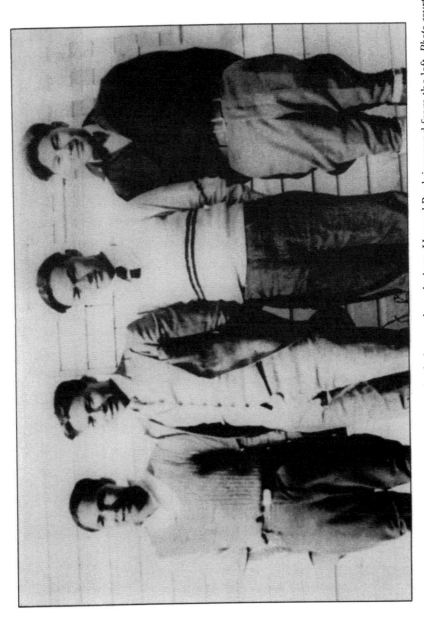

DRESSED FOR SUCCESS White Mountain students pose in their store-bought best. Howard Rock is second from the left. *Photo courtesy of Mamie and Frank Pickett.*

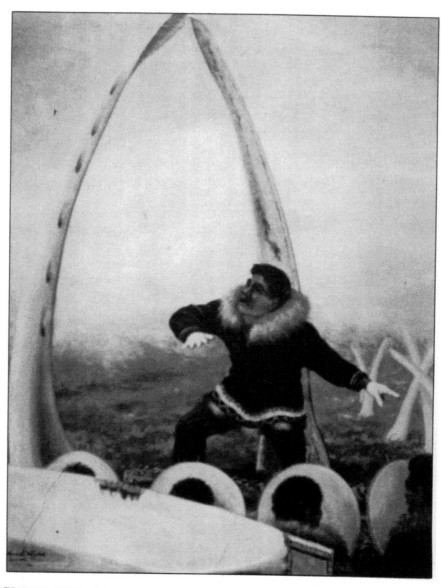

WHALE DANCE Painting of a traditional whale dance being peformed by Howard's brother Allen after he captured the largest whale ever taken at Point Hope, in 1961. *Anchorage Museum of History and Art*

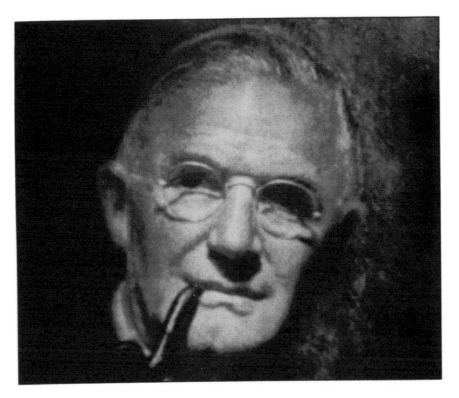

MAX SIEMES   A Navy photographer during World War II, Siemes was also an accomplished artist who made an excellent living doing scenics and portrait work in Trail, Ore. Howard served as his apprentice from 1934 to 1936. *His self portrait is courtesy of Mrs. Gladys Tuttle of Trail.*

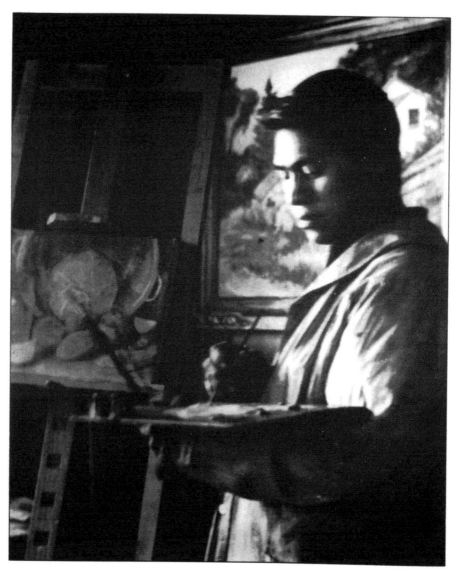

ROCK AS AN ART STUDENT This photo was taken by Ruby Dingee, who helped Howard enter the University of Washington art school.

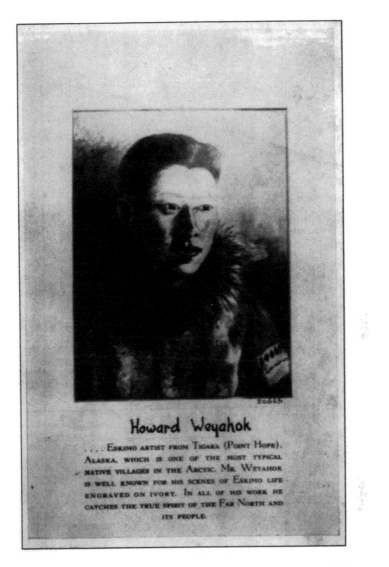

Howard Weyahok

. . . Eskimo artist from Tigara (Point Hope),
Alaska, which is one of the most typical
native villages in the Arctic. Mr. Weyahok
is well known for his scenes of Eskimo life
engraved on ivory. In all of his work he
catches the true spirit of the Far North and
its people.

SELF PORTRAIT   Howard Rock did this painting of himself under his Eskimo name, Weyahok, which means "Rock." The portrait was used to illustrate a book that featured up-and-coming Alaska Natives and was copied for a postcard by Kaeser & Blaire, Inc., Cincinnati, Ohio. *Courtesy of James Bush.*

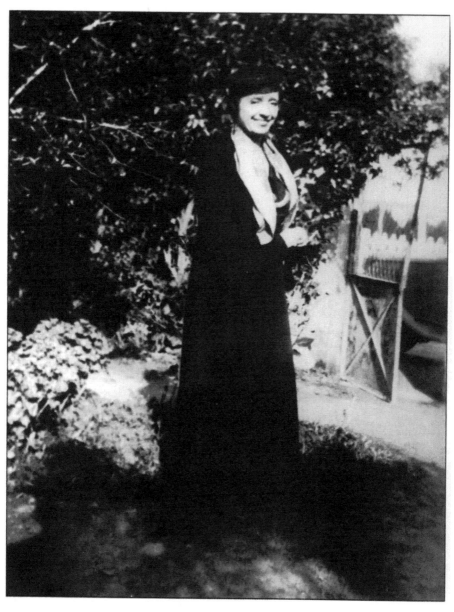

THE LOVE OF ROCK'S LIFE   Madelaine Faulcon, a wealthy French woman living in Tunisia, captured Rock's heart when he was stationed in North Africa with the Army Air Force during World War II. *Photo courtesy of Priscilla Faulcon Girardot.*

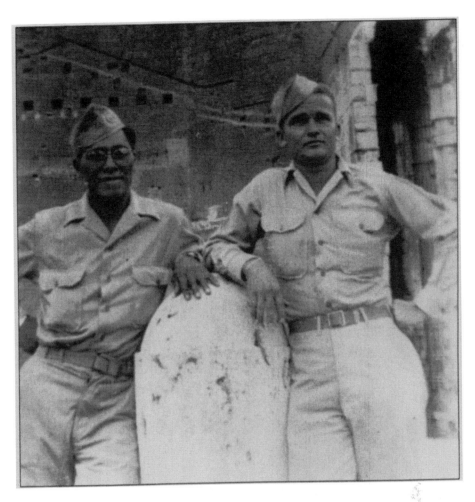

TOURING ROME Howard Rock and his Air Force buddy, Charlie Brooker, toured Rome on leave from their base in Tunisia in 1943. The war-torn country didn't offer much in the way of art, but Rock enjoyed the ancient buildings. *Photo courtesy of Charlie Brooker.*

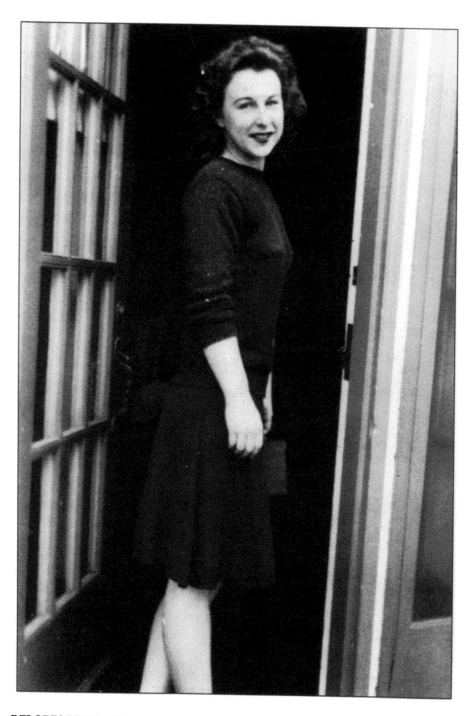

DELORES BROE   This photo was taken when Delores was a schoolgirl at Eklutna. Later she married Howard Rock in Seattle. The union lasted just a few months and Broe asked only for the return of her maiden name when she divorced him. *Photo courtesy of Mrs. Ruth Wallace.*

10

Evening The Score

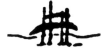

RAIN CAME IN GUSTS with the wind, drenching unfortunates on deck, and the mood inside the pilot house of the *Sampan* was even bleaker. Howard slumped over the helm staring glumly into the murk beyond the riverbank. George sat on a passenger bench playing absently with his penknife.

"Tough on McCollester," George said, breaking a long silence.

"They didn't fire him. The record reads, 'Resigned without prejudice,' "[1] Howard pointed out.

"That doesn't seem to make much difference."

"No," Howard conceded.

Since no transport but the school boat was available, the older boys had been required to escort McCollester and his teachers to Golovin to catch the steamship *Sierra* for the States. Now they were left to deal with their consciences as they waited for incoming replacements to debark from the same ship.

McCollester had called White Mountain home for six years. The school had been his dream. He'd built it almost single-handedly, but he boarded the *Sampan* to take his final turn at the helm without looking back. Family and staff crowded in sullenly behind him, scarcely speaking, leaving at the end of what seemed an interminable trip without good-byes. It was the height of the Depression and they had nothing to say to a scruffy league of half-educated Eskimos who had shattered their careers.

Methodically, McCollester shut down the engine as Howard had seen him do a hundred times, and reached for his slicker.

"She's all yours, boys," he'd said in a natural voice. And then, almost inaudibly, "Good luck to you."

"You, too, sir," George had the presence to answer, but the old man was already gone.

Eugene clambered in from the deck, dripping.

"The new teachers are coming!" he yelled. "Arthur's helping them with a ton of luggage."

"What are they like?" George asked.

"Can't be worse than that last bunch."

"We did what we had to do," Howard snapped. "Let's get on with it."

The newcomers clamored aboard laughing and joking in marked contrast to the passengers who had just left. Last on deck was a tall, balding man, almost as old as McCollester, who looked familiar.

"William Neeley, your new superintendent," he said, pushing through the crowd and offering his hand to Howard and George.

"Neeley ... " Howard puzzled.

"You probably knew my son, Everett," the older Neeley smiled. "He talked so much about the school, I just had to come and see it for myself."

"He was one of the best, sir," Howard said with a surge of relief.

Neeley Sr. was accompanied by his wife—a straightforward woman with an unusually high forehead like the models favored by old masters, Howard thought fleetingly—and their daughter, Wilma, who was about his own age and looked terribly sad. The other teachers were young. Frank and Mamie Pickett were newlyweds. The Goodrich couple could not have been married too long for their daughter was only a toddler.

"Does that do it? Everybody accounted for?" Neeley asked as George, Eugene and Arthur scrambled for the ropes. Howard started the engine, shoved it into reverse.

"WAIT!" came a bellow from shore.

"Martha!" Mrs. Neeley remembered. "She went back for her medicine kit."

"How could anyone forget Nurse Parrish?" Goodrich chuckled, and they docked once more. The woman's face was lost in the shadows of a dripping felt cloche but her hands were large and capable, her stride wide and her figure imposing.

"Leave me on the dock will you, you ingrates," she yelled cheerfully, shaking a dripping fist. "Who is going to nurse you through the pneumonia you're bound to catch from all this liquid Alaskan sunshine? Who is going to birth the babies and carry the lamp? ..."

George moved to help with her dunnage.

"Thank you, young man, but I prefer to carry my own medical bag," she said gruffly. "If you dropped it, I'd be forced to shoot you."

"Yes, ma'am," George said, backing off.

"You may cast off now, gentlemen," Neeley said with the faintest of smiles. "Our little company is definitely complete."

The following morning Howard and George appeared nervously in answer to Neeley's summons.

"Boys, you know that Mr. McCollester left this job on short notice," he began. George stopped breathing and Howard twisted his cap. There was an awkward pause.

"The point is that my teachers and I have no one to indoctrinate us in school routine," the new man continued, apparently unaware of their discomfort. "You are the longest-tenured boys. I know it's a lot to ask but we have no choice. We'd like you to familiarize us with school—study hours, curfews, the plant, everything."

George let out a sigh of relief.

"Yes, sir," Howard answered smartly.

"Unfortunately, in the confusion of leaving, the old staff neglected to order supplies. Mrs. Neeley and Mrs. Goodrich took stock last night and report that about the only goods left in the pantry are canned tomatoes, hominy, rice and beans. We're ordering by phone from Nome today, but there's no telling how long it will take to barge the groceries in."[2]

"We're used to making do, sir," Howard volunteered.

"So I hear," Neeley said.

On return from his summer in Kivalina, Mickey had purchased cigarettes from a steamship crewman and after supper he shared his good fortune with Howard and George in the shadow of the gym.

"Camels are the best!" Howard congratulated him. "When I get rich I'm going to buy Camels by the gross."

"You fellows missed your chance today filling Neeley in," Mickey said, leaning back against a tree and inhaling deeply. "You should have told him that a smoke break after supper was part of our routine, along with Tuesdays and Saturdays off."

"And maybe I should have put Camels on that grocery order," George grinned. "Sure would be a lot handier if the school supplied them."

"What do you think of this new group? Strict as the last ones?"

"Perhaps, but they're talking about piping in water. Mr. Neeley was surprised that we were still hauling it in this day and age," Howard reported. "Pickett's planning central heating and cold storage so the girls won't have to do all that canning,"

"Geeze, that would cut our workload in half," George figured.

"Then they'll hire us out to the Highway Commission again," Mickey speculated. "Don't get your hopes up."

But before freeze-up they piped running water into the kitchen and laundry room and were laying heating ducts. No one was hired out to the road commission. Instead, the new teachers worked hard to fill spare time with recreational activities—sled dog racing, hunting and trapping. Spanish and Oriental dances were introduced along with the Highland fling in gym class. Neeley's daughter, Wilma, overcame her shyness and managed to teach Howard to dance. There were military drills and a continuing round of skits and entertainments. Even classes were more fun.

"Sears and Roebuck is going to be one of your textbooks this semester," Mrs. Pickett announced, early on. "I figure anyone who graduates from the eighth grade should be able to order from this catalogue for a mother, father and a boy and girl. That will be your assignment."[3]

"Could we really do it? Really order something?" Arthur asked eagerly.

"If you have any money you can," she said. And suddenly she had their fullest attention. Everyone had a hilarious time with the make-believe family order: a lace-up corset for mother, short pants for junior, a bow tie and fedora for dad, diapers and a doll for baby. And when they passed that test, the older boys filled in their own wardrobes with the money they had earned longshoring.

"I ordered the dress shoes with the wing-tips," Howard told Arthur when they met after supper for their accustomed smoke. "It took all the money I'd saved."

"All mine, too," George sighed. "No more cigarettes for a while I guess, but it will be worth it. Imagine this handsome Eskimo in a real fedora."

Mickey fished an unopened pack of Camels from the pocket of his jacket.

"How'd you manage to get those?" Howard asked.

"My credit's good with Pop Hansen," he grinned. "Help yourself."

"Aren't you going to take one?" George asked.

"Nah, I just don't feel much like it," Mickey shrugged. "Maybe when I shake this cold."

"Maybe you should see the nurse," Howard suggested.

Early in the winter, Mickey had been mushing dogs with Robert Sunnyboy and cracked his ankle. The break wouldn't heal properly and the cold set in shortly thereafter. It seemed minor. Mickey didn't think much of it, but Martha Parrish noticed his cough and continuing limp and asked him to stop by the clinic.[4]

"When Mickey Downey doesn't want to smoke it's got to be serious," Howard decided. "I don't blame you for not wanting to face Nurse Parrish alone. But look, we'll all go up with you. Safety in numbers."

"Safety in numbers," Mrs. Parrish chuckled good-naturedly when she saw the small delegation of students on her doorstep that night. "Make yourselves at home, gentlemen. The tea kettle's on. And you, Mickey

Downey, come into my office. I won't keep you long."

But she did. When Martha Parrish emerged an hour later, she came out alone and unsmiling.

"I thank you for bringing him in, boys. He's far sicker than I thought. George, is there TB in the family?"

George nodded miserably. Parrish looked grim. There was no test she could give, but she'd seen enough cases to know consumption when she saw it. At her urging, Neeley chartered a plane to rush Mickey to a hospital but he was dead within the month.

"They're burying him in Nome. No way to get him back to Kivalina," George told Howard dejectedly during an evening walk.

"You know, he'd just turned 20 ..."

Howard dug in his pocket and pulled out a rumpled package of Camels.

"These were his," he said offering George the pack. "I saved em."

George accepted the token absently. They lit up.

"To Mickey," Howard said, exhaling a cloud of smoke.

"And to Pop Hansen whom *I* now owe for the pack."

With spring, student activities increased to a fevered pitch for the upper grades were producing a school yearbook "by direction of the Secretary of Interior, Office of Education, Washington, D.C."[5] Howard's panoramic sketch of White Mountain was selected as the cover design; his amusing account of reindeer herding with George became a leading feature of the book. And, since he was among the fastest and most accurate typists in Mrs. Neeley's business class, he was also drafted to reproduce the final 14-page manuscript for mimeographing.

As preface, students chose a quote from "Gentlemen Unafraid" by Barret Willoughby, an Alaskan writer who had become a national best seller.

Life is a wonderful gift in sunny Alaska and I have little sympathy with the unvarying grim and gloom tales of the 'silent, snowbound North'—tales that have made the very name of our country a synonym for cold and ugliness. To me Alaska stands for youth, romance, beauty. It stands for ships of adventure sailing into the sunsets trailing their wakes of amethyst on quiet amber seas. It stands for my motherland, gracious, flower-crowned, holding aloft serene pure peaks that are alabaster altars to God.

They called the yearbook "Nasevik," the Eskimo name for White Mountain which means "lookout."

"It is to be hoped that the name may be somewhat symbolic of the work of the White Mountain Industrial School," the young editors explained.[6]

>We realize that times have changed and that it is no longer possible for the Eskimo to live as he once did. The cream of the hunting has been skimmed and it is necessary to push farther back to obtain furs and food. The fur business has become a market wherein keen competition must be met. Barter can no longer be the sole idea in exchange. The Eskimo's association with the white man has created new tastes in food, in clothing, in manner of living. Sometimes this has been to the advantage of the Eskimo. Sometimes it has been to his disadvantage. Be that as it may, the problem exists and its solution lies with the younger generation. In its solving and in dealing with other problems constantly arising, it is necessary to keep in mind Nasevik—a wide look—a broad view of the whole situation.

George took over Howard's job as chief mechanic during the publishing effort, helping ready the school's construction equipment for the busy summer ahead. A new tractor had been ordered but they were also counting on the old Fordson and he elected to stay and overhaul it instead of going to Golovin on the *Sampan* with his friends to meet the first mail boat of the year.

The boys returned armed with packages.

"What ya got?" asked Harry Apodruk who turned out on the riverbank with a crowd of youngsters to welcome them back.

"Our stuff from Sears," Arthur told him excitedly. "Where's George? This bundle has his name on it."

Harry scratched his head.

"Gee, I haven't seen him all afternoon. He was up in the shop working on that engine."

Armed with his package, Howard tore up the hill to the shop.

"George, you handsome devil, your fedora has arrived!"

The door was closed. Howard pushed it open, blinking into the darkness.

"George?"

The place reeked of gasoline. They found George sprawled under the Fordson, out cold. Given fresh air he came to quickly and his friends kidded him about sleeping on the job. He was the biggest and healthiest boy in the school and nobody gave the accident much thought.

"You still look kind of gray," Howard observed, as his friend adjusted the brim of his new fedora. "But it makes you look like a bank president."

"We *all* look like bank presidents," Arthur insisted, consulting his new pocket watch. And they did.

Newspapers that came in the spring mail boat were full of stories about the stock market crash and the great Depression, but White Mountain remained strangely isolated from the national tragedy. Congress had actually appropriated money for expansion—another large schoolroom, shop, woodshed, even a new scow—so 1930 was to be their most ambitious building season. Frank Pickett helped draw up the plans, but family business called him outside for the summer and he singled out George for a little pep talk before he left.[7]

"You know as well as I do it's going to be tight. You've got maybe three months of good weather in which to build," he warned. "You're one of my most capable boys. I think you have future in this business, George. But you just haven't been carrying your own weight lately."

George stared down at his workboots. It was true. He'd taken to loafing without even realizing it. He'd try harder, he promised.

Later Martha Parrish took him aside.

"You smoking again, George?" she asked straight out.

"Can't afford it at the moment, Mrs. Parrish," he said with an honest grin. They'd guessed Martha smoked herself, against the rules of the school.

"Well in this case I'd rather hear you were inhaling a couple of packs a day," she said thoughtfully. "I don't much like that cough you've developed."

To her surprise, George answered he summons to the clinic meekly, for there wasn't much fight left in him. The bout with the gasoline fumes had apparently damaged his lungs.[8] Tuberculosis set in. It was already in the advanced staged and she told him frankly there was no hope.

"Do you think, maybe, I could go home?" he asked. "I keep thinking about Mickey, being buried in Nome among strangers..."

"We'll get you home," she promised, swallowing hard. "You'll have some time with your family before ... before you have to give up."

Howard built George a stout box for his things in lieu of a suitcase and helped him pack. His clothes hung loose on him now and he was forced to lean on Howard en route to the river where the float plane had landed. Other students crowded around, unknowing, wishing him well, laughing and joking as the pilot prepared for take off.

"All right, gang, time to go," the flyer announced. Everyone moved aside except Howard.

"Tell the boys to be good—Arthur and Eugene and Harry," George said in a husky voice, clutching his treasured fedora. "And be good yourself, Howard, Be the *very best*. You have to do it all and see it all for me."

Howard nodded, grateful that the roar of the engine overcame his own muddled words. Awkwardly he groped for his friend's thin hand, then backed off so the others wouldn't see his tears. The plane roared away in a cloud of spray. All eyes were on it.

It was a singularly fine day. The crest of the riverbank was bright with flowers. Snipes called to one another in the tender young grasses and Martha Parrish lingered after the crowd had gone, watching a solitary straggler. She had served in the front lines in France during World War I and she had lost her husband and her brother in the same day's battle. She understood grief and she knew time healed. But she had never seen anyone as desolate as the Rock boy at the loss of his friend. What would become of him, she wondered?

The summer was a continuing series of 12-hour shifts, raising the school addition, lining out the new woodshed, camping in Golovin to build the new scow. Howard was the first to volunteer for overtime, the last to lay down his tools each night.

Word came in September that George was dead. Howard heard it from barge crewmen who had just come down from Kivalina. It was early afternoon. He'd just been paid for longshoring so he took his money to Pop Hansen's store. Pop was in the midst of telling a yarn to some locals—talking nonstop as usual—and Howard waited quietly in a corner. The locals left.

"What can I do for you, Howard?"

"Last winter you gave Mickey Downey credit for some Camels?" Howard said.

"Why yes ... Mickey was always good ..."

"George was planning to pay it off."

"Say, how's George doing?"

"Same as Mickey." Howard said flatly. "I'd like to pay you for those Camels."

"Howard, you don't have to ..."

"Yes, I do, Pop," he said. And Hansen rang up the sale without another word.

11

Direction at Last

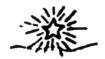

AMONG THE NEW TEACHERS that Neeley hired were Ruby and Cola Dingee, who served as house parents. Mr. Dingee proved easy to work with as a shop teacher and students just naturally called Mrs. Dingee "Ma" although she was no older than other house mothers with whom they'd been more formal. She was a squarish woman with glasses. Pleasant enough, Howard thought, but he took no particular notice of her until the afternoon he found her ensconced with oil paints and easel, rapidly transferring one of his favorite views to canvas.

"Why, you're really good!" he blurted out.

"Tolerable," she allowed. "And improving."

"Do you mind if I watch," he asked.

"Suit yourself," she said.

Ruby Dingee had 37 dormitory students under her charge and she wasn't about to play favorites. She was a brusque, practical woman, but she loved art and with a minimal amount of training had become a fine painter. Howard, who'd never seen her equal, shadowed her until she relented and asked to see his work.

"I know it's a poor start ..." he apologized as she leafed wordlessly through his sketchbook.

"Nonsense, young man," she finally declared. "I'd say there isn't much you couldn't do with a little training."[1]

Without further prompting, she set out to give it to him—making time in each busy week, financing oil paints, proving both a stern critic and a staunch backer—and Howard progressed rapidly. With the death of George Downey he had distanced himself from his friends. Art filled the void.

Expanded facilities at White Mountain drew new students in 1931, among them two lads from Nome who had been tried and found guilty of stealing a car. Mr. Neeley was outraged. The yearbook specifically stated that his school had been established to give training and encouragement to "exceptional young people," but the judge insisted that "industrial school" was just a pseudonym for reformatory.

To make matters worse, the ringleader, Joe Bill, was the only Indian in the student body. Big, bright and belligerent, he was as reluctant to join their ranks as Neeley was to have him. About the only thing that interested him was cowboy movies. He affected Western dress and seemed to be spoiling for a shootout.[2]

Howard first encountered him in the school music room. Everyone else was at a basketball game when Bill stalked in armed with a stack of country western records and demanded use of the Victrola on which Rock was playing Beethoven.

"I won't be much longer. Ever listen to the classics?" Howard asked, looking up from his sketchpad.

"I been watching you," Bill glowered. "You're the one who's always patting paint all around. I think you're a pansy, that's what!"

Howard had never heard the term "pansy" used to refer to someone who was effeminate and the idea of comparing himself to one of those monkey-faced windowbox flowers made him laugh out loud.

"Don't you dare laugh at me! You're all down on me because I'm Indian and I've had a belly full of it," Bill yelled. Then, without warning, he socked Rock squarely in the jaw. He was tall and packed a good punch, but Howard reacted instinctively, flooring the newcomer with a single, well-placed blow. Bill wobbled to his feet, gingerly felt his jaw and backed off.

"The first Indian I ever met was named Harper and he'd just climbed Mt. McKinley. Hardly what you'd call a pansy! Now, you can stay quietly and listen to Beethoven or you can leave," Howard declared. And to his amazement Joe Bill laughed and sat down to listen.

Another newcomer to the dormitory that year was Mary Ellen Ashenfelter, a bright, vivacious village girl. Her father, George, had come to the area from Germany as a mining engineer and supported his large Eskimo family in style until it was discovered he was dying of cancer. His move to Anchorage for treatment left his wife, Mary, with seven children to support. Their oldest son, Alex, returned from Chemawa Indian School in Oregon to help but the family was forced to seek government board for Mary Ellen. Although only 14, the girl was mature with a stunning figure and Howard's immediate attraction to her caused comment.[3]

"He told me the other day he admired her *pluck*," Bob Sunnyboy told

Lilly Nash when he noticed Howard helping the newcomer with her homework. "I thought he was going with Esther Apodruk."

"He is going with Esther if he's going with anyone," Lilly defended, "but Howard wants to make something of himself before he gets involved. That's what he promised poor George Downey. Maybe he really *does* admire Mary Ellen's pluck."[4]

Howard did, indeed, have ambitions beyond the wildest dreams of his peers. He was at the head of his class and had just won the territory-wide essay contest conducted by the Alaska Department of Forestry. His paintings were selling for the unheard of price of $2.50 per canvas. Mrs. Dingee was encouraging him to become a professional artist and, for the first time, he considered higher education.

Dr. H. Dewey Anderson and Dr. Walter Crosby Eells, Department of Education, Stanford University, had teamed to survey Native schools throughout Alaska. They were funded by a Carnegie Foundation grant backed by the United States Commissioner of Education. Their assignment was so important that a joint session of the Territorial Legislature was convened to honor them. But Howard had ample chance to talk to Dr. Eells when they were stranded on the mud flats of Golovin Bay in the *Sampan* for several hours en route to White Mountain.[5]

"What would be the chances of an Eskimo attending a regular college ... not a special Indian school like Carlisle or one of those religious institutions, but a real college like Stanford?" he asked. Eells, who had not quailed through the storm that battered their boat or their long stranding, suddenly looked ill-at-ease.

"Tough, boy," he answered honestly. "That's not to put down your teachers here. They're good, well-meaning folks. But with the emphasis on shop, skin-sewing and all your other work like, er, boat salvage ... well, there's just not enough time for the academics."

Frank Pickett whooped with pride, waving a rotting incisor aloft and the patient, a grizzled prospector, sighed in relief. With a two-hour short course from his dentist back in Washington and a set of wooden-handled tools (recently outlawed because they could not be sterilized), Pickett had extracted 268 teeth from grateful students, miners and villagers who had no other alternatives. Martha Parrish became expert at administering Novocain and Howard developed flair as a dental assistant, for there were no bona fide dentists or physicians within 80 miles.

TB continued to haunt them. Nurse Parrish wrongly suspected Joe Bill might be a carrier and confined him for some time to a tent outside their tiny clinic with Isaac Eralook, who was infected, but she failed to note symptoms in a girl named Mary Ann who came to them that year from Nome.

"Do you know anything about that child, Martha?" Mamie Pickett asked one evening over supper. "The girls and I were hiking up on the hill today and she began dancing around the cemetery. Actually dancing on the graves." [6]

"One of the students tells me she nursed her brother-in-law until he died of TB, but she doesn't appear to have it," Mrs. Parrish worried. "If only we had a test ..."

No one was particularly surprised when Mary Ann was buried a couple of months later near where she'd danced. As was their custom, the younger children hauled their sleds up the hill to the cemetery and slid back down after services. Somehow it didn't seem much like a funeral.

Decidedly more devastating was the flu epidemic that followed. It began with a church conference attended by delegates from throughout the arctic. Each family took in visitors, few of whom had brought provisions, and when sickness struck, White Mountain was almost out of food and firewood. [7]

Every dormitory student and most of the staff were stricken and the village death toll began to mount. Grace Downie, their youngest teacher, stayed on her feet along with Martha Parrish and Mr. Dingee, although they were all infected. Mrs. Pickett, Ma Dingee and Mrs. Neeley remained healthy and cooked endless buckets of stew for villagers who sent two men up each day for the much-needed rations.

The church became a morgue. Frank Pickett and Cola Dingee went to Solomon for a box of dynamite and returned to blast a hole in the frozen ground to serve as a mass grave. Older boys struggled out to help Pickett build coffins—six for villagers and a small one for a young student named Peter. [8]

Numbed by the earlier deaths of his sister and his closest friends, feverish with the nameless malady the churchmen had brought, Howard hammered coffin nails with the rest. There seemed no rhyme nor reason for it. Isaac Eralook, a brilliant young Eskimo who'd entered White Mountain with him half a decade earlier, had survived the flu but would soon die of consumption. It was enough to shake one's faith.

The Rev. Pearson, their local preacher, argued passionately that God was on the side of his Swedish Covenant Church. Visiting Friends missionaries insisted He stood with the Quakers and was against dancing. Methodists claimed God belonged to them and had no quarrel with dance.... If there *was* a Supreme Being, Howard found himself wondering, was he paying attention? "Blasphemy," he thought, alarmed, and dutifully hammered on, humming a favorite hymn.

Warm weather wafted in on the heels of the disaster. Wilma Neeley was intrigued to find herself playing horseshoes in the snow with Eskimo friends on May 20 and several picnics were organized despite lingering drifts.[9] Everyone bet on the day, hour and minute when the ice would roar out of the Fish River. And Howard Rock, age 20, sat down to prepare a valedictory address titled "Our Obligations," for his eighth-grade graduation. Ethel Smith, who had given him inspiration for the speech, was now back in Kivalina teaching school alongside Tony Joule, and Howard wondered fleetingly where his own obligation lay.[10]

Although White Mountain offered no regular high school program, Howard elected to stay on. Mr. Neeley, who was an excellent history teacher, tutored advanced students in that subject and algebra. Mr. Dingee and Frank Pickett offered additional shop training. Poetry was one of the subjects of Mamie Pickett's English course that semester and Howard tried his hand at verse, choosing "The Loon" for his publishing debut in *Nasevik*:[11]

Spirit of Wilderness-
Song of Desolation –
Rover of the Deep thy
Mournful cry I hear.

Through the still air,
When the day is dying
In the western sky;
Thy monotonous cry
Sounds long and drear.

When dawn streaks the east,
And my dreaming eyes
Are scarcely awake
Still I hear thy cry
Through the murm'ring sky.

Child of the Desolate Lands –
Rover of the wildest Strands-
Thy cry of distress can dart
Cold chills through the stoutest heart.

The most valuable instruction Howard would receive was a two-week course in ivory carving from Norman Lee, a slight, genial Eskimo who came as a special guest from Nome.[12] With distaste, Howard had watched Native carvers hawk crude artifacts on Nome street corners and he was engrossed in learning to paint. Still, Lee was an excellent craftsman and Howard worked hard to please him.[13]

"You could become a fine carver," Lee told him toward the end of his stay.

"Thank you, sir," Howard said, choosing his words carefully, not wanting to hurt the neat, old gentleman. "But I really love working with oils … something more modern."

Lee had admired Rock's canvases. He understood. "But sometimes it's difficult to get established as a painter," he noted practically. "Good, traditional carving skills are like money in the bank."

Ruby Dingee had 59 children under her charge that year and little free time, but she encouraged Howard to try portraiture.

"Maybe if I started with a dog," he suggested. "If it doesn't work out well, a dog isn't going to complain."

Wilma Neeley's beloved German shepherd, Jock, had been killed by a pack of malamutes and, recalling his own sadness at the loss of a pet, Howard labored to bring Jock to life on canvas. Both artist and owner were delighted with the results and Howard began to look for more challenging subjects.[14]

"Esther Apodruk's grandfather, Tom, is going to sit for me," he announced happily one day after school.

"Goodness, old Tom's got more crags and valleys on that face of his than Mt. McKinley," Ma Dingee warned. "He may not be as charitable as the lamented Jock." But a handsome portrait resulted. Even school superintendent Leigh Robinson was impressed.

In many ways this was White Mountain's best period, for teachers, worried by accounts of the Depression, elected to remain at their jobs far longer than was usual, providing the boarding school with real continuity. Many students had called the place home for five years or more and there was a strong sense of family.

There were several Indians now and the outgoing Hunter family, Athabascans from Fortuna Lodge, was quick to fit in. Donald Hunter had served as a mess boy on the steamship *Yukon* and Howard and Arthur, who'd worked the boats before coming to White Mountain, welcomed his company. With Fred Chaney and Robert Sunnyboy, who also hailed from the river region, they formed a formidable crew for the *Sampan* and turned up proudly in real Navy uniforms—Howard and Robert as officers,

Arthur, Frank and Donald as common seamen—for the school's masquerade dance.[15]

Even Joe Bill settled down. With the announced goal of becoming a movie star, he distinguished himself as their smoothest ballroom dancer. He also captained the winning spelling team and lent a hand with the yearbook—writing in praise of classical music, no less.[16]

In mid-winter Warren Oakes, vice president of American Airways, was storm-bound for several days at White Mountain. Time hung heavy on the hands of the New York executive. He gave a talk to the student body on his flight from the East Coast to Alaska, got to know them on a first-name basis and left promising to send the shop boys an airplane engine on which to practice flight mechanics.[17] Arthur was overjoyed because he'd made up his mind to become a mechanic. He had just been named class valedictorian and Howard envied his sense of direction.

The Dingees did not extend their teaching contract the following year which meant the end of art lessons. Howard considered applying to one of the Indian schools outside the Territory but Abraham Lincoln, who'd attended, said they were little different from White Mountain. Nick Gray, a villager who had returned after long years of traveling in the States, urged Howard to "see the country and get involved." Gray—who was part Eskimo and part Jewish—had become dazzled by the Indian lawyer from Juneau, William Paul, who was battling for Native rights. But Howard was more concerned about making a living.[18]

At the time, a crew from Metro-Goldwyn-Mayer Studio was wintering in Point Hope to film "Eskimo," a movie featuring a local man called Mala. The star, who was Howard's cousin, had asked Eebrulik Rock to play his second lead and Howard's brother had acquitted himself well. Now, according to newspapers, Eebrulik had been invited to Hollywood to appear at the movie's lavish premiere.[19] Joe Bill, who worshiped Mala above all his celluloid heroes, was wild with envy. Howard found the idea of Eebrulik rubbing shoulders with Hollywood greats amusing for he remembered him as a gruff, no-nonsense hunter. But privately he had to admit that the thought of his virtually unschooled sibling's cosmopolitan success was galling.

Then, while working longshore, he learned his brother Rupert, 15, had died in a fall. The boy was the family pride— personable, strong, a good hunter and, some claimed, every bit as fine an artist as Howard. His mother would be devastated, Howard realized.

Briefly he considered going home, but to do what? He couldn't become a storekeeper like Andrew Frankson. Math was his only poor subject.

Nor did he fancy becoming a schoolteacher. He was on the verge of giving up his studies and going to sea when a letter arrived with the best news of his life.

Ma Dingee had contacted Max Siemes, an established artist near her home in Trail, Oregon, who agreed to take Howard on as an apprentice in exchange for help on his farm. She'd also written Charles Wesley Hawkesworth, who was acting chief of the Alaska Bureau of Indian Affairs, to inquire if Howard might work his passage to Seattle on the *North Star*. Hawkesworth was a fine man and she was certain he'd work something out. The only hurdle was raising the train fare from Seattle to Medford, Oregon, near Siemes home.[20]

Howard took her letter to Mr. Neeley who seemed every bit as pleased as he was, but who had no idea how to raise the money. A nationwide bank holiday in March had frozen his savings and the school had no contingency fund. In desperation Neeley called Superintendent Robinson in Nome and Howard listened in anxiously.

"Ruffle? What do you mean have a ruffle?" he heard the line buzz and crackle. Neeley shook the receiver angrily. He and the boys would probably have to go out and repair the cables again.

"Oh, raffle. What a splendid idea!" he beamed. "If Tom Apodruk doesn't object ... If you can handle the tickets in Nome."[21]

Grandfather Apodruk graciously allowed them to raffle off his portrait and was more than a little amused to see it prominently displayed in a bank window in Nome. The venture raised almost $100. Grace Downie arranged for her mother to meet Howard in Seattle. But the *North Star* failed to pick him up.

The winter that followed was disheartening, not only for Howard, who had stayed on at White Mountain for want of anything better to do, but because it was learned that the school would close. Stanford University researchers had published a report that gave it low marks scholastically and alluded to the scandal of McCollester's firing.[22] The killing factor, though, was cost of maintaining their isolated facility in face of the Depression. Exceptional youngsters would be transferred to the orphanage at Eklutna near Anchorage. The rest were to be introduced to types of work best fitted for local villages.[23]

Students were stunned. No one wanted to go "back to burning seal oil and melting ice blocks for showers," as Lorena Lincoln put it. Still, they had a year to prove they were the best and the brightest.

The 1934 White Mountain yearbook was the group's most ambitious effort and Howard Rock typed the finished manuscript with satisfaction.

His cover, depicting two seals on an ice floe under a snow-capped *Nasevik* logo, was a noticeable improvement over years past. So was his writing in praise of the traditional Eskimo igloo.

His disappointment at missing the boat was tempered by a letter from Ma Dingee assuring him Mr. Siemes would keep his apprenticeship open. Charles Hawkesworth arranged for late summer passage south on the *North Star* and Howard was glad he had not missed the final year of school.

Suddenly, everyone was making commitments. Lilly Nash and Frances Walker were married at the school in the first formal wedding anyone had ever attended with Howard serving as best man.[24] Esther Apodruk fell in love with a reindeer herder who couldn't read. Eighteen students, including Arthur and Mary Ellen Ashenfelter, had been accepted at Eklutna. Lorena Lincoln, who'd been Neeley's secretary, got a job in the hospital at Nome. And many looked farther afield. Irene Schaeffer, who had been Howard's girl briefly before transferring to Ferris Institute in Grand Rapids, Michigan, was doing well as a student teacher in the States.[25] Harry Apodruk dreamed of becoming an artist in Seattle and Mary Ellen swore she'd live there one day, too.[26]

Those bound for Eklutna sailed in early summer. Only ten students were left. The dormitory seemed like a ghost town. Summer dragged on with the dreary task of closing down the school.[27] Then, at last, the *North Star* pulled into Golovin and Howard was on his way. He'd heard nothing recently from Ma Dingee and was uncertain who would meet him in Seattle, but he wasn't really worried. He was 22 years old. He could read and speak English with the best of them. And he had money in his pocket.

12

The Makings Of
An Artist

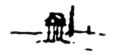

HOWARD TOSSED another perfectly peeled spud into a rapidly filling pot. No waste, pits or gouges. Truly the work of an artist.

"Good job, Rock," the steward agreed, hauling in an unopened crate of vegetables. "Only 10 more pounds to go and you've won yourself some shore leave. Should drop the hook off Point Hope about 11."

Howard had taken demotion from captain of the *Sampan* to kitchen boy on the *North Star* in good grace. Boat fare was $1.10 per day and the trip to Seattle might take 50 days or more. By working passage he could preserve his savings and the cook, Jimmy Kalerak, had promised him a crewman's share of whatever cash was left over from the mess fund to boot.

The ultra-modern *North Star* seemed like a cruise ship in comparison to the old *Boxer* which she had been built to replace in 1932. She measured 225 feet and boasted a 1,500-horse diesel engine that hustled her along at 12 knots under sail. In addition to her enormous hauling capacity there were 18 staterooms which meant 40 or 50 people to feed. But Howard had learned well on kitchen duty at White Mountain. It was obvious that the quiet Eskimo who ran the *North Star's* galley liked his work, and Howard enjoyed the job because it gave him time to think.[1]

Like the heroes of the fairy tales with which he had once entertained his family, Howard had been away from home for seven years. He was to have one day's shore leave in the village and he grew increasingly nervous as they neared the flat, rocky coast.

Would they even remember who he was?

Skies were somber; the wind brisk. The lumbering umiak rose, disappeared and rose again on leaden swells. Howard scanned the faces of the paddlers and found his father among them. He hurried down the weaving rope ladder of the ship, connecting neatly with the skin boat as it topped the crest of a wave. Samaroona made room for him, putting a steadying arm around his shoulder.

"Welcome home, my son," Sam Rock said, extending his big, calloused hand. Swallowing hard, Howard took it. It would not do to let the men see the tears of love and relief he fought.

Then he saw his father's eyes were also wet.

The village had changed little; a few new houses, but his own looked just the same. Nor did he have trouble identifying the tall, dignified woman who awaited them, although the years had taken their toll on his mother. Her dark hair was nearly white, her face lined and drawn.

"Howard…" she said, embracing him briefly but firmly.

"It is good that you…"

With a shout of genuine delight, Mumangeena waddled up full speed.

"Mother!" she exclaimed, hugging him around his middle which was as high up as she could reach, then holding him out at arms length to admire him. "How big you've grown and how strong you look! Not that I ever doubted for one minute… You must tell me everything…."

"Let him at least catch his breath, sister," Emma admonished, smiling in spite of herself. "He will die of hunger before you let him get to the meal I've prepared for him."

As if on cue, everyone came trooping into their house—friends and neighbors; his sister, Helen, and her family; Ruth who had grown into a lively 14-year-old, and Allen who, Howard observed with a twinge of jealousy, was much like their father.

Questions flew. Where was this "Or-re-gone" and why would anyone want to go there? Howard produced his sketch book and was pleased at the murmur of approval it created.

"But how can anyone feed themselves by drawing pictures?" his mother asked.

"Sikvoan predicted he would be different," Mumangeena defended. "What do you know about Or-re-gone, anyway? Maybe pictures sell just as well as fox skins there."

To Howard's relief, his father intervened. The boy had been allowed to work passage on the government boat, he pointed out. He might find a permanent position there should this job called "artist" fall through.

Later, walking across the tundra to the Episcopal mission with his father, he inquired about Eebrulik who, rumor had it, was lost in a small plane on his return from Hollywood. Sam Rock's laughter immediately put his mind at ease.

"Your older brother is herding reindeer right now. Although the plane he was traveling in was missing in 60° below weather, he finally got home and you wouldn't believe the things he brought. He has 12 suits—one with short, baggy pants that button below the knees that he tells me people wear just to hit a small, pitted ball with a club—they call it 'golf.' And he has a flat hat with a useless brim and lots of fancy neckties and shirts."[2]

"Why did he buy such things?" Howard puzzled.

Sam hesitated, then reminded himself that Howard was, after all, 22. "He told me that the beautiful, blonde movie star, Miss Harlow, and others, too—one named Miss West—took a great liking to him. They did everything they could to make him happy, which is why he stayed there so many weeks after the other Point Hope people came home."[3]

"I saw a picture of Eebrulik in the Seattle newspaper." Howard recalled. "They said he was good in that movie...."

"Well, now he is a reindeer herder again and he is good at that, too. But I am glad he had a chance to travel." Sam's eyes took on a distant look. "Once I had a chance to visit the world of the white man and I turned it down to marry your mother. I do not regret this, but I have always been curious. Now you will go and see it and perhaps you will come home again some day and tell this old man what he has missed."

It took the Rev. Goodman a long time to answer their knock.

"He gets lost in his translations," Sam explained.

"Sometimes we even have to remind him that it is Sunday, but he is doing important work."

"Sam—and Howard, my lad!" Goodman said warmly, ushering them at last into his book-littered study. "I hear you are headed for the world outside. I have friends who can help."

Goodman spoke fluently in Eskimo which was a disappointment to his returning student who had hoped to impress him with *his* firm command of English. In fact, Howard found a constant barrage of Eskimo tiring after so many years of disuse.

The day flew by. There was supper with Mumangeena and Nayukuk which included dessert of canned peaches. His aunt chatted on about her friend who married a white man. Nayukuk did not look well, Howard thought, although his pleased smile was in itself worth the trip.

Then, all too soon, it was time to leave. Sam readied the umiak. Howard stopped for a round of good-byes and, glancing up to check his father's progress, noticed a toddler wandering out into the surf. Dashing after the child he snatched her from a crashing roller and returned her to her mother. As he did so, a fat louse from the child's clothing settled on his hand and Howard almost dropped the baby in his haste to rid himself of the parasite.

"Not all Point Hope housekeepers are as dedicated to the use of soap and water as your mother. But I hope you will not be ashamed of your people," Sam observed on the trip to the ship.

"We have survived here where few others could. We may be slow to adopt refinements of the white man's world, but we have become Christians and we have done our best."

Howard crawled gratefully between the clean sheets of his bunk on the *North Star* that night, but sleep was long in coming. Although he was pleased with the reception of his loved ones, he'd felt uncomfortable in their cramped, airless homes. Even the cleanest reeked of rancid seal oil, uncured hides and urine used for tanning. The lack of refinements his father defended bothered him more than he cared to admit. He knew he must look to the future, not the past. But even as a small boy, he had never felt more confused and homesick than he did that night.

The busy routine of the *North Star* brightened Rock's perspective. Loading and unloading cargo gave him an opportunity to visit villages all along the coast, and even the long days at sea offered variety.

Dumping the garbage astern one morning, he stopped to watch porpoises playing tag with the ship's churning wake.

Albatross circled idly overhead. Wind carried the scent of land. He could not see the island that lay to the west but he knew exactly how it would look, for Samaroona's saga of the Eskimo's travels along the Aleutian Chain proved stunningly accurate in describing each land mass. It was amazing how oral history had preserved to the tiniest detail what must have been a true adventure from another century.[4]

"Not a good sign," someone muttered.

Thinking he was being reprimanded for daydreaming, Howard jumped to attention, but crewman Charlie Salenjus was eyeing an evil-looking formation of clouds.

"The barometer just dropped past the point of no return. I'd guess we're in for it unless we can run for Dutch before it hits."

"What do you think our chances are, sir?"

"Dismal, boy. Give you a real test of your sea legs."

To his credit, Howard didn't get seasick, although the vegetables he chopped for fish chowder were more often in mid-air than on the block. Meals were minimal, anyway. Most of the passengers remained in their bunks. Off Korvin Head the wind shifted abruptly and the ship turned into monstrous waves causing her timbers to groan and shudder.

Howard staggered topside lugging a bucket of garbage and worked his way to the stern. Congratulating himself as egg shells and peelings flew aft, he turned into the wind for the return trip, just as a freak wave crashed down nearly washing him overboard. He managed to grab a cleat, then inched his way to safety where he blundered into the captain.

"There's stiff penalties for abandoning ship, lad," the old man said sternly.

"J-just sort of got taken by surprise, sir," Howard stammered. "D-do you think we're going to make it through all right?"

Whitlam had sailed more than 30 years in the arctic and was one of the most respected seamen of his day.

"Not so bad as the time I put the *Boxer* up on Unalga Island," he considered. "Worse than when we went aground in the Straits.

"Say, you're not scared, are you, son? This is what I call 'conversion weather.' "

"Conversion, sir?"

"Weather like this converts more sinners than a boatload full of missionaries."

In Juneau, the ship was met by a bear of a man with a cherubic face who introduced himself as Charles Wesley Hawkesworth and invited Howard home to supper.

"If you've got anything you want screwed up, just give it to Charlie and tell him it's vitally important," muttered a crewman, and Howard recalled all too well the disappointment of depending on Hawkesworth for transportation the year before. He had no choice but to accept the supper invitation, though. And he was glad he did.

Hawkesworth and his wife were a delightful couple who had lived in Alaska for 30 years. Their adopted daughter, Florence, was half Eskimo— orphaned during the flu epidemic in Solomon.

They were interested in White Mountain School and they also quizzed him on the course he hoped his life might take.[5]

What can we do to help?" Mr. Hawkesworth asked.

"Really, sir, you've helped already by getting me on the boat."

"You are well outfitted," Mrs. Hawkesworth said, noting his mail-order suit with approval. "What about a suitcase?"

"A suitcase?"

"You know, to carry your belongings on the train?"

"But do we have an extra one, dear?" Mr. Hawkesworth asked doubtfully.

"Of course not, Charles," she said brightly. "He'll have to borrow yours."

Southeastern Alaska's Inside Passage, through which the *North Star* traveled, was awesome with lush rain forests and glacier-decked mountains. Deer grazed at the water's edge, driven down from the hills by early snows. Bald eagles perched by the dozens at stream mouths, attracted by masses of spawning salmon.

Humpback whales, larger even than bowheads, cruised the waterway in search of food. Sometimes they could be seen mating, leaping out of the water towards each other and coupling with showering splashes.

"Now that is love!" Jimmy Andrews sighed.

"Reminds me of Creek Street in Ketchikan," Joe Bush said, rolling his eyes heavenward.

"What's Creek Street?" Howard asked.

"Where men and salmon go to spawn," Jimmy explained delicately.

"The red light district there is built on a boardwalk over a creek," Joe said. "It's really something to see."

They traveled by taxi to visit the girls and the trip itself proved the highlight of Howard's evening in Ketchikan. He had never seen a taxi. As for the ladies of the evening, they looked fine, but were unquestionably beyond his budget. Besides, he had yet to resolve a few moral questions and he was bothered by memory of a motion picture on venereal disease that McCollester had insisted on showing the older students. Still, the girls were good sports about the whole thing and he thanked the crew heartily for introducing him to the big city.

Ketchikan soon paled in comparison to Seattle. Nothing he'd read prepared Howard for that first sight of its vast harbor—lined with endless docks crowded with freighters bigger even than the *North Star*—backed by a mind-boggling network of busy streets, tall buildings and urban sprawl.

Mr. Hawkesworth had promised someone would meet him. No one appeared and he'd decided to join the crew in hiring a taxi when he heard someone call his name.

"Sir?"

"You are Howard Rock, aren't you?" a bespectacled, gray-haired man asked, sounding sure of himself.

"How did you know, sir?"

"I knew your father when he was about your age," William Lopp explained, introducing himself.

"This is a real honor, sir," Howard said, in awed surprise.

Everybody knew who W.T. Lopp was. The Eskimos of their coast had named him "Tom Gorrah" (meaning "good man"), many years before the famous educator became a regular in *Who's Who*.

When the Indiana-born, Presbyterian missionary came to Alaska in 1890, he was stationed in Wales, just south of Point Hope. Natives were prejudiced against outsiders for a sea captain had killed 13 Eskimos there, but the newcomer appeared to be no threat.

"Too poor to trade, too stingy to marry and too effeminate to hunt," they joked, but Lopp proved them wrong on all counts. For starters he married petite Miss Ellen Kittridge, also a teacher, and took her by dog team and kayak on a honeymoon trip to Point Hope to meet his friend, Dr. John Driggs. In the course of the 500-mile journey, the Lopps became the first whites on record to cross Kotzebue Sound over ice and the Eskimos of Point Hope welcomed them warmly.[6]

The next year the couple was overseeing a reindeer herd at Teller, when Wales Eskimos murdered a teacher named Harrison Thornton. The Lopps dared to replace him, bringing peace to the troubled settlement and staying on through the birth of six of their eight children. Later Lopp traveled from Wales to Barrow on a mercy mission, driving a reindeer herd to feed sailors from a shipwrecked whaling fleet. And by the time he was appointed to replace Sheldon Jackson as head of education for Alaska, the Eskimos thought of him as their own.

Supper at the Lopp's proved an extraordinary experience for, although Lopp was close to 70, his rambling house in the University District was full of boisterous young people.[7]

Mrs. Lopp was a short, easygoing woman who was unperturbed by unexpected guests. Although several times a grandmother, she was enrolled at the University of Washington and also spent considerable time doing excellent charcoal sketches. Housekeeping was not her bent, but she cooked up a splendid supper with no fuss and even managed to join in their fun.[8] Howard woke next morning in the basement room which served as a bunk house and discovered his sides were sore from laughing.

"Rise and shine," Mr. Lopp was saying in Inupiaq, and the Eskimo braced himself for another round of the same.

In comparison to the Lopp household, downtown Seattle seemed peaceful. By way of introduction, his host took him to the Smith Tower, 42 floors above the ground. Cars swarming on First Avenue looked like bugs and the harbor was a mirror dotted with moving specks.

"Easy enough to find your way. The main streets are in numerical order," Lopp pointed out. "And you can remember the cross streets with the blasphemous little sentence—*Jesus Christ Made Seattle Under Protest.* That's the way the streets line up—Jefferson, James, Cherry, Columbia, Marion, Madison, Spring, Seneca, University, Union, Pike and Pine."

En route to the railroad station, Howard noticed a long queue of people and asked about it.

"That's a bread line."

"We read about the Depression but somehow it didn't seem real."[9]

"It's not real until you experience it with your stomach," Lopp observed.

The train was crowded and dirty. Howard hated the noise and the smell and the motion and he decided Medford would look good to him no matter what kind of a place it was. It proved an attractive town set in wooded hills and valleys, but the temperature was at least 90° in the shade. Sweating profusely, Howard inquired about bus connections to Trail.

"You missed it by about 30 minutes," the agent informed him. "Nothing going that way now 'til tomorrow morning."

Howard knew no one in Medford. Ma Dingee was traveling and Siemes didn't have a phone.

"You might try hitchhiking, son," the clerk said, noting his dismay.

"Hitchhiking?"

"You know, just go to the side of the road and stick out your thumb. Someone's bound to give you a lift."

"Best-dressed hitchhiker I ever see," the farmer said, looking Rock over as he stowed Mr. Hawkesworth's suitcase in the back of his truck. "Pretty hot to be wearing a three-piece suit, ain't it? Got anything in that bag might be cooler?"

"Mostly overalls," Howard said, wishing the stranger would mind his own business. Invasion of privacy was apparently the price of a ride.

"What are you, anyway, a Jap or what?..."

"I'm *Eskimo.*"

"One of those meat-eating Eskimos who live in snow houses?"

"That's what some people think," he answered, struggling to keep his temper.

"Boy, now wouldn't one of them snow houses be handy on a day like today!"

"If I had any idea how to build one ..." Howard began, then let the subject drop.

Downtown Trail consisted of a post office. The woman who ran it was curt.

"Siemes… two miles down the road, on the right," she said. "Dreadful man!"

Hoping that the directions were accurate and the postmistress's opinion incorrect, he set out on foot. Trail Creek rippled merrily just below the shoulder of the road and jays screamed alarm from the thick forest through which it ran. A profusion of wildflowers decorated the roadway. The air was spiced with pine scent.

Rock had covered about a mile and a half when he noticed a tall man approaching with long, rapid strides. He was arrestingly handsome with sharply chiseled features and a muscular body clad in spotless khaki.

"Know where you're going, young fellow?" he demanded.

"I think so, sir," Howard answered, taken aback by his briskness and his European accent.

"You must be the Eskimo," the stranger guessed, pulling wire-framed glasses out of his pocket for a closer look.

"Probably the only one in town," Howard blurted out, and Max Siemes dissolved in laughter.

"I was just headed down for another battle with the postmistress, but that can keep," the artist said after dispensing with introductions. "I've got lemonade cooling in my root cellar and I'll warrant you could use a glass." [10]

Siemes' 40-acre homestead with its rustic cabin, pools and careful landscaping of transplanted wildflowers, lay beyond the next bend like a magic oasis. A hand-carved sign, "Dripping Rock," hung from a vine-wrapped arch that served as the entrance. Just to the right was a whimsical gazebo.

"It looks like something out of the Brothers Grimm," Howard exclaimed. "Why do you call it Dripping Rock?"

"That's the main attraction," Siemes said, leading him down a shady path to a series of pools that apparently sprung from a mossy boulder.

"Is it natural?" Howard asked, intrigued.

"Like everything else here, I have engineered it to appear so," the builder confessed. "I pipe the water in, but that is a secret that I trust you will protect."

Siemes proceeded, skirting gardens and pastures, to a subterranean root cellar which contained fruits and vegetables in amazing variety, bottles of homemade wine and a crock of excellent lemonade.

"We're self-sufficient here," he boasted. "About the only things I have to buy at the store are salt, sugar and a lemon or two. No electricity. No indoor plumbing. But I think you'll find it comfortable."

Rock suppressed a smile. He'd traveled all this way to live in a place that had fewer 20th century amenities than the arctic. Even Point Hope had a light plant! Still, he liked what he saw.

The outhouse was an ode to cleanliness. Siemes had built the cabin with double, sawdust-filled walls which insured warmth in winter and kept out the worst of the summer heat. Interiors were quaintly charming with well-filled bookcases. An Enrico Caruso classic issued from the Victrola.

Supper included rye bread, cheeses, sausage, beer and fruitcake, all of Siemes' making.

"I intend to live to be 100. Am seven years over the halfway mark now and I still have all my own teeth," he announced as he uncorked a bottle of Marsala wine as an after-dinner treat. "The secret is eating right. No store-bought bread or candy; plenty of vitamins and roughage. Learn the basics, lad, and you can aspire to a productive old age."

"And liquor, sir?" Howard had never seen alcohol served in a private home.

Siemes snorted.

"I suppose all those confounded missionaries have been warning you about the evils of drink. Well, actually, it's good for the circulatory system—taken in moderation, of course. I, myself, make it a strict rule never to imbibe before two in the afternoon and I expect you to do the same!"

Howard scarcely knew what to think of his host until they moved from the supper table to his studio where a dozen or so paintings were in various stages of completion. Intently the student examined the canvases—fresh, impressionistic, not unlike Renoir or Monet but truer somehow, more vital.

"Well?" Siemes demanded when at last Rock had circled the room.

"I think I shall have to work very hard to be one-tenth the artist as you are, sir," he answered with humility.

Siemes grafted his own fruit trees, maintained a vineyard, raised livestock for meat and fished from the local creeks.[11]

Howard was assigned to work the vegetable garden, a task he enjoyed, but he was also responsible for herding cattle.

"No different from reindeer," Siemes reasoned. "Not much bigger either," but Howard didn't trust them. Especially Mad Martha with her crumpled horn.

"Have you heard the story about the butterfly that went to sleep on a daisy and while it slept a cow came by and ate the flower?" Siemes asked soberly one morning as he took his accustomed place on the milking stool and his apprentice nervously ushered in a skittish heifer.

Howard shook his head, never sure of what might come next.

"Well, she woke up terribly frightened in that warm, moist, noisy darkness of the cow's belly, but having nothing better to do, she went back to sleep and when she woke up again the cow was gone!"[12]

"I prefer chickens," Howard grinned. But having Max for a teacher definitely made up for the skirmishes with Mad Martha.

At age 15, Holland-born Siemes had been sent to England and then to uncles in New York City to learn the family brewing business. Hating the work, he ran away. During the Spanish-American War he became the U.S.Navy's first official photographer and by the time he retired in the late 1920s, he'd seen and photographed most of the world.[13]

He discovered Trail following an old stagecoach route in his Model T, and offered a reward of $100 to anyone who could find him a good piece of land there with water on it. He had staked his homestead in 1929, before the highway came through, when wolves were a menace.

Although Siemes claimed to have no formal training, he displayed superb command of the fundamentals of art and his dazzling scenics sold well, even during hard times.

"Never mind buying paint tubes of magenta and the indigo blue. All you need is the four basic colors," he told Howard practically at the onset of his training. "There is not one hue you cannot mix if you use your eyes and your head."[14]

Howard did his best but Siemes, who was light years ahead of him in technique, often grew frustrated and cursed his student.

"You cannot force it," he insisted after Howard spent six hours working on a simple scenic that eluded him. "Let things fill your imagination and ferment. See them in your mind's eye."

"But in my mind's eye it is always so brilliant, so much more beautiful than it comes out," the young painter despaired.

"Take a break!" Siemes roared. "Stop fiddling around with those brushes. Let your *subconscious* do the work!"

"How?"

"There's a dance tonight at the Rogue Elk. The band is tops. Red Chamberlain's going to call. I guarantee any serious thinking you do will have to be subconscious.... You do dance, don't you Rock?"

"About as well as I paint, sir."

"That should be perfectly sufficient," Siemes snapped, turning on his heel, and only belatedly did Howard realize the artist had paid him his first compliment.

Imposing Rogue Elk Inn had been a favorite hostelry of writer Zane Grey in the 1920s and was still going strong despite the Depression.[15] Siemes was a favored customer for he generally hired a whole table and filled it with friends. A confirmed bachelor but by no means celibate, he attracted an interesting coterie of admiring females that Howard found fascinating.

A marvelously freckled redhead named Effie Lou took an immediate fancy to the young Eskimo and asked him to dance. At first Howard thought she was just being polite. Uncertain on how to conduct himself, he'd kept pretty much to the sidelines, studying Siemes' debonair European manners. But when Effie nibbled at his ear during a slow waltz and whispered that she'd love to have him come home for the night, he realized her interest went beyond the realm of simple kindness.

He was tempted. He could have gazed happily into Effie Lou's emerald-green eyes for hours. The golden freckles that dusted her cheeks mesmerized him, as did the alluring curves of her angora sweater. But, certain that his host would disapprove of the dalliance, he regretfully declined.

When at last they closed the Rogue Elk, Siemes had a woman in tow. "Have you met Frieda?" he asked casually, holding the door of the Model T for the pretty brunette.

"No," Howard said, somewhat confused.

"Frieda is going to vacation briefly at Dripping Rock," Siemes said, like that sort of thing happened every night.

Frieda giggled.

Painting lessons were temporarily suspended. Dabbling away on his own, Howard was amazed to find that his "subconscious" readily defeated the problems of the scenic that had been giving him trouble and produced an excellent painting. Max congratulated him roundly when they returned to their regular routine.

"Do you think you'll marry Frieda, sir?" Howard mustered courage to ask.

"Frieda already has a perfectly good husband," Siemes answered blithely. "He just happens to be out of town at the moment at a pharmaceutical convention."

"But that's adultery!"

"Damn it all, Rock, any artist worth his salt can see the world isn't all black and white but a thousand shades of gray!"

Howard nodded thoughtfully. In philosophical argument, he'd found his teacher to be a fervent atheist. Siemes had his own strict code of ethics but he was what he called a "Bohemian," which apparently gave artists special license.

"I'm not totally sold on everything the preachers say," Howard defended. "But adultery—well, I don't think I could come to grips with it."

When Effie Lou suggested Howard slip away from the dance with her the next Saturday night—ostensibly for some lemonade spiked with gin— Howard did not hesitate. He was inexperienced in some matters, but Effie Lou seemed to know exactly what she wanted and he learned the basics in no time. Her wonderful freckles were universal and Howard set out to kiss them one by one. Time passed quickly. He missed his ride home.

Max was cooking breakfast when he trudged in.

"You look like a man who's just made an important discovery," he noted.

"Well, I'm beginning to understand your philosophy, sir," Howard allowed with a giggle. "Effie Lou says I'm an 'exotic'."

"Discretion, young man. You just let Effie Lou do the bragging."

"Yes, sir," Howard said, embarrassed. "I'm pretty new at this."

"Well, it would be practical to keep in mind that Effie Lou's husband stands about six feet two and weighs . . ."

"Husband! She didn't tell me about any husband!"

Howard was irrevocably smitten but Effie Lou, fickle creature that she was, transferred her affections even before her spouse returned. When next he saw her at the Rogue Elk, she was nibbling the ear of a short, swarthy Italian who seemed to have endless amounts of cash. Howard was crushed. He had no money to win her back and no prospects of getting any. Bitterly he resolved to become rich and famous.

Ruby Dingee shuffled canvases, pausing over a pastoral scenic. Howard held his breath. She had returned from her travels to her home at the far end of their valley a month earlier, but this was the first visit she had paid them.[16]

"A glass of wine, Ruby?" Siemes offered.

"No thank you, Max. You know I don't touch alcohol."

"This isn't *just alcohol*," Siemes bristled. "This is my finest Marsala."

"How's the boy behaving himself?" she asked, taking the proffered glass.

"Mulish. Devilishly mulish and dunderheaded," Max complained without hint of a smile. "But I agree with you, Ruby. He's got talent."

"Then you'll take him on for another year," Ma Dingee said, settling back in her chair as if the matter were cut and dried.

"Certainly I'll take him," Max agreed.

Irwin Howe was a member of the GOP, which assured his appointment as postmaster of Trail when Republicans were in power, and his wife, Rena, was a registered Democrat who got the job in off elections. Siemes had no quarrel with the system nor with Irwin, but for reasons long forgotten he loathed Rena, and his daily arguments with her were high drama.[17]

"I'll live to dance on her grave!" he muttered, stamping out of the post office after one particularly vicious set-to. "I'm 57, I still have all my own teeth and I'll live to dance on her grave."

Howard nodded absently. He was engrossed in reading a letter from Arthur Upicksoun who was still studying at Eklutna. Mary Ashenfelter had gotten a part-time job as Mr. Neeley's secretary, he wrote. Some teachers had offered to bring her to Washington when they came next summer and Arthur, himself, was planning to work his way to Seattle on the boats.

Howard seldom got news from home and it was welcome. He missed Alaska and he missed the boats. Trail was miles inland and it occurred to him that it was a strange place for Siemes to settle after spending years at sea.

"Do you ever miss the Navy, sir?" he asked. "You said you enjoyed sailing."

"Homesick, eh, Rock?" Siemes observed, not without sympathy.

"Yes, I liked being at sea but that was another life. What's behind you ceases to exist, son."

Springtime at Dripping Rock was a heady experience. Howard gave himself over to it, seduced by the perfume of the apple blossoms and the joyous songs of nesting larks. Max was spending a week in Medford, a trip prompted no doubt by another pharmaceutical convention, and Howard worked feverishly on a painting with which to dazzle him on return.

The painting was a tribute to the new season, bright with blooming fruit trees yet masterful in its restraint. Howard considered it his best work and he was crushed when Siemes viewed it with distaste.

"I've been robbed," Siemes grumbled.

"Robbed, sir?"

"You've copied my technique so well I almost think I painted this myself."

"But ... but I meant to..."

Siemes shook his head.

"I know you mean it as a compliment, boy, but you have a style of your own."[18]

"Primitive. My style is primitive."

It's *unique!*" Siemes bellowed.

They both sat down.

"Look, Howard, I'm not condemning you, although I'm amazed at the thoroughness with which you picked up my methods."

"I'm just using what you taught me," the student defended.

"Exactly! And I can teach you no more!"

Rock was thunderstruck. "No more..." he echoed.

"There is nothing more I can teach you. You'd be wasting your time here...."

"But . . ."

"Don't interrupt," his mentor said sternly. "What I'd suggest is that you enroll at University of Washington School of Art."

"But that's one of the finest schools in the country!"

"And you should settle for nothing less," Siemes insisted.

13

University Days

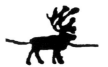

IT WAS MORE THAN A LITTLE CRAMPED with three of them wedged into the single seat of the Dingee's Ford coupe but Howard was grateful for the transportation. After Charles Hawkesworth had arranged for the Bureau of Indian Affairs to grant him a college loan of $900, the Dingees volunteered to take him to Seattle to enroll. It was a distance of almost 500 miles. They traveled at a leisurely pace, camping like gypsies at any scenic spot that took their fancy. The jagged shoreline was often fringed with handsome surf. There were bright, star-smeared nights and warm, misty mornings that turned the world into pastels. It was a wonderful trip but bad news awaited them in Seattle. The University refused to accept Rock because he didn't have a high school diploma.[1]

"Neither did Michelangelo. That's what I told 'em," Charlie Hawkesworth recounted with a snort of indignation. "The registrar is a hard-nosed woman so we'll just have to go higher up."

"But Howard will miss the first semester," Ma worried. "What will he do with himself?"

"That's one problem I have managed to solve," Hawkesworth grinned. "Cap Whitlam will take him on the fall run of the *North Star*. It will give you a chance to see your folks, son. And he's going to pay you a regular wage!"

The ship wasn't due to leave for a couple of weeks and Hawkesworth invited Howard to room with him in the interim. He was on temporary duty in the Seattle office, away from his family, and welcomed the company. Politics was his passion and Rock proved a good listener.

"Seems like I'm always getting appointed 'acting' supervisor whenever they've got a hole to fill, like this summer," his host complained. "Ran the Alaska bureau for years, then they brought in Claude Hirst over me. But considering what they did to Tom Lopp, I guess I'm lucky to be employed."

It was Tom Lopp who'd given Hawkesworth his first teaching job. The men were close friends, Howard learned, and as Lopp had moved up in the ranks, he'd taken Hawkesworth with him. Then, in 1924, Lopp was forced out.

"They had to abolish the Bureau of Education to get rid of him," Charlie noted glumly. "The *Alaska Weekly* called him a 'victim of odorous politics' right in a headline. But, by damn, I can learn to play that game, if that's what it takes."

Howard suppressed a smile. He knew little about politics, but the thought of a man as guileless and fair as his host joining the ranks of "odorous" politicians defied imagination.[2]

Hawkesworth believed so passionately in equal opportunity that he treated even drunken Eskimos on Seattle's skid row with deference. Howard was disgusted by his first exposure to the down-and-out Natives who panhandled for a living along Alaskan Way. He saw them as a discredit to his race, but Hawkesworth argued that they'd never had a fighting chance.

"They were cheated out of their birthright, robbed of their lands, given a second-class education and no vote," he defended. "Most of them come here to better themselves, to find work or to go to school, like yourself. But they buckle under the continued humiliation of white bigotry. It's no wonder they just give up."

Having been carefully sheltered from discrimination by his benefactors, Howard had little idea what Hawkesworth was talking about but his host offered some provocative ideas on Indian rights. At the time, Hawkesworth was backing the Duwamish Tribe in asking $4,158,000 for the site of Seattle which had once been theirs, and the Snoqualmie who sought $9 million in compensation for timberlands relinquished by treaty in 1855.[3]

"Indian treaties were made to be broken," Hawkesworth mused, en route to deliver Howard to his ship. "Usually it's the government that breaks them but there must be some way around that."

"Did Alaskans make treaties?" Howard asked.

"They never had to, son. They were never defeated in war so, the way I see it, they still own their land. Problem is, they don't have title to it in the American courts."

"Well, you've given me an education in political science, sir," Rock allowed. "Even if I never get into the university."

"Don't worry about a thing, young man. You have friends in high places!" Hawkesworth assured him blithely.

Trying to paint in an ill-lit bunk room on the *North Star* proved impossible so Howard planted his easel on deck during off-hours when the weather was fair. He was executing a study of an Eskimo driving a sled deer and sometimes passengers came to watch.

"Excellent. Just excellent!" declared a well-dressed man who spoke with a broad southern drawl. "You must be the chap we're sending to art school."

"We, sir?"

"Oh, the Bureau," the stranger said, taken aback. "I'm Claude Hirst."

"Yes, sir!" Howard snapped to attention. Hirst was the man who had passed over Hawkesworth to become director of the Bureau of Indian Affairs for all of Alaska.

"What do you do when it storms?" Hirst was asking.

"I hope it doesn't," the artist answered with resignation. "There's just no place to work inside."

"Nonsense," the director said. "Plenty of empty staterooms. I'll see that you get one. And, in return, you'll hang this fine canvas in the social hall." [4]

"I'd be honored, sir," Howard said, wishing Charlie Hawkesworth could overhear.

As usual, Howard worked longshoring on the *North Star's* many stops and landing at Wainwright he was surprised to see Aunt Mumangeena in the crowd. She was visiting her friend, Ellnou, who was married to a well-heeled white trader named Jim Allen.

"But where is Uncle Nayukuk?"

"Buried," his aunt replied.[5] "*Now*, perhaps, your mother will admit he was sick!"

Again Howard managed a day's shore leave at Point Hope and spent most of the time with his parents. They had hung a painting he had sent them in a place of honor and Sam seemed well-pleased with the gift of a new dictionary.

"Perhaps you might use it to write me a letter," Howard suggested.

"But this old man's grammar is so poor. You would be ashamed."

"I will never be ashamed of my people," Howard promised, remembering his father's dictum word for word.

At Nome, a bunch of students boarded the ship en route to Eklutna along with travelers stranded by a shipping strike. Every bunk was full. Howard was forced to relinquish his stateroom, but there was no time to paint, anyhow. He was up to his elbows in dirty dishes when steward Sig Sumdt appeared with a gangly Eskimo lad.

"Clint Gray, working his way," Sumdt announced, unaware of the charming rhyme. "Your assistant."

Gray, who was well-dressed and spoke unaccented English, appeared less than enchanted with the prospect. He was the brother of Native rights advocate, Nick Gray, who was now mayor of White Mountain. Like Howard, Clint had obtained an education loan from the government and was on his way to Oakland, California, to attend diesel engine school.

"Don't you find this work demeaning?" he demanded, as he set to with a dish towel.

"No," Rock said, looking him straight in the eye. "It's just a job."[6]

Tom Lopp met Rock when his ship returned to Seattle.

"Has the University admitted me?" Howard asked, anxiously.

"It doesn't look good," Lopp reported. "Claude Hirst has been lobbying on your behalf but he hasn't gotten anywhere."

"Mr. Hawkesworth said he had friends in high places ..." Howard recalled.

Lopp smiled, embarrassed. "I'm afraid he meant me," he said.

Following his ouster as head of the Alaskan Bureau of Education, Lopp had been hired by the Hudson's Bay Company to work on reindeer ventures in Canada and similar projects in Norway and Lapland. He'd also served successfully as a lobbyist in the nation's capitol.[7] Although retired, he still had considerable influence, and when he returned from a chat with officials at the University of Washington, Howard Rock was admitted as a freshman.

Reporter Ann Wilson looked up from her typewriter and blinked. The smartly suited Eskimo standing in front of her desk was possibly the handsomest young man who ever hit Seattle, she thought. A heartbreaker.

"Miss Wilson?" he asked shyly, apparently unaware of his charm. "I'm Howard Rock, the artist Mr. Lopp told you about."

"I'd expected someone ... well, someone a little more ... er ... primitive," she stammered.

"I paint under Sikvoan, my Eskimo name, but Eskimos aren't much different from anybody else."

"Of course," she shook her head. "Let's just start over. I understand three of your paintings are to hang in the social room of the *North Star* next season. We'll want a photo of you with one of them and a good rundown on your career."

Back in Juneau, Charlie Hawkesworth read the interview headlined, "ESKIMO ARTIST ANXIOUS TO STUDY AT UNIVERSITY," with satisfaction.[8]

"I need much more training (but) when I have studied longer, developed the necessary technique, I want to specialize in Eskimo art," Howard was quoted as saying.

"Eskimos are much more artistic than generally is given them credit. Long ago they developed an art of their own which is crude, but which, in the youths of the village, is being improved."

Since Howard was unfamiliar with the University District, Mr. Lopp agreed to help him find a room there, but it was hard going.

"No Orientals!" the first landlady said, slamming the door in their faces.

"I don't take Japs," snapped a second. Others simply eyed the Eskimo nervously and lied that they had no rooms.[9]

Howard, garbed neatly in his three-piece suit, said little, but something inside him died. At last he understood what Nick Gray and Hawkesworth had tried to tell him. No matter how well-dressed or well-educated one might be, many white people considered those of other races loathsome and inferior. He wondered if it was true. And Lopp, who was no less staggered, finally suggested they consider another approach.

"No, I won't have him," Mrs. Lopp said firmly when Tom broached the subject of taking the Alaskan in on a permanent basis.[10]

"He's a fine young man, Nelly, and he will pay his own way."

"It's not that, Tom. You know I enjoy his company, but we have a houseful. Besides he's 25 years old and too handsome for his own good. It's inevitable he'll get into trouble, and I don't want to ride herd on him."

"Oh, Nelly, if you could have been with us today and listened to the insults. He seemed to take it in stride but it was just brutal."

As a young woman Ellen "Nelly" Lopp had elected to teach at a missionary school for blacks in North Carolina and experienced discrimination on a grand scale.[11] Later, some of her Eskimo students at Wales had returned from Carlisle Indian School unfit for village life and equally ill-equipped to deal with the harsh realities of white society. She was ambivalent about government acculturation programs.[12]

"Howard is different, Nelly," her husband insisted. "He has more talent than most and a real chance of doing something important for his people."

"You just want someone to practice speaking Inupiat with, Tom Lopp," she kidded him. But ultimately she agreed to take the artist.

The University of Washington campus was an imposing quadrangle of ivy-covered brick. Registration took place in old Meany Hall. Howard met several faculty members and came away impressed. Some of the most respected artists in America would be his teachers—among them landscape painter Walter Isaacs and Dudley Pratt whose fantastic granite friezes decorated many local buildings including the university library.

The Art Department was relegated to the garret of Winlock M. Miller Hall, a neo-Gothic marvel decorated with dark woodwork and leaded stained-glass windows. Administration, including the office of university president, occupied the ground floor, engineering was on second and an incongruous mix of home economics and architectural students filled the gaps.[13]

Classes were informal. When models took a break, students did likewise, wandering into other classes, finding their own company amusing. But Howard made no close friends. His mid-year entrance was a deterrent and the disastrous hunt for lodging had made him painfully aware of his minority status. Living with the Lopps, on the other hand, proved a richly rewarding experience for he found himself, for the first time, in the midst of a large, loving family.

As Nelly had suggested, Tom Lopp longed to brush up his Eskimo. The educator was writing a children's book titled "Eskimo Robinson Crusoe," and having an eager informant delighted him. Often Lopp would rise early, cook breakfast for the two of them and, as they came to know each other better, their talks broadened.

In contrast to Max Siemes and his vehement declarations of atheism, Lopp believed strongly in the church. Rock found his moral dictates restrictive after the art teacher's free-wheeling Bohemian style, yet Lopp was always open to discussion. Talking with him helped Howard sort through some of the conflicts he found within his confusing new world, and a unique closeness grew between Eskimo and educator.

The rest of the family, Nelly Lopp, daughters Alice and Mary, who were living at home, and son, Dwight, who lived nearby, treated Howard as one of the clan. The girls delegated him kitchen chores and dragged him to church socials. With Dwight and Nelly he shared an interest in art.[14]

Then there was Melba Call, an Eskimo from the Alaska Peninsula, whom the Lopps had helped raise. Blind since the age of three but chronically cheerful, she had won a scholarship to Perkins Institute in Massachusetts and, after two years of post-graduate work, returned to Alaska to teach. She came home for vacations, and Howard found her amazing.[15]

"Where are you going?" he asked one afternoon when he discovered her alone, hauling on her overshoes and coat.

"To the movies," she answered matter-of-factly. "Alice is going to meet me at the theater. It's Clark Gable."[16]

"But how will you get there?" he asked, incredulous.

"By bus, ninny," she said with an infectious smile. "You don't think I would walk?"

The family also encouraged Howard's friends to visit. Clint Gray spent a few days. Arthur Upicksoun lived there for a month while he worked at the Ballard shipyards. It was not unusual for casual acquaintances to stay on for weeks. More than once, when Nelly Lopp ran out of beds in which to put them, Howard found her sleeping on the floor.

"Miscounted and I was the last one up," she would explain. And she remained unflappable, even in the face of gross breaches of etiquette.

Paul, an extremely bright but unsophisticated Eskimo from a remote village, arrived well-scrubbed and suited for supper one evening and managed to field the required social niceties until Tom Lopp unwittingly asked if he cared to clean up before supper. The visitor nodded gravely, was escorted to the bathroom and did not return.

"Maybe you'd better check on him, Tom," Mrs. Lopp suggested after 15 minutes had passed. "The roast is getting cold."

Lopp returned shaking his head.

"He's taking a bath," he reported, scarcely knowing whether to laugh or cry. "He thought my asking him to wash up meant he didn't meet our standards of cleanliness."

Mrs. Lopp sighed heavily but when the visitor returned, she proceeded with her usual grace to offer him the serving platter of roast beef.

"Thank you," he beamed, setting his own plate aside and taking the platter in its stead. And, without missing a beat, the hostess returned to the stove and filled a second dish for the family.

Each summer, with visitors in tow, the Lopps moved to Rolling Bay on Bainbridge Island. Preferring the outdoors, they'd built their vacation cottage without glass in the windows and Howard loved it. Days were filled with swimming, clam digging and picnicking and, in early evening, they would watch for the ferry to see if Mr. Lopp was bringing company home. Guests always stayed overnight and the whole experience was a continuing beach party.[17]

In August, Howard sailed again on the *North Star*, reclaimed his stateroom and painted some of his finest canvases between turns in the galley. He spent his Point Hope stopover sketching, and in Wainwright he divided shore leave between his aunt and Arthur Upicksoun who was planning to travel to Seattle that fall to look for a job.

"Mary Ellen Ashenfelter has already got one, as a switchboard operator in Pasco, Washington," Arthur reported.

"How did she do that?" Howard wanted to know.

"Teachers paid her way out like they promised. They kept saying that she could pass for white. She wrote me it wasn't that easy."

"Would you do that? Pass for white if you could?"

"Would you?" Big Boy countered.

With bitterness Howard recalled the trouble he'd had finding a room, but he shook his head.

Ashore in Seward for the day, Howard spotted a masterful oil painting of Mt. McKinley in a shop window.

"The artist, Sydney Laurence, has a studio in Anchorage," the woman behind the counter said, surprised at the Eskimo's interest. "He came to Alaska as a prospector in 1904."

"But he must have had training..."

"He certainly did," she laughed. "Edward Moran, Coni Robert Flori, Ecole des Beaux Arts in France. His paintings hung in the Louvre. But when I first met him he was down-and-out drunk. I had to supply him with paint."

The shopowner was Mrs. Goldie Blue, a portly brunette who was a longtime resident. Her business was woman's and children's wear and imported decorative goods, but she had encouraged many local artists.

"Some of the passengers from the *North Star* were telling me about your paintings," she said when Howard introduced himself. "What would you say to my exhibiting your work?"

Howard had never had a show of his own. He was thrilled, and his new patron did an elegant job of it, even standing the expense of an ad in the local paper. The *Seward Gateway* critic referred to him as a "gifted young man"[18] and his story sparked the interest of the Juneau newspaper.

"Sikovan Weyahok travelled 3,000 miles this summer and fall to spend one single day with his parents—and when he reached his home, he spent all the time sketching the faces of his mother and father and his two brothers and sisters," the Juneau *Daily Press* reported.[19]

Well-accustomed to interviews by now, Howard allowed himself some gentle levity when the journalist insisted on an English translation for his Eskimo name (which was ultimately misspelled).

"His native name—Weiyahok—means 'rock', so thus his English surname," the reporter noted dutifully, "but Sikvoan in the Eskimo dialect does not mean anything, so Rock took the name of Howard, because that doesn't mean much of anything, either, he says."

This story, picked up in turn by the *Christian Science Monitor*[20] and *Alaska Life Magazine*, stood the fledgling artist in good stead.[21] Frances Kittridge, Mrs. Lopp's sister, asked to see his new portfolio and commissioned him to do 12 canvases illustrating Eskimo seasons for stories she was writing. The idea of being published in a widely circulated magazine that featured Miss Kittridge's writing was exciting and, although she was in her 60s at the time, Howard found her amusing to work with. She had begun her career as a school teacher, moved to the arctic to help Mrs. Lopp take care of her large brood of babies and returned to Washington State to run a chicken ranch.[22]

Howard still spent most of his time with the Lopps, even attending their University Congregational Church. The pastor, Dr. Clinton Ostrander, had been recommended by Rev. Goodman at Point Hope and Howard joined his young people's group.[23] But he also liked to party with his shipmates and some of the freer spirits he met in the University District who did not always meet the Lopps' approval.

Stopping for coffee one afternoon at Dick Wiseman's Cafe on University Way, he noticed the attractive, dark-haired girl sketching a well-dressed man in a nearby booth. She was quick to catch the likeness and when she had finished she showed the portrait to the flattered stranger who plunked down four bits for her efforts.

"How about you?" she asked when she returned to her stool. "Care to sit for a portrait?"

"I can't afford it," Howard smiled. "I'm a starving artist myself."

"I'll do you anyway," she said, deftly sketching his profile before he could object. "You know you remind me of Mala in the movie, 'Eskimo'."

He was surprised and pleased. Most people mistook him for an Oriental or asked tasteless questions.

"He's my cousin," he said.

"Have you seen his new movie, 'Hawk of the Wilderness'?"

Howard shook his head, then remembered that good models held still.

"It's O.K. I'm finished," she announced.

"Really, I've never seen anybody work that fast—or so well."

"Your good looks inspired me," she laughed. "Say, want to go to that movie?"

Howard was acutely embarrassed.

"I spent my allowance on art supplies for school and I'll be broke until next month," he admitted uncomfortably.

"I'll make you a loan," she offered. "Starving artists should stick together."

Everyone called her Jerry but, although her last name was Irish, she confided to Howard that she was part Russian and asked him to call her Jerinka. She was intrigued by the Communist Party of which he knew little and cared less, but otherwise he found her stimulating company.

The ease with which she had picked him up led Howard to hope she might be a woman of casual morals, but Jerinka insisted theirs be an "intellectual" relationship. Occasionally she invited him to her small apartment for a beer and kissed him good night at the door, but mostly they talked art or argued politics.

Jerry seemed to know everybody and one day, when he was waiting for her to finish her quick-sketch routine at Wiseman's, she introduced him to Tom Clark, a tall, lanky farm kid who had the job of dishwasher.[24] Clark was struggling to work his way through the university as a journalism major and when Jerry left for an appointment, Howard stayed on to talk.

Alaska fascinated the farm boy but he confessed he knew little about the territory. Howard drew a map on a paper napkin and held forth on geography while Clark plied him with free coffee. It was payday at the cafe and after work Clark invited Howard to have a beer with him at Bailey's. Howard was broke again. Clark volunteered to buy and, snacking on free popcorn, enjoying several rounds, they discovered they had similar dreams. Just as Howard was going to be a rich and famous artist, Clark was determined to be a rich and famous writer. He was particularly interested in Indians and asked Howard endless questions.

At length, they were interrupted by a burly workman and his girl who had passed up an empty booth in favor of theirs.

"I don't like Japs or Chinks or Goo-Goos and I especially don't like four-eyed queers that associate with them," he said glaring at Clark. "So why don't you guys go outside and get some fresh air so a couple of good, white Americans can have a booth for a change?"

Rail-thin, wearing thick glasses, Clark knew he was no match for the intruder but Howard took up the challenge.

"Whoever or whatever you are, Mister, I don't like you either," he said quietly.

"Says who? I never saw a Jap or Goo-Goo, whichever you are, that could fight his way out of a wet paper sack. Let's see how good you are before you go mouthin' off, Buster."

Howard let fly with a punch that caught the troublemaker on the chin and laid him out cold in the clutter of stale popcorn and cigarette butts. The bartender, who'd been monitoring the bout, came round with a pitcher and filled their glasses.

"On the house, boys. Thanks for doing my dirty work for me," he said cheerfully.

At closing time Clark invited his new friend back to his two-dollar-a-week room to continue their conversation.

"How do you keep in shape?" he asked.

"Well, one thing in Eskimo country is the high kick."

Clark had never heard of it so, taking a flat-footed stance, Howard demonstrated, jumping to touch an overhead light fixture with his toes. The bulb just brushed the top of Clark's six- feet-two-inch frame and the feat astonished him.

The two students continued to meet at local taverns and Nelly Lopp protested. Although liberal on most accounts— tolerant even of the suggestive nudes Rock sculptured in her basement—she was vehemently against drinking. On more than one occasion she refused to allow the Eskimo in her house because she smelled beer on his breath.

Fortunately, school kept Howard too busy to get into very much trouble. In addition to regular studies, Dr. Melville Jacobs, assistant professor of anthropology, had asked him to record the Inupiat dialect and serve as informant to produce a phonetic alphabet and grammar. It was painstaking work but Jacobs, who had studied under Frans Boas, offered considerable insight into aboriginal custom. Howard enjoyed the man and Jacobs was so charmed by the bright, articulate student, he told a staffer from the school paper that even if he never used the Rock material the project had been fun.[25]

Through Jacobs, Howard met anthropologist Erna Gunther, a contemporary of Margaret Mead, whose field was Alaska. A pedantic woman of little humor, she was, nonetheless, dedicated to careful research and when she asked Howard to work with her building a diorama of a Native village for the university museum, he was honored.[26]

He also began to form friendships with his art instructors, particularly Ambrose Patterson who often shared lunch with favored students of his life-drawing classes. Patterson was the picture of an absent-minded professor. But he offered them dazzling accounts of his early days as an artist on the Left Bank of Paris, recapturing one of art's most romantic eras.[27]

"We spent every waking moment painting," he recalled, still radiating boyish enthusiasm. "We even resented having to stop for meals. For the first year or so, we did still life. I trod the same streets and probably sat in the same cafes with Braque, Dufy, Matisse... ."

Patterson was a great admirer of Monet, Renoir and Pissarro. Endlessly he would discuss their merits, their use of color to depict light and other changes which had a permanent effect on his painting. Listening to him, Howard was in his element. And the Eskimo grew closer to other serious students with whom Patterson surrounded himself—Herbert Carlson who had the makings of a commercial artist; Irwin Caplan, a talented cartoonist; Fred Anderson, who stood out at life drawing and Shozo Kaneko, a talented Japanese who could turn his hand to anything.

The avant-garde among them rankled Howard sorely, however.

"By the time I get through listening to some of those fuzzyheaded professors talk about modern art, I don't know up from down," he complained to Tom Clark as they hoisted a few after class. "When I paint a picture of the sunrise on Mount Baker, all I can do is copy what it looks like—not what it feels like as they say you're supposed to do. I'm just not going to draw a bunch of colored squares and triangles and cubes and cylinders and call it a snow-covered volcanic mountain. That's not the way it is."[28]

Even Jerinka was trying to get him to change his style of painting and she was also nagging him to join the Communist Party.

"Supposing I was interested. With classes I wouldn't have time to join," he protested, but she dragged him to a small, dirty little hall downtown where a handful of people—mostly unkempt and wild-eyed—spouted well-rehearsed rhetoric about sharing wealth.

"It sounds all right when you're broke, but if I'm lucky enough to acquire any wealth I don't think I'll want to share it," he told her later that night when she invited him in for a beer. "I don't understand what you see in that organization."

"It takes awhile to get used to that kind of thinking," she admitted. "You have to learn to think on a level of world good. Sharing can be a wonderful experience."

As if to prove it, quite unexpectedly, she hauled him off to bed. Howard had to admit that kind of sharing *was* a wonderful experience, but he found her love-making a little bizarre. Watching fires turned her on, she explained. Not having a fireplace, she occasionally built them in her bathtub and Howard grew increasingly nervous as the number of unexplained blazes in her neighborhood increased beyond all previous record. Sailing on the *North Star* that summer offered him welcome reprieve.

"Jerinka says she's moving to San Francisco," Tom Clark informed him as they hopped a street car for the Ballard Docks. Howard chuckled with relief.

"They're famous for fires in San Francisco," he considered.

Howard had hoped Cap Whitlam would hire Clark to sail with them but the answer was no.

"He didn't want to sign me on because I was white."

"It's the first time I've ever known that to count against you," Howard said ruefully as they shared a pitcher of beer back at Bailey's.

"Well, I'm doing all right at the cafe. It's just that it isn't much of an adventure and I do so want to see Alaska."

Howard sighed and poured himself another beer. Clark raised a cautioning hand.

"Damn, I don't care what Nelly Lopp thinks. I'm 26 years old, for God sakes! I'm so tired of being dependent on other people, worrying about what they'll think. I swear to you Tom, I'm going out on my own and do well at it, no matter what it takes!"

When Howard returned from Alaska, Tom Clark was hospitalized with a hernia engendered by an unsuccessful bout with Wiseman Cafe garbage cans and complications resulting from nearly having starved to death during the first half of the Depression. Renewing his vow to succeed, Howard threw himself into his classes at the university and did some of his best work. Two of his oils were exhibited at the Seattle Art Museum[29] and Grapha Techna fraternity asked him to join their ranks. Their goal was bridging the gap between school art and the outside world. Frederick Anderson, Irwin Caplan and Shozo Kaneko were among the founders, and Howard pledged gladly.[30]

Aside from fraternity meetings and a few tours of the waterfront with comrades from the North Star, Howard partied little that year. But he did join fellow students occasionally at the home of Professor Ray Hill. Critics usually found Hill's work aggravating—"hitting consistently high standards, just missing real excellence," as one reviewer put it. Hill would not reach his peak for a decade or more but he was an inspiring teacher and Howard agreed with his philosophy of art.[31]

"Nature is my source of inspiration ... in this respect I am a realist," he lectured, wandering absent-mindedly out one door of their classroom and returning by another as his words echoed down the hall. "Lighting, color, texture heighten the design and mood. Mood seems to me to be the first and lasting response to the thing seen."

Hill's evenings with the students were homey affairs, livened somewhat by sweet kosher wine manufactured by his mother.[32] No one, least of all Howard, drank the cloying brew to excess, but Mrs. Lopp got a whiff of his breath after one such soiree and bawled him out so unmercifully that shortly thereafter he rented a room downtown. Although he remained on good terms with the family, Rock decided it was high time he was on his own. An artist needed his space and besides he was darned near 30 years old.

14

Big Money And
Big Trouble

It was late, or early, depending on how you looked at it. Howard and Moe had closed Jerry's Place at 1 a.m. and, although they'd been drinking ten-cent beers since seven, they'd paced themselves, dancing off most of the excess. As usual, they'd gone after the same girl. It was a friendly contest and tonight Moe's Clark Gable good looks won out. They stood about 50/50 on that score. No hard feelings.

Big, gruff, soft-hearted Cecil "Moe" Cole had become Howard's closest friend. They'd met back in '37 when Rock visited the *Boxer* which was up for winter repairs. Cole, who was white, had signed on as dishwasher and flunkie—the same job the Eskimo held on the *North Star*. On his own at age 15, so broke he had to fill the holes in the soles of his shoes with newspaper, Cole had battled his way to respect on the Seattle waterfront. Howard regretted that he'd never sailed with Moe, but they did plenty of cruising together when they hit port.

Usually they'd go to the bars favored by Native Alaskans, making a stop at Jerry's Place. Or maybe they'd look in on Dick Hall who lived aboard the arctic trading schooner *C.S.Holmes*. Like Hall, who was in his 70s, the ship was pretty much tied to the dock and, if they were lucky, Jim Allen might be visiting him from Wainwright. The two old whaling men were always trying to outdo one another with wild yarns.[1]

Moe knew everyone along the Alaska coast. He would give a buddy the shirt off his back. If Moe was broke, he'd borrow money from Howard and vice versa. If they both were broke and Cap Whitlam wasn't around to touch up, they'd get a loan from Jerry, the bar owner, or Mrs. Jerry, his wife. Nice to have friends like that, Howard thought warmly as he headed for his hotel at Third and Pike. And it was absolutely *wonderful* to be out on his own.

True, he missed the Lopp family and returned often to visit. But to come in at 2 a.m. with no explanations, just a wink to the room clerk ...

Not that he spent all his time carousing. During the winter of 1938-39 Rock signed up for his heaviest class load: drawing and painting, drawing from life, sculpture, and English composition which was giving him fits. In addition, there were fraternity meetings and time out for any paying jobs he could hustle.

The *North Star* had been chosen as flagship for Admiral Richard E. Byrd's expedition to Antarctica. Several of the regular crew planned to sail with her, including Moe and Charlie Salenjus, but Howard did not consider it. Instead, he got a job designing dress material. That failing, he worked part-time in an art store and sold sketches for greeting cards.[2]

Because of his $900-a-year government loan, Howard was better off than many of his classmates. Fred Anderson was fielding five or six jobs— everything from washing dishes at night to a stint as janitor at the YMCA. Others were forced to fall back on the National Youth Administration which paid the grand sum of 25 cents for 30 hours' work.[3] Mr. Roosevelt's New Deal seemed especially designed to train artists to starve, they joked, but at least they were starving in the company of talented friends.

In April of 1939, Tom Lopp died suddenly of a stroke. It was the end of an era, the local papers noted in their lavish eulogies, and Howard felt a door had closed for him as well. Lopp had been as much of a father as he'd ever known. With his broad understanding of all that was Eskimo, he'd proved a sound advisor and a wonderful friend. Muddled by grief, Howard went straight from the funeral to the Eskimo exhibit at the university museum where he often wandered aimlessly when he was homesick or out-of-sorts. The whole world seemed to be falling apart, he thought glumly as he stared at the dusty kayaks and arctic apparel of listless, long-dead furs. Not just his world, but the *whole* world.

Talk of another war was growing. The German Army had marched on Prague and Poland while the Japanese brazenly threatened the west. And Howard was beginning to feel the brunt of public backlash.

"Get off this bus, you yeller Jap!" a passenger snarled at him that night[4] when he boarded to go to a fraternity meeting. It happened so often he was becoming resigned to it. Stifling his resentment, he took a distant seat. Shozo Kaneko was probably having an even worse time, he thought. Kaneko was an American citizen, as patriotic as any, but already there was talk of putting "foreigners" away in camps.

Japanese art was much in vogue at the time. Its subtleties, which flew in the face of conventional rules of perspective and accuracy, were influencing leading artists. Someone brought the irony of it up that night and Howard warmed to the subject.

"Art is a link that knows no discrimination; a spiritual link between people, no matter who they are. It is universally understood between Indian and Eskimo, European and Chinese," he maintained.[5]

"Too bad Hitler wasn't a landscape artist instead of a house painter," Fred Anderson suggested.

One night after work, Howard stopped at Jerry's tavern by himself. Moe was out on the high seas so he shot the breeze with Jerry and Mrs. Jerry. Business was off. He was enjoying the quiet when a chunky young woman claimed the bar stool next to his.

"What'll it be, Billy?"

"The usual. A boilermaker," she said, flipping a five on the counter and lighting a cigarette. "Place is deader than Warren G. Harding. What ya celebrating?"

"The demise of the American economy," Jerry said, plunking down a beer with a jigger of whisky on the side. With an off-beat smile the girl settled the whisky, jigger and all, into her beer schooner, watched it sink and took a healthy swig.

"Thank God my old man's rich. How about your old man?" she asked turning casually to Howard.

"Whales," he replied.

"The Prince of Wales?"

"No, real ones."

She looked puzzled.

"His father is an Eskimo whale hunter," Jerry explained.

"Sounds like one whale of an occupation," she chortled at her own pun. "Buy that man a drink and I'll have another."

He'd never met a woman with a penchant for boilermakers. She was outrageous but she was quite amusing and, although he never asked her out, he began to look forward to their chance meetings.

Then one night when he was complaining to Jerry about the cramped dankness of his hotel room, Billy jokingly suggested that he move in with her.

"Can you cook?" he asked in mock interest.

"Of course not, ducky. Why do you think I want a roommate?"

The more they kidded around with the idea the more it made sense. She lived in a pleasant flat over a pharmacy near the university. The kitchen, though dusty from disuse, was serviceable. The sunny living room had good light by which to paint. And, much to Howard's surprise, the relationship turned into romance.[6]

It didn't bother Billy that he hammered away at soapstone carving on her dining room table or that his paints and easel cluttered up the living room. She considered him dashingly handsome. He had exquisite manners and, in the beginning at least, he was most attentive.

She was at least 10 years his senior and not, by current standards, a good-looking women. Judged by the criteria of the Old Masters, however, she was pleasingly Junoesque and just plain terrific in bed. Obviously she cared about him. It was the first time anyone really had, and Howard settled in tranquilly to unwedded bliss.

Mrs. Lopp was appalled at the news.[7]

"Howard, how could you?" she anguished.

"But why do you object?" he asked, puzzled. "She's very good to me."

Moe was slightly more enthusiastic.

"So she ain't no beauty, but it sure must be nice to have someone cook your meals and warm up your bed every night."

"I cook the meals," Howard allowed, "but there's lots of Billy to warm up a bed."

Howard now owed the government close to $2,000[8] in student loans. Although he had ranked high in the most advanced art classes he was woefully short of academic credits and had only sophomore standing after three years of school. Times were getting tougher. High paying part-time jobs were hard to find. And, in the summer of 1939, Rock considered dropping out of school.[9]

He had made enough of a name for himself as an artist so that he was to be included in the forthcoming *Who's Who in Northwest Art,* but he couldn't earn a decent living as a painter. No other line of work appealed to him, but Dell Thomas, a fellow parishioner at the University Congregational Church, made him a provocative offer. Thomas was a watchmaker who had done well importing cultured pearls and ivory. He found a lucrative market in Alaska which, though small in population, attracted a good many tourists.[10] Now he was seeking art items to sell them and he asked Howard to experiment with etching on ivory.

The Eskimo carvers who worked for Thomas knew nothing about engraving. Jimmy Houston, Thomas' son-in-law, had gotten Rock's name from anthropologist Erna Gunther who recommended him highly. Thomas was a friend of the Lopp family. His company was well-respected and Rock accepted the assignment.[11]

Progress was worse than slow. The blade of his penknife made unpredictable detours on the hard, slippery surface of the walrus tusk. Jimmy Houston watched nervously. He was an artist in his own right, a charter member of the Northwest Watercolor Society, and he was moving to become a partner in the family business.[12]

Howard threw the knife aside in exasperation. "It just won't work," he complained.

"I can see that," Houston said. "And if it did, it would be so slow we'd all go broke. Say, how about a dentist's chisel or some engraving tool?"[13]

"Maybe a dry point," Howard suggested.

Working with a point it took Rock two days to execute a simple drawing of a reindeer pulling an Eskimo on a sled but, filling in the etching with India ink, he was more than pleased with the results. As he was finishing, the rich bellow of a powerful baritone announced the arrival of Mr. Thomas. There were folks who claimed Thomas was crazy because of his sudden outbursts of song in public—not to mention his outspoken tirades against President Roosevelt—but the old gentleman had an affinity for Alaskans[14] and Howard genuinely liked him. Wordlessly, he handed Thomas the finished tusk.

"Wonderful!" the jeweler exclaimed. "I can sell a thousand of them. How long will the manufacture take?"

"That's the problem," Houston fretted. "This one took two days, although I will say it's worth it."

"Howard's a clever boy," Thomas considered. "He'll speed up with incentive. Something like 25 cents for a small finished bracelet piece?" the jeweler suggested.

Howard quit school to work full-time at the end of that semester. From the beginning he made $2 or $3 dollars a day which was considered good money. Then, with practice, he tripled his output and Houston suggested they promote the new line. Publicity photos were needed. One hot afternoon Howard donned his fur parka while Houston readied his camera.[15]

"Look off into the distance, like you were scanning the horizon for polar bears," Jimmy suggested, squinting into the viewfinder.

"All I can see is the University Way bus," Howard giggled. "I feel like an idiot."

"Hold your head up. I got to cut out the telephone wires," Houston called.

"And the sweat running off my nose!"

"Don't sweat, Rock. I'm going to make you rich and famous overnight," Houston insisted, and he wasn't joking. Almost overnight, photos of the handsome, parka-clad Eskimo appeared in jewelry store windows from Alaska to California, and orders came pouring in. By the fall of 1940 Rock was making $200 or so a month, more than four times his *North Star* salary.[16] He purchased a new wardrobe, began to patronize good restaurants, indulged himself and Billy in splashy evenings on the town. There was but one major drawback. He didn't enjoy the job.

Rock's original designs proved so popular that he was required to duplicate them hundreds of times. The work was dull and repetitious. Not caring to associate with Thomas' other Eskimo employees who seemed to be forever running afoul of the Seattle police, Rock began working at home. Starting after the bars closed, fortified with enough beer for a pleasant buzz, he discovered he could dash off pieces with precision that was painlessly automatic. In fact, if he drank *enough* beer, his wonderful paycheck almost seemed like found money.

In September, London was hit by the Nazi blitz and Rock was called to register for the "peacetime" draft. To his relief he was classified 4-F due to poor eyesight, but Dell Thomas assured him if Roosevelt won re-election he could "expect to pack his kit bag and go off to a full world war."

There was also threat of war on the domestic front for Billy had decided Howard should marry her. When he showed no enthusiasm, she began drinking in earnest. Warily he broached the subject.

"Boilermakers for breakfast ..."

"I just don't give a damn," she said flatly.

"Well, it doesn't add to your charm."

"Look who's talking!" she retorted. "Up on your high horse because you never take a drink before two in the afternoon. Well, you catch up fast enough when you're working. If you keep it up you're going to be just another drunken Eskimo in Dell Thomas' stable...."

Which is when he hit her. He did it without thinking and repented for weeks, but he had hit her as he would hit a man. Her ample jaw turned black and blue and she headed to her parents' home to think things over.

At first the respite was welcome. With school chum Herbert Carlson, Howard spent the weekend with the Lopp family at Rolling Bay.[17] They did not talk much about art. Although he was making more money than any of his classmates, Howard felt he'd sold out. One of these days, when he got a little ahead, he would go back to oils, he said. Easygoing Carlson let it ride. They dug clams, talked about old times and considered the time well spent.

After a week by himself, however, Howard welcomed Billy's return. He had missed her and told her so. Moved by his concern, she promised to cut down on her drinking.

Moe returned from the Pole. It called for a celebration and a follow-up celebration. Moe and Howard got in the habit of touring the night spots without Billy for she had little in common with their friends from the arctic coast.

One of the regulars in the Alaskan crowd was Anne Bernhardt from Teller. Howard had met her father, a red-haired German working longshore, and her mother was from Point Hope. There were 16 children in the family, little money and plenty of hard luck.

"Anne's got real spunk," Howard told Moe one night, as they watched her take to the dance floor with a friend.

"More than spunk," Moe acknowledged. She was a handsome woman and they vied for her company.

"Billy claims he can smell Anne's perfume every time I dance with her."

"Woman!" Moe sighed.

Howard ordered another beer.

Strangely, it was on an evening when he'd elected to stay home that the trouble started. The nation was still reeling from the Japanese attack on Pearl Harbor. War had been declared and Howard made the mistake of bringing up Dell Thomas' prediciton that he would soon be drafted. "They just feel your skin and if you're warm, you're in," Thomas had said.

Billy was appalled.

"You're an artist. They can't send you to war."

Howard shrugged. The military had jobs for artists. "Maybe I can go into camouflage. You know, design all those green and brown and black blobs that make men look look trees." he chuckled at the thought.

"Dependents get to stay with their men. They have housing for couples..."

Howard groaned. She'd been drinking and when she drank their conversations always took this bent.

"Billy, I'm not cut out for marriage and neither are you. I don't want to talk about it."

"But I love you," she wailed. "You're everything to me."

He didn't want to hurt her. "Hey, let's put on a record and dance..."

"Go dance with one of your *klootches* at Jerry's," she snapped.

Howard's eyes went hard. "Klootch" was the most degrading thing you could call an Eskimo woman.

"What does that make you?" he challenged. "I've got work to do. When you decide to sober up, give me a call."

Instead he heard her rattling bottles as she retired to the bedroom. Grimly he settled down with his work and forgot about her until sometime in the early hours when he heard a scream.

"Damn her anyway," he said, laying aside his dry point. He should have gotten the bottle away from her.

"Billy!"

Not a sound.

Wearily, he checked the bedroom. She was nowhere in sight. Confused, he noticed an open window, went to close it. Then he saw her sprawled in the alley one floor below. She was in her nightgown. He grabbed her coat and hurried down. She didn't move. There was no pulse. Her neck was broken.

Rock called the hospital and the hospital called the police.

"You just visiting or what?" the officer asked him.

"I live here," Howard said dully. "She's dead, isn't she?"

"That what you wanted?"

Howard stared at him.

"She was my girl ..."

"Little long in the tooth ..."

"Just got a reading on her folks," a second officer interrupted. "She comes from money. What's the Jap doing here?"

"Claims he lived with the woman. Looks like he mighta given her a shove."

Howard sat down heavily. How could anyone kill themselves by falling from a second-story window? Had she jumped? Had she meant to hurt him so?

Rock was suspect, but they didn't book him. He called Jimmy Houston and explained the situation. Houston asked no personal questions and was supportive. Miserable with guilt, Howard kept to himself. He might have stopped her, he thought. He should have loved her more. He grew angry at her for leaving him suspect. He faced jail or worse and, although the autopsy finally cleared him, he realized there would always be a question of his innocence.

"How could anyone even suspect such a thing?" Moe asked when Howard reappeared at Jerry's.[18] That had been Dell Thomas' reaction, too, but Howard knew he had sorely disappointed many who trusted him. How could he ever face the Dingees and the Lopps?

It had long been his goal to prove their faith in him by establishing himself as a famous artist, becoming an inspiration to his people. But in reality that dream had died even before Billy's fall. After all his work and study, he had become just another Eskimo in Dell Thomas' stable. There was no point in trying to perfect artistic techniques when he could use the time to make big money. He still longed to return to the arctic in triumph, but he found himself consigned to the demi-world of Alaskan expatriates, with a blot on his name.

Old friends were caught up in the war effort and he saw less of them. Moe went into the Merchant Marine. Herbert Carlson took paratrooper training. Irwin Caplan landed a plum assignment as cartoonist for *Yank* magazine. Tom Clark and Fred Anderson headed to Alaska with the military. [19]

Suspected of being a Nazi, Max Siemes was required to teach at an internment camp to retain his homestead. Shozo Kaneko lost his property and was also interned.[20] But Howard stayed in place and got lucky. Sales snowballed as thousands of souvenir-hungry GIs were deployed to Alaska. Rock's income increased accordingly and, since he'd already disappointed his backers at the Bureau of Indian Affairs and war made the future uncertain, he decided to enjoy it to the hilt.[21]

First among the new friends he made was R.S."Deke" Brown, son of pioneering Alaskans, who worked for a jeweler in Juneau and often traveled to Seattle on buying trips. And Alaskan Natives began to drift south, in for training, attracted by jobs connected to the war effort. Among them were Harry Ptarmigan and Emery Hunter from White Mountain days, and Tommy Richards of Kotzebue who had been an Eklutna student. Howard was delighted with their company, and together they formed the nucleus of a closely knit group. It was like old times but a lot more fun, and they lived as fast as they could on borrowed time.[22]

15

Love In Tunisia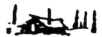

On december 30, 1942, Howard Rock was called into the Army Air
Force. He explained to his draft board that he was an artist and an Alaska
Native. Logic suggested that they train him in camouflage and send him
to the Aleutian Islands, but instead they dispatched him south.

The temperature was 15° the morning he left Fort Lewis, Washington,
and 85° when he arrived at Clearwater, Florida, three days later. He
literally sweat out training in St. Petersburg, but basic was no real hardship
for, at age 31, he could still leave his footprints on the low barracks ceiling
demonstrating the Eskimo high kick.[1]

In off hours, he corresponded with friends, most particularly Deke
Brown, who kept him abreast of what was happening in Alaska. The vulnerable Arctic Coast had been left unguarded by military planners, but
Marvin "Muktuk" Marston, who'd traveled the country as a prospector,
had formed a Territorial Guard of Eskimo volunteers which turned into a
formidable defense network. Allen Rock was among the first to join,
Brown reported. There were Native guard units in even the most primitive
coastal villages which meant there would be little chance for Howard to
land an Army assignment near home.[2] Still, thousands of men were being
sent to the Aleutians and Rock held out hope he would follow. Diligently
he applied himself to long hours in stuffy classrooms and a bewildering
barrage of aptitude tests in which he scored high in instruments.[3]

"Sioux Falls, South Dakota! What's in Sioux Falls, South Dakota?"
"It's sort of a kindergarten for radio operators," explained a buddy
who had been ordered to the same base.
"What's the population?"
"I'm not sure there is one."
"That bad?"

"Nah ... it's right up there behind Rapid City. You'll love it. And we get another train ride, too."

Rock groaned. "Are you sure we joined the Air Force?"

At least Sioux Falls was cooler. It reminded him a little of Alaska and he made friends with some local people—namely Sally who worked at a liquor store near base and introduced him to rum and coke. He was a lowly private first class and his paycheck of $60 a month didn't stretch far, but that didn't worry Sally and life looked brighter.

School proved engrossing. Back when he'd sailed on the *North Star* he'd often hung out in the radio shack, puzzling over the dit-dar-dit-dar of the wireless. Now he mastered Morse code, graduated with the top of his class and, in the early spring, was ordered to Truax Field in Madison, Wisconsin, for specialized training as a high-speed operator.

Time raced by. The Wisconsin temperature, so right in spring, turned miserably hot in summer but Howard scarcely noticed. He had become engaged in a personal war with a typewriter. To graduate as a high-speed operator he was required to receive 25 words per minute and he couldn't get past 21.

"I've been hung up for a month now, and there's less than a week left," he worried. Eddie, a classmate, had hit the magic 25 mark only the day before and understood how he felt.

"It's psychological," he insisted. "Once you get over 21 you won't have any trouble."

"But they keep sending impossible names like 'Chiang Kai-Shek,' words with a million hyphens...."

"You can do it, Rock. I've seen you pounding the sender and I know you're good. So does the CO. It's all in your head."

With three days left, Rock cracked 21, hyphens and all, and easily increased his speed to 25 in time to graduate.

His new post in Tennessee was hell-times-six hotter than Madison, and this was *winter.* He hadn't moved a muscle, not so much as a pinkie towards the typewriter on the classroom desk before him, and already his uniform was soaked through with sweat.

Smyrna must be a Greek name, taken from the classics like the ornate pillars of the stately mansions one occasionally glimpsed behind the tall, locked gates of the town. Most of the local folks were friendly, though. They'd even thrown a picnic where the good ladies of the Smyrna Congregational Parish introduced the Eskimo to southern fried chicken.

He met a cute little girl during a pleasant leave in Nashville. At her suggestion they went to visit the capitol building. Her interest in government surprised him but he went because he was, after all, a tourist and to his astonishment discovered numerous young couples necking behind the lavish shrubbery on the capitol lawn. It was amusing to make love in such an auspicious setting and he would remember the novelty of it long after the name of the girl was gone.

There were other girls, too, real southern belles, a few carpetbaggers and a USO dancer named Gigi who traveled from camp to camp. Of them all, he liked Gigi best.

"Good girls get to go to Heaven," she said. "Bad girls get to go everywhere!"

There were "For Whites Only" signs all over Tennessee, but nobody bothered him. Perhaps they mistook him for Chinese. Certainly the uniform helped. He went where he pleased and did what he liked, except that school took up an enormous amount of time.

He was learning to transmit code; pounding the single key— long holds for dashes, just a tap for the dots—his brain racing ahead of his flying fist. If he did well with the codes, he hoped he would get an Alaska assignment. The men who graduated just before him were sent there, but when his turn came he was dispatched to Camp Patrick Henry in Newport News, Virginia, to join a convoy headed for North Africa.

It was November of 1943, the worst possible season to sail the Atlantic. Soldiers were packed into Liberty Ships to a point that it was difficult to turn around. Most were ill during the stormy 12-day crossing and the stench of vomit was all-pervading. Howard did not get seasick but he felt queasy watching them. Deck space was restricted but he managed to find a spot at the rail where he could stare out at the angry seas.

"You're not one of the puking masses," a stranger with officer's braid observed, apparently glad to have some company.

"Not usually. You?"

"No, I was a seaman. Thought the Air Force would be a pleasant change, but I have yet to fly anywhere."

Howard noticed their ship followed a zig-zag course.

"Where's all the debris and the oil slick from?" he asked.

"Seven of the ships in the convoy ahead of us were torpedoed," the man said. "And five behind us, also, I hear."

"German U-boats?"

The officer nodded. Yet, miraculously, their convoy of 80 ships was never hit and Howard managed to enjoy some of the voyage. Actor Mickey Rooney was aboard, fresh from filming "The Human Comedy," and did his best to entertain the troops on a tossing stage. He was not nearly as tall as Rock, who regarded himself as a short man, and the Eskimo was intrigued by the amicable confidence with which the entertainer moved among them.

The food was bad, even by Army standards. One evening a man auctioned off an apple for $125. Bootleg Cokes were available for 10 times their original price but otherwise the black market appeared to be as limited as the cook's larder.

About eight days out, part of their convoy veered off for England, but Howard's ship pushed east, sighting Gibraltar four days later. The famous rock proved disappointing for it was just a rock and not a big one. But the Mediterranean, whose portals it guarded, was a beautiful body of water, even when you knew that German submarines lurked within its azure depths. In contrast to the violently heaving Atlantic, this inland sea would calm to a point that the horizon mingled water with sky until it was impossible to tell where one started and the other left off. A constant escort of dolphins hitched rides in the bow wake or frolicked astern. Rainbow-hued flying fish flashed in the sun, arcing and diving and flying again with stunning grace.

Although their ship stopped briefly at Gibraltar, it wasn't until they reached Oran, Algeria, that the men were allowed ashore. Despite Allied and German bombing, much of the port remained intact and on the outskirts they were accosted by a ragged Arab child armed with a bunch of newspapers.

"*Stars and Stripes*, two francs, fuck you! *Stars and Stripes*, two francs, fuck you!" he yelled, apparently well-grounded in the business by American GIs who proceeded them.

"It's gonna be just like home," muttered Eddie who marched at Howard's side.

"Well, his English is better than my Arabic," conceded Rock, who had managed to trade cigarettes for a newspaper.

They spent Christmas restricted to base in Oran. There was turkey and cranberry sauce and some of the guys in Howard's unit worked up a vat of home-brew to make it a passable celebration. Rock had been assigned to the 18th Airways Communication Squadron, detached to the Eighth Air Force. Their destination was Tunisia, but apparently Rommel, the Desert Fox, had yet to give it up. They marked time for more than a month.

"Howard, we got orders for Tunis!" The southern accent of Charlie Brooker echoed down the barracks hallway. "We're leaving in the morning."

"Then my unit can't be far behind you," Howard said. He was finishing a sketch of Eddie which his buddy intended to send home as a belated Christmas present. "Are you going by train?"

Brooker's group—half of it—had traveled over the Atlas Mountains from Casablanca, jammed like sardines into railroad cars built during World War I to accommodate 40 men and eight horses. The rest of the convoy had gone on by ship and was never seen again. Charlie, barely 21, was shaken by the experience. Howard hoped the youth wouldn't have to sail until things calmed down.[3]

"We're gonna fly!"

"No kidding?" Eddie marveled. "Hey, maybe we really joined the Air Force after all!"[4]

They did fly, landing first in Algiers, which was by far the largest city Rock had ever seen. Then on to neighboring Tunisia with its pristine sandy beaches and sprawling palaces of intricate stone lacework. No wonder the Germans had been reluctant to leave, Howard thought. Tunis was a real vacation spot. But although the elegant city with its broad, tree-lined boulevards remained almost unscathed, El Aouina Air Field a few miles distant had been bombed into oblivion. Bedraggled sheep grazed among acres of wrecked German planes. There were no roofs on the barracks; no toilets other than bomb craters. French and Arab workmen were rebuilding, but in the meantime troops made do.

Brooker saved Howard a bunk.

"It lacks comforts," he apologized as he escorted his friend to the flimsy shell of a charred building, "but what ventilation!"

"The floors wash automatically when it rains," Howard observed, glancing at the placid sky that served for their ceiling.

"Well, at least, summer's coming on."

"How hot does it get?" Rock asked.

"Not exactly Eskimo weather," Charlie grinned, "but there are compensations."

Even at 110° in the shade, the dry Tunisian heat proved tolerable, and access to a makeshift Noncommissioned Officers Club located on the Mediterranean close to the ruins of Carthage made it more so. During the height of the summer Howard swam until he was water-logged, staying in all day long. When the evening cooled there was a band and French girls, Italian girls, Sicilian girls.[5]

"So many girls," Charlie Brooker sighed. The kid was from Jupiter, Florida, population 350, where the choice of women could not have been dazzling. He looked like a movie hero—tall, blond, curly-haired—and his popularity was exhausting.

"War is just hell, Charlie," Howard chuckled, floating on his back, balancing a glass of beer on his chest.

"Actually, I think I'll be glad to get back to work," the youngster said.

El Aouina Air Force Base was being set up as the hub for all primary communications between the European Theater of Operations and the United States. There were 17 men in Howard's division with young Brooker as their chief. Rogers, their commanding officer, was seldom seen and they answered to Sergeant Anderson, who was gruff but fair.

Shifts were six hours on, twelve off, which was grueling. Messages were in code so translators had no understanding of content, but each was classified according to importance. Often urgent communiques took so much time, those of lower priority never got sent. Luckily, the station was equipped with semi-automatic sending keys which transmitted a solid dash when one side of the paddle was pressed and a dot with the other. This was a vast improvement on the old system but operators still emerged from their shifts with spinning heads.

Field Marshal Erwin Rommel, Germany's most popular war hero who based his Afrika Korps at Tunis, had treated the local populous extremely well. Many hated to see the Germans go and, fearing reprisals, conquering American commanders would not allow their troops into the city for four months. Even wireless men were armed with handguns and required to take a refresher course in their use before they were given leave.

"I can just see myself gunning down some Tunisian housewife," Eddie said as a heavily veiled Arab woman darted in front of their jeep, driving a herd of goats before her. Men wearing black tasseled red fezzes and dark capes gave them evil looks.

"We fly under the flag of peace," Vanmeter, the jeep driver, reminded them. "And our money's just as good as anybody else's."

Tunis was two cities. One was an ancient walled fortress built by the Arabs with winding cobblestone streets and open markets with names like Kasbah and Bab Souika; the other, classic European designed by French colonials who had taken the small country on as a protectorate in 1881. Since the base had recently been troubled by Arabs who were Nazi sympathizers, Howard's group bypassed the unique bazaars of the old town to enter Port of France with its broad esplanades and brightly lit sidewalk cafes. There were no incidents. They scrambled about locating French and Italian bars, learning there was no whiskey to be had at either. But there was cognac and muscat, a sweet, musky wine, and green beer, and those who were not friendly were at least not hostile.

On their second trip, Howard and Charlie discovered the Cafe Royale, a once-elegant delicatessen which still featured white tablecloths and old world dignity. It had none of the usual bar girls or noisy souvenir hawkers and they sat quietly, drinking green beer and eating hard-boiled eggs with fresh sliced tomatoes.[6]

"Boy, I could go for this as a steady diet," Brooker said.

"Can't remember the last time I had a fresh tomato," Howard agreed. "Even the green beer is not so bad."

"I have four brothers, all overseas and in action," Charlie considered. "Looks like I drew the best duty of all."

"I too wasn't anxious to join," Howard admitted. "I was making good money. Having fun for the first time in my life. But sometimes the things you fight the most, turn out for the best."

Conversation rested. The two men could sit for an hour or more and feel comfortable saying nothing. Brooker was 10 years Howard's junior, fresh out of school with no experience except odd jobs and a brief stint working for his father, building a house. They had little in common except a strong bent for honesty and an appreciation of things not said, but that was bond enough.

There was not a single customer at Cafe Royale when Howard returned alone with an afternoon to kill a week or so later. After the noisy clatter of the code room, inactivity was welcome and he relaxed with a glass of muscat, studying his surroundings.[7]

Cafe Royale was in the heart of town, next to the ornate Theatre de la Ville de Tunis and not far from the French Embassy. Most of the architecture was 1890s, amusingly rococoed with birds and flowers and simpering cherubs. The cafe, by contrast, was pure Art Nouveaux, built in the 1920s with hand-carved wood, floral murals, a gleaming pastry bar and an elegant curved counter. There was even a dance floor.

With laughter and a flurry of French conversation, three women settled at the table next to his. They were a study in contrasts—one quite tall, one average-sized, one petite despite the fact she wore the highest of heels. Howard could understand little of what they were saying but they seemed to be arguing. Once in a while he'd catch the word "American" and see them glance his way. Finally the tallest of them, a well-tailored young woman, approached his table.

"Pardon Monsieur, but do you have zee American cigarettes?" she inquired.

"No, no, no!" the shortest of them jumped to her feet. "It eez very forward. It eez very embarrassing to talk wez you. Forgive us!"

Howard was highly amused.

"It is all right," he assured her. "Of course I have American cigarettes. I have Camels. I have lots of Camels."

Grateful, mindful of manners, they inquired politely where he was from and the smallest of them, particularly, seemed intrigued to discover he was Eskimo.

"I have never seen one," she said gazing at him intently. "You must tell us all about zees Alaska."

"Do zee Eskimos swap their wives, like we have heard?" one of her companions inquired.

"No more than the Frenchman, I think," he said, and the ice was broken. When he had covered the subject of Alaska, they asked him about Washington, D.C., New York City and Chicago. Never having visited any of the three, there was little he could tell them, but they seemed delighted simply to practice their English. The afternoon flew by. Rock was due back at the base for a night shift. Reluctantly, he rose to leave.

"Wait, Monsieur," the little one who spoke the best English followed him to the door. "My name eez Madelaine Faulcon and it would be very nice to see you again some time. I own zee Hotel le Bordeaux near zee cafe. Here eez zee address."

Howard stared at the paper. She was the last one of the three he would have expected to be so forward but, in truth, she was the only one he had really looked at since they entered the cafe. Scarcely five feet tall with carefully arranged long auburn hair, large brown eyes, and an absolutely stunning figure, she was easily the most attractive woman he had ever met. She was also charming with elegant manners. Never would he have found nerve to ask her out.

"I have leave on Friday," he managed to stammer.

"It eez settled, then," she said, and it was.

Howard said nothing of the incident to young Brooker, but made discreet inquiry among the older men. Hotel de le Bordeaux was, described delicately, a place for "rapid rendezvous" and Madelaine Faulcon a lady of formidable repute. She was as wealthy as she was beautiful and, early on, she had caught the eye of a French general who was a powerful friend of the Governor of Morocco. There were others, too, all influential men. She could pick and choose.

"But a word to the wise, Rock," his informant warned. "Go easy."

Howard stiffened. "You mean because I am Eskimo?"

"I mean because our commanding officer has been courting the fair Madelaine ... rather unsuccessfully ..." he added with a wink.[8]

The hotel was a modest affair just a block from the Cafe Royale and not far from the opulent Majestic Hotel where Rommel had made his headquarters. The lobby was hung tastefully with oil paintings. The room clerk directed him to a well-furnished apartment on the ground floor.

"Good evening, sir. I'm Patrick," said the self-assured 14-year-old who answered his knock. "Mama will be with us soon."

It was not exactly the reception he'd expected from a reputed vamp. Family photos decorated the apartment. There were shelves full of books, more oil paintings, antique glass. Classical music drifted from an unseen record player.

"Mama tells me you are a painter," Patrick was saying.

"Before the military made me a soldier," Howard smiled at the youth's manful effort to make conversation.

"I have been hoping to learn," Patrick told him. "But it is difficult to teach oneself."[9]

They were engrossed in Patrick's sketch book when Madelaine arrived with a mesh bag full of groceries and a long loaf of French bread. She paused in the doorway, listening to them talk. The Eskimo's accent was charming when he tried to speak French and he had such a gentle way with the boy.

"Patrick, you will be late," she interrupted. Startled, they both scrambled to their feet.

"My poor friend, Henri, will think I have been hit by a tank," the boy said, grabbing his hat, still mindful of his manners. "My pleasure, Monsieur. I hope we will meet again."

"If your mother will have me," Howard smiled.

"Oh, she will," the boy assured him gravely. "She is cooking supper for you which means you are special. Mama does not generally cook."

Supper was "cous cous," a Tunisian specialty involving a heady blend of lamb, grains, vegetables and spices.

"That was just beautiful!" Howard declared when at last they adjourned to the living room for small cups of strong coffee.

"Patrick eez right. I do not often cook. I never had to," she admitted. "But when there eez one special, I very much enjoy."[10]

Running the hotel, he learned, was the first real work Madelaine Faulcon had ever done. The pampered daughter of French nationals living in Algeria, she married a wealthy man who became a director of General Motors in Switzerland. Upon his death in 1939 she found herself worth one-million gold francs but most of her assets were frozen in Switzerland. The hotel in which she invested in Algiers was taken over as district headquarters for the British Army. Her mother and sister were living in Tunis, and after its liberation from the Nazis she had come to join them, moving in with the sister and brother-in-law.[11]

"They had zees pet monkey. It was everywhere, zee monkey, and it drove me crazy," she recounted, wrinkling her delicate nose at the thought. "So one day I came to town and buy zee hotel and, voila, I am zee working woman."

The absurdity of it amused him. The diamond she wore on her right hand would have kept an ordinary family in comfort for a year. So, he guessed, would the antique broach at her throat.

"I know what you think," she guessed, fingering the broach. "But I will not sell zee jewels. I would rather starve."

"I can see you are a stubborn woman," he said, half teasing.

"And you?" she asked. "Are all Eskimos zees well educated? What eez your family like? Do you have any little boys? I want to know everything."

And suddenly he wanted to tell her everything—about his family and Point Hope and White Mountain School and people who had been important to him like Max Siemes, Ma Dingee and Mr. Lopp.

Unaccountably, he found himself recalling the time he and Tom Clark had been called ugly names by the bully in the bar. How much it had shaken him to have someone belittle his ancestry. He told her how his people had coped with the severe conditions of the arctic. It took great skill to deal with the frozen country and the animals and the currents and the winds, he maintained. It was something to be proud of, no matter what anyone else said.

At length he looked at his watch in embarrassment.

"I'm sorry. I had no idea of the time. I must be boring you."

She shook her head, but he was certain of it. She did not drink alcohol. He'd had a little muscat, but very little. He wasn't sure what had come over him. He seldom talked that much.

"Bad enough to be rambling—but in English, a language that must tire you to listen to. How I would love to know French."

"Zee best place to learn zee French eez in zee bed," she said, looking him squarely in the eye.

And he signed up straight-away.[12]

She set aside a room at the hotel especially for him. When he mentioned that he had no pillow at the base she sewed up a lovely one of kapok, trimmed with a pretty border of hand-embroidery.

"It's beautiful, Mineu, but I can't take it back to camp with all that fancy trimming on it," he protested. "The guys will tease the hell out of me."

"Ef you do not like zee pillow I will take it back. But I will not take zee border off," she said stubbornly. "You will take it or you will not take it but ef you do not take it, do not come back here any more."

He took it, of course, and all the ribbing that went with it, because suddenly—for the first time in his 33 years—he was irrevocably and totally in love. And Madelaine Faulcon loved him in return. She made him part of her little family and she wrote her married daughter, Priscilla, in Paris asking her to come and meet this Eskimo who was "tres gentil." Rock translated to "roche" in French and the soft-spoken Alaskan was just that, a sturdy, tranquil island in her turbulent life.[13]

When she was young, Madelaine's parents had arranged for her to marry a wealthy man much older than herself, a match so painful that she had finally divorced him despite her Roman Catholic faith. Her second marriage had been happier but her husband suffered a head injury and was ill for some time before his death in 1939, and the war that followed completely tore her life apart.

She was older than Rock; how much older, he did not care to ask. The age difference (11 years) was one reason he was attracted to her, for she was wise and sophisticated beyond any woman he had met. When he doubted himself, felt inferior because of his primitive beginnings, she gave him "beaucoup courage," as she was wont to put it.[14] And the fact that he had supplanted numerous generals and his own base commander in the affections of such a beautiful woman was not lost on him, either.

Mail call brought a letter from Deke Brown who had just traveled to Point Hope to buy whale bone and baleen baskets:

> I asked for Sam Rock, all right, and he came out with a shotgun about a mile long with a bore about as big and the front sight was missing. But he was going out hunting for eider ducks and I don't have to tell you he got some.
>
> Well, I told him you were in Africa and he didn't understand me worth a damn so he got ahold of this Eskimo kid and asked me to tell the same story again with an interpreter. He was sure interested in his son and he wanted to learn all about you and Africa and I've never been to Africa but I tried my best and he went away satisfied.
>
> He certainly is a good-sized man. You'd have to be a good-sized man to shoot that gun.[15]

Howard chuckled and tucked the envelope into his pocket to show Madelaine. They'd been together a year and a half now, and she enjoyed his letters from home. But Madeline was not her usual gay, amusing self that night. She seemed terribly worried and he noticed that she was pale.

He'd gotten a pay raise with his recent promotion to corporal. He wanted to take her out, but she did not care to go.[16]

"Mineu, what's wrong?" he pleaded.

"Oh, Howard, I am going to have zee baby," she said putting her arms around him. "And I am very, very much afraid of zee local people when they find about zee baby. And I have been thinking very, very much that zees baby will not be born."

He was speechless. The idea of a baby thrilled him beyond anything he had imagined. It was clear she wanted the child as much as he did. She was Catholic which made the decision doubly difficult. But he had seen enough of her class-conscious, French community to realize it would be impossible for her to buck. It was not simply that he was an Eskimo, but that he was an American soldier of no real status.

"I have zees friend in Algiers. A woman doctor friend and I will fly to see her," she was saying. Howard nodded dumbly, holding her, feeling her tears—and never in his life had he known such sadness.

16

Au Revoir

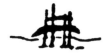

HOWARD HAD NEVER SEEN a thunderstorm from the top. It was a spectacular thing, but he would have enjoyed it more with oxygen. The B-47 in which they'd hitched a ride, had climbed to 30,000 feet to get above the ceiling. Some of the boys were already giggling inanely which was the first warning of oxygen sickness. The pilot would have to take them down soon or they'd all be in bad trouble. Charlie Brooker wasn't laughing but his complexion had turned puce.

"Some vacation!" he groaned.

"Mt. McKinley is 20,320 feet tall. I figure we must be about 10,000 feet over the top by now," Howard said, delving into memory of White Mountain geography class in an attempt to distract his friend.

"Hand me my ice ax," Charlie said weakly. "I want down."

Madelaine was still in Algeria when Brooker engineered a trip to Nice, France. Howard welcomed the diversion, but the trouble-plagued flight was more than he'd bargained for. They broke through the murk just as the pilot skirted the midsection of a formidable mountain. Lightning flashed around them and below, scarcely more than a minuscule scar, was a short rocky strip.

"This is not Nice!"

"Either way you want to pronounce it," Brooker grinned.

But they landed, triumphant, in a hail of stones.

Rock and Brooker ended up at Monte Carlo, Monaco. Although the casinos were closed, the bars of the extravagant hotels were noisily operational and there was no lack of diversion for visiting GIs. Then one of their group learned that a Mitchell B-25 was headed for Italy. They took it. Howard, who was older than the rest and not quite as enthusiastic about ogling girls, hoped to see the wonders of Rome. He talked Charlie into a walking tour of the Coliseum which they found open and empty, but there was little left of the art treasures of which he had read so much. Much of Italy—especially the Boot which they traveled by train—had been flattened by bombs. People were buried in the rubble by the hundreds and the stench was overpowering.[1]

Madelaine was not well when she returned to Tunis. She had lost considerable weight, was moody and sad, but after a while things went back to a happy norm. She began planning to buy a hotel at Bizerte, a coastal resort town about 25 miles from the city. It had been leveled by bombardment but the hotel, which stood on the outskirts, was only slightly damaged. She would repair it and furnish it with rugs and furniture from Paris.

"When zee war eez over many tourists weel come," she predicted. "And you weel be zee manager. You weel look so handsome in zee three-piece suit."

"But I'm an artist," he protested.

"Oui, but zees ez only in zee beginning. You weel make zee fortune and paint to your heart's content."

"And you will become the hotel cook," he teased her. "But that is still a long way off."

Then, suddenly, it wasn't. There was a flurry of excitement when Roosevelt, Churchill and De Gaulle visited their base en route to a conference at Yalta. The Germans surrendered. The atom bomb was dropped on Hiroshima. El Aouina communications center exploded, also, with top priority communiques, and Japanese surrender followed eight days later.

"We're going home!" Eddie whooped. "The war is over!"

No provisions had been made for travel to the States. Each man fended for himself and Howard and Charlie Brooker remained in Tunis long after most of the troops had departed. Women was a topic the two friends never discussed but Howard suspected that, like himself, the youngster had someone he found difficult to leave. Then Brooker, too, packed his duffel.

"Guess it's time," he said as they shared one last green beer at the Cafe Royale. "Some of the guys think it's possible to connect with a Liberty Ship out of Algiers. Want to come?"

"I'll wait until after the rush," Rock answered, although they both knew the rush had long since passed.

Come winter, El Aouina Air Force Base was nearly deserted and there was no more excuse to delay. Madelaine was still making plans for their future. She would buy a store for him. The sizeable Italian community and the French were fond of Nordstrom shoes and Parker pens and Gillette razor blades. She would import these things and Howard would be store manager. He protested that the plan wouldn't work.

"It's hard to say which is worse, my math or my French, and I don't know one word of Italian," he pointed out. "I would be a disaster and I cannot live on your money."

"Zen we weel think of something else," she insisted. "You weel be back in Tunis and we weel be very, very happy."

She threw a brave little farewell party in his honor, inviting her sister and brother-in-law and Patrick and a few friends. There was black-market pink champagne and all Howard's favorite dishes, but it was an occasion devoid of laughter.[2]

"No one weel ever love you more than I do," she whispered when she saw him to the door shortly before dawn of the next day. It was cold. She shivered in the winter air. She seemed so small and childlike with her auburn hair unknotted, falling in rich waves to her waist.

"I find it so hard to leave you ..." his voice broke and he realized he could never tell her how much a part of him she had become. How weak he felt without her.

"Beaucoup courage!" she smiled.

17

Marriage

"Home in time for Christmas." The man who issued discharge papers
beamed as if he personally had made it all possible, but Howard had no
home to go to when he walked out the gates of Fort Lewis, Washington,
December 18, 1945. Beds were scarce. He was grateful to get back his
dingy room at the rundown hotel on 3rd Avenue while he waited for
veteran's housing.

His former employer, Dell Thomas, had sold to partners Johnson,
Trinell and Houston, but they welcomed Rock back. In fact, he had no
choice but to work for them because he had earlier signed a five-year
contract without realizing how binding it was.

"How ironic that hundreds of thousands of unemployed veterans are
desperately seeking jobs and I—who want only to return to you, my Mineu
—am tied to one that pays me exceptionally well," he wrote Madelaine.

Yet, much as he missed her, it was great to be back.[1] He marveled at
the big, well-stocked department stores with their extravagant Christmas
displays; at the seemingly infinite variety of fresh meats, fish and vegetables at the Pike Place Market. He preferred the tall spruce of Washington State to paltry palms. When it snowed he was ecstatic.

Moe Cole had married and settled down. Howard missed his company,
but Jerry and Mrs. Jerry were still in the bar business and the Alaska crowd
was back with reinforcements. Tom Richards and Tony Joule's son,
Reggie, were in Seattle training to be airline pilots. Anne Bernhardt came
by occasionally with her sister, Betty, or Dorothy Leask from Annette
Island whose brother, Wally, played basketball at University of Washington. Harry Ptarmigan was passing himself off as a Chinese waiter while he
attended barber college. Even Harry Apodruk had gotten himself out of
White Mountain.

"Came south at the beginning of the war. Drifted into logging because it paid good money, but now I'm going to Edison Tech to become an advertising artist,' he told Howard proudly.[2]

"What about your cousin, Ester?"

"Happily married with a mob of kids, and Mary Ellen Ashenfelter is married, too. I think she has a little girl. Lorena Linclon worked in the Eskimo Village of the World's Fair in New York City before she came home to marry Clint Gray. And Arthur Upicksoun has a great job as mechanic for the FAA."

Howard was always pleased to hear good news of White Mountain alumni.

"Everyone seems to be doing O.K."

Harry looked surprised. "Didn't you hear about Joe Bill? They hung him at Walla Walla penitentiary last September."

"For what?"

"He raped and killed a little girl."[4]

Howard stared at his drink, remembering how Joe Bill had won all the spelling contests; how elegantly he had danced with Mamie Pickett, how much he had wanted to succeed.

"Are you sure it was the same Joe Bill?" he asked.

Harry nodded. "Joe always wanted to make the headlines."

Howard had loved Bainbridge Island ever since he'd summered there with the Lopps, and when a housing project opened up in Winslow he took am apartment there. He liked commuting by ferry and he especially liked the distance it put between him and his job.

James Houston had invented a machine that would etch basic designs on ivory using templates. The process, which was strictly mechanical, was turned over to some hireling and Howard was given the task of filling in the outlines by hand. Since Houston did many of the original designs, there was little rom for creativity. Rock despised the work more than ever but the increased output fattened his paycheck.[4]

Having paid off his college loan, he spent most of his money entertaining himself. He still loved Madelaine but he could not understand her passionate letters without the help of an interpreter which he was embarrassed to seek. He was not free to go to Tunis, nor could she come to the States, and he began dating other women.[5]

Everyone but Howard seemed to know the petite, pale-skinned girl with chestnut hair who stopped by Jerry's one evening in June of 1946. There was a round of friendly hellos as she settled on a stool next to Emery Hunter.

"Who is she?" Rock asked Tommy Richards.

"I keep forgetting you didn't go to Eklutna with us. That's Delores Broe."

"She went to Eklutna? But she looks white?"

"As white as they make 'em. Her family had a homestead up there."

"What's she like?"

"OK, I guess. She was all hung up on Emery's brother, Bruce Hunter, who was going with Mary Ashenfelter," Richards recalled.

"She's a beautiful girl."

"Reminds me a little of the Wicked Witch of the West ... or was it the East?" Richards shrugged.

"Delores Broe never said anything bad about anybody," Harry Apodruk spoke up.

"I never said she did." Richards defended.

Rock introduced himself. Emery obligingly made room for him. "I feel like I know you," she smiled. "The girls at school were always talking about you. They said you were the brightest boy at White Mountain and a wonderful artist and that you were the handsomest boy in Alaska—with John Starr second."[6]

"I never met John Starr," Howard chuckled.

"I don't care to, now that I've met number one," she said breathily, and of course he asked her to dance. She was shorter, even than Madelaine, and there were light freckles like melting snowflakes on her milk-white skin. Her eyes were the clearest blue and there was a naivete about her that enchanted him.

Delores Broe had suffered a rotten childhood. Her natural father, a Hollywood moviemaker, deserted when she was tiny and her stepfather, Sig Broe, was a master of subtle child abuse. When Delores lost her mittens down the well, Broe lowered her in a bucket to retrieve them. He forced her to drown a litter of kittens she had tried to adopt and her dreams were cluttered with other macabre memories of her foster parent's attempts to "make her strong."[7]

Broe had lost a fortune in the Depression and their homesteading venture in Eklutna was his attempt to recover. Delores' mother was a fine commercial artist and she hated the harsh life. Delores was required to work hard, too—feeding the stock and helping with the haying in addition to the usual household chores. But her stepfather did allow her to keep a horse which made it all bearable.

On Broe's death in 1937, Delores' mother opened a hat shop in Anchorage and later married a well-to-do Oregonian. Delores returned to her stepfather's family long enough to graduate from high school at age 16, then struck out on her own for Alaska where she landed a good job as secretary for the Corps of Engineers in Anchorage. Eventually she managed to buy back her horse which had been sold despite her mother's promises to the contrary, and, with two partners, founded the North Pole Riding Academy. The pioneering venture ultimately folded, taking all her savings, but she was gamely planning to start over.

Howard found Delores boundlessly optimistic and fun to be with. They made a handsome couple. Heads turned when they walked into a room. And, discounting her passion for horses, they seemed to have everything in common. She, too, loved art, music and books. She adored a good party. They danced and drank and necked passionately whenever the opportunity arose and three weeks after their first meeting, Rock proposed.[8]

"I'm not sure," she said.

"But I thought you loved me," he stammered.

"I do," she confessed. "But I love Bruce, too."

"Bruce Hunter?"

She nodded.

"Well, then, marry him."

"He refuses," she sighed. "He's got TB and he's going to die. He says it's not fair to me. But I'm not sure it's fair to you, either."

Delores had been in love with Hunter since the age of 12 when she discovered the handsome Athabascan in the superintendent's office at Eklutna, crying his eyes out because his mother had just died of consumption. Being older, Hunter paid little attention to the compassionate adolescent. He was enamored with Mary Ellen Ashenfelter, but Delores returned to Alaska in hopes of winning him. When Bruce contracted TB and was sent to Toppenish Hospital in Washington State in 1942, Delores followed and when he was transferred to Tacoma she moved there, too. Years dragged by. Hunter's condition worsened. Delores pressed for a commitment, but he flatly refused her.

Howard thought of Madelaine. He thought of her more often than he cared to admit although her letters had long since stopped.

"Certainly it is possible to love two people at the same time," he suggested, gently. And Delores' beautiful blue eyes were so trusting, he was certain their marriage would work.

He did not write of their plans to his parents for it would pain them that he had not married within their race. Later, when he could take Delores to them, they would understand, but it was simply too far to travel without proper planning.

Delores' mother was also against mixed marriages and she did not care how charming, well-educated and financially secure the Eskimo might be. In hopes of placating her, Howard decided upon a church wedding. Mrs. Broe did not soften but for once her daughter proved equally stubborn. Delores was 23 years old and she saw Rock as her last chance at happiness.[9]

Jimmy Houston agreed to be Howard's best man. Norma Whitney Hurley, who had worked with Delores at the Corps of Engineers, was her matron of honor. There were no others present when the Rev. Clinton Ostrander united the couple at University Congregational Church on a Friday morning, July 19, 1946.[10]

Howard was enormously proud of his beautiful bride. Making a good, Christian marriage compensated somewhat for the bitter humiliation of Billy's death and he planned their honeymoon around visits to Mr. and Mrs. Neeley at South Bay, Washington, and Max Siemes and the Dingees in Trail.

"Well, what do you think, Max?" Howard asked when he and Siemes settled in for the afternoon with some home-brew. Delores had decided to go riding alone because earlier attempts to teach Rock had proved a dismal failure and he was too lame to try again.

"I think you're never going to cut it as a cowboy," Siemes replied, deadpan.

"No, seriously, what do you think of Delores?" Both the Dingees and the Neeleys had seemed pleased for him, but Max remained noncommittal.

"Well, she can sit a horse and she's a bright, good-looking woman," the artist allowed, frowning slightly. "But I haven't changed my views on marriage, Howard. I still hold with writer Guy de Maupassant that it's a long dull meal with the dessert at the beginning."

"I should have known better than to ask a confirmed bachelor," Howard laughed. But, in truth, even dessert had been somewhat of a disappointment.

Delores's innocence was one reason Howard had chosen her for a bride, but in contrast to the sensual sophistication of Madelaine their lovemaking was lackluster. He found his attention straying to other women even though he was determined not to cheat. Hurt and bewildered, Delores retaliated by comparing him unfavorably to Bruce and by flirting outrageously with any attractive man who happened by.

"What the hell do you think you're doing?" he demanded as he hustled her out of a cocktail lounge shortly after their honeymoon. "I come out of the men's room to find you dancing cheek-to-cheek with some longshore-man."

"We weren't dancing cheek-to-cheek. We were just dancing," she defended. "Besides I saw you talking to that blonde at the bar. Tommy tells me you used to go with her."

"So what? We're still friends, but I'm not about to cheat on you, Delores. Is that what you think?"

"I don't know what to think," she answered miserably. "Bruce never pushed me around and yelled at me."

"Bruce never married you, that's why!" he shouted. "You're my wife and I want you to act like a wife!"

But Delores was naturally friendly and outgoing. She craved attention and Howard gave her less of it as he settled back into his habit of working on ivory etching in the wee hours of the morning. Flirting with others was the only way she could be certain he still loved her, but unfortunately it threw him into increasingly jealous rages.

"I'm sorry," he said stiffly, after he'd nearly throttled her on the kitchen floor following a particularly vicious verbal battle. "I love you so much that I just go crazy when I see you with anyone else."

"Love me ... you damn near killed me," she said, shaken to the core. "Last week when you blacked my eye you said it was an accident—that nothing like that would ever happen again. Well, I've read about shell-shocked veterans but you weren't even in combat, Howard Rock. You're just plain crazy!"[11]

It lasted less than a year. She left with only the clothes on her back and shortly thereafter Rock received divorce papers which stated her views with clarity:

> The defendant has been and is guilty of cruel treatment toward the plaintiff and of personal indignities toward her which render her life burdensome. The defendant is of an extremely jealous nature and unjustly accuses the plaintiff of improper conduct and of being an unsatisfactory wife and by his actions has caused the plaintiff mental and physical distress and has caused her to feel humiliated.
>
> The actions of the defendant have caused the plaintiff to lose all love, affection and respect for the defendant and has made it impossible for the plaintiff to again live with the defendant as husband and wife.[12]

Rock did not contest. The only property settlement Delores sought was return of her maiden name. Divorce was quickly granted but he left her clothes hanging in his closet for more than a year after the decree was final.[13]

"Happy 1947!"

At closing time Howard and fellow Alaskan refugees had moved their New Year's party from Jerry's to someone's apartment. Howard sat moodily nursing a beer. The music was country western—something about being lonesome in the saddle—and he wished he'd stayed home. Nearby he noticed a dark-eyed girl who was considerably younger than the rest of the crowd and looked every bit as lost as he felt.

"Where you from?" he asked.

"Nome," she said, brightening. "White Mountain, really, but they threw my father out of there because he was white. Harry Apodruk's a relative of mine."

Her name was Betsy Peterson. She was bright and funny, but painfully unsure of herself. He remembered that feeling all too well.

"Do you have a job?" he asked.

"At a dry-cleaning shop, but I'd rather not think about that," she said, wrinkling her nose in distaste. "Where do you work?"

"I'd rather not think about that, either," he grinned.

The gang at Jerry's was easygoing. Nobody dated anybody and they usually trooped off to supper as a group. Being at loose ends, Betsy Peterson got into the habit of tagging along and Howard worried that she would end up in some kind of trouble. Not that he was interested in her romantically. The girl was scarcely out of her teens and he had established beyond all doubt that he preferred experienced women. But she reminded him of his sister, Ruth, and he became increasingly concerned about her.

"How much do you make at the dry-cleaning place, anyhow?" he demanded when she dragged in discouraged from a hard day on the job.

"I don't even want to think about it," she grimaced.

"Look, my wife has left me and I need a housekeeper and cook. You could come over on the ferry in the afternoons and leave when supper's ready, if you like. I'll pay you what you're making at the plant—maybe a little more."

She looked at him in surprise.

"Why did your wife leave you?"

"She liked to ride horseback and I didn't," he said, pleased with the partial truth of the explanation. The idea of Howard on horseback made her giggle and Betsy's giggle was infectious. "But Howard, I don't have any idea how to cook," she suddenly recalled.

"That's all right. I'll teach you."

It couldn't have worked out better. Betsy's comings and goings put some order in Rock's haphazard life and she kept his house tidy. She was, indeed, an awful cook, but she improved. He allowed her to bring friends over to party but kept a fatherly eye on them. Occasionally he scolded her and she argued that he was too tough on her, but a deep feeling of trust grew between them.

Still, Rock was careful to keep his personal life to himself for it was becoming increasingly wild. He made friends with many island residents and in the summer of 1947 he joined Colen Hyde American Legion Post #172, which sponsored weekly dances and a lively bar. There was a scandalous divorce rate among the membership and Rock was rumored to be involved.[14] He also frequented a Bainbridge bar called the Bucket of Blood where wives of shipyard workers often came unescorted to cash their husband's paychecks and again it was suspected that the handsome, well-mannered Eskimo was the breaker of homes.[15]

During this period most of the Native crowd with whom Rock had chummed returned to Alaska. Tom Richards and Reggie Joule became bush pilots; Emery Hunter and Arthur Upicksoun got work with the Federal Aviation Agency.

Still, Howard occasionally dropped by Jerry's and he befriended several newcomers including Arthur Upicksoun's younger brother, Joe, who was a crewman on the *North Star*. The two teamed to go drinking or play miniature golf when Upicksoun was in port.

Rock also looked forward to Deke Brown's newsy visits and kept a sharp lookout for other Alaskans. One of the best places to find them was Pike Place Market which sold fishheads and other Eskimo staples. Howard made a habit of shopping there and one morning he was rewarded by a shy greeting in Inupiaq.

"Eskimo, maybe?" a pretty young woman was asking.

"Yes, Eskimo right here," Howard answered, delighted. "Every time I come here I run into someone."

"Angelia Davidovics from Kotzebue," she said when he introduced himself. "Your family used to stay with mine when they came to Kotzebue to trade each spring. I knew you when you were a little boy."[16]

He remembered Angie, too, for she could drive a dog team as well as any boy and was kinder than most to outsiders. She was married now to a GI, had grown into a good, sensible woman and he felt comfortable talking with her.

Her early memory of him was as a jolly little fellow and she was saddened by the changes that she saw. It was obvious, despite his financial success, that Rock's life was not going well.

"If you're not too happy, why don't you go home? Go back up home and get yourself a good wife," she ventured. "I'm going back just as soon as I can."

"Well, Angie, I'd love to live there again but I'm so used to modern conveniences I don't think I could stand that any more," he admitted. "No toilets, no running water. I'm used to all that and I like this life."

Still, her suggestion stuck in his mind. He hadn't seen his parents in almost a decade. They were in their 60s. It would be good to go home and make his peace with them. If things worked out, perhaps he would stay.

Tommy Richards had earned a good reputation as a pilot and Howard was happy to fly with him to Point Hope from Richards' base at Kotzebue. It was a lovely day just after spring whaling season. Below them the ice of the Arctic had broken and floated in patches that looked like lace.

"Do you make this run often?" Howard asked.

"Never have," Richards admitted. "There's one little problem with it."

"What's that?"

"There's no airstrip at Point Hope," Richards answered blithely.

They landed nose in, but Richards did a neat job of it. The villagers, who viewed the accident as routine, repaired the propeller and had the plane ready to go in half an hour.[17] In the excitement, Howard had little chance to greet his family. Now Sam welcomed him warmly in Inupiaq and, beaming, he attempted to answer in kind, but no words came. Although he could understand everything that was said to him, he'd lost forever the ability to speak his native tongue.

It was, nonetheless, a wonderful reunion. The presents he brought them—watches and jewelry—were well received. And they seemed genuinely glad to see him. To Howard's amazement his father remained so strong that, at age 65, he accidentally broke the neck of a catsup bottle whose stubborn cap he was attempting to remove. And Emma appeared to have mellowed.

"I see now you have learned a few things more than what you learned on that first day of school," she laughed, recalling how proud the youngster had been at not having farted. "You must tell us about all the things you have seen."[18]

The first thing he had to explain was Africa for his father was still puzzling over Deke Brown's report. Howard drew a map and spoke at length about the curve of the earth and they drifted into a long philosophical discussion about scientific theory versus the Eskimo way of thinking. They talked happily for hours—Sam with his pipe, Howard with his Camel cigarettes—and Emma seemed not to mind that the air around them turned blue.[19]

The village was little changed—too little. Mumangeena was in Wainwright and there was a new crop of young people, but other than that, they were living in the past. The Rev. Hoare's light plant had long since failed. Oil lamps were back in fashion. Water was hauled from three brackish wells or melted from snow. There were 17 frame houses, 22 sod-insulated igloos, 36 families and 304 dogs. There was a struggling cooperative store, but no economic base beyond hunting.

Allen had moved to Fairbanks to work construction and Eebrulik was talking of following, for Point Hope's average yearly income was less than Howard made in a month.[20] Nor was government aid much in evidence, even for the village school which ran out of books at the seventh-grade level.

Luckily Mae, his precocious young niece, was headed for White Mountain School which had recently reopened.[21] Sam and Emma had informally adopted the child from his sister, Helen, which gave her an edge. Sam had even gone to the trouble of figuring out square roots on his own, so he could help Mae with her homework.

"I could never master math, even with a teacher," Howard marveled.

"Grandpa's pretty smart," Mae allowed with a cocky grin that won his heart. "After all, he picked me out of the litter."

Unfortunately, her sister, Irene, had not been so lucky. The girl was equally bright and personable, but had been offered no chance at high school, and Howard agreed to lobby for her.

He did his best to settle back into village life, attending church, even teaching a Sunday school class. He began dating Hilda Kunik, a local girl, and it seemed a happy match. But he grew increasingly restless.[22]

En route to Point Hope, Rock had stopped to visit his old teachers, Mamie and Frank Pickett, who strongly urged him to help his people.[23] But what in the name of heaven could anyone do for them, he wondered? Most stood by their hunting traditions and seemed unconcerned about poverty and the backwardness of their village.

He decided to touch base with his brother, Allen, who had moved to Fairbanks and appeared to have a foot firmly planted in both worlds. Allen had started working for contractors when the military built a Distant Early Warning station at Cape Lisburne and easily found work as a cement finisher between hunting seasons. Howard noted with approval that Allen dressed and spoke well.[24] After a pleasant supper with his family, the two brothers struck out alone to get reacquainted. The evening was genial until Allen asked about Howard's marriage. They were sharing a bottle of whisky Howard had stashed in his suitcase. Both had more than enough to drink.

"Aren't Eskimo women good enough for you?" Allen needled. "Why do you embarrass your people by marrying a *tanik?*"

"I've gone with a lot of women, white and Eskimo," Howard said, trying to hold his temper in spite of his brother's use of the derogatory Eskimo term in referring to whites.

"So I hear. I also hear you're making thousands of dollars down there, but we don't see any of it. You must know Father and Mother have been on welfare for the last eight years."

Howard was stunned. It never occurred to him to ask. He had been adopted out. Only now, after all this time, was he beginning to feel a part of the family.

Allen was too caught up in his angry denouncement to listen to anything Howard might say in his own defense.

"I send our parents money. Eebrulik hunts for them," he was shouting. "And you—you who have become nothing but a *tanik* yourself—live in luxury in Seattle, playing around with your white whores ..."

Allen was taller than Howard and in good shape, but the bitter fist fight that ensued was a draw. No discussion followed. And Howard returned to Seattle discouraged.

18

The Downhill Slide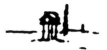

A DISPROPORTIONATE NUMBER of Seattle's skid row derelicts were Alaskan Natives. Howard avoided the district whenever possible but Ed "Buck" Weaver had asked to meet him there saying he needed moral support. Weaver, who had a cement finishing business on Bainbridge, had served as fire chief and marshal in Fairbanks in the 1940s, and Rock had taken an instant liking to him when they met on the ferry. Buck introduced him to Ted Lambert, a popular Alaskan artist whom Weaver had helped put through school, and they had other friends in common.[1]

The subject of Weaver's waterfront quest turned out to be a brilliant Fairbanks attorney—a white man who had gone out of his way to prove that Eskimos had no monopoly on alchoholism. They were old friends, Buck told Howard. If he could find the lawyer, he thought he could rehabilitate him.

"Hey, brother, you got money for a cup-a coffee?" Drunk though he was, one of the winos recognized a fellow Eskimo and he hung desperately on Howard's sleeve. "Look, ol' buddy..."

"I'm not your buddy," Rock said, brushing him off distastefully, quickening his pace. Buck reached for his wallet. Howard shook his head. "You do that, and we'll be besieged."

"Sorry to drag you here," Buck apologized. "Why do you suppose booze hits them so hard?"

It was a question Rock had often asked himself. There was a theory that Eskimos couldn't drink because of their physical makeup, but he had matched many a white man drink-for-drink. He had Max Siemes to thank for his well-studied introduction to alcohol and he was always careful to buy nothing but the best liquor.

They found Weaver's friend under a pier, out cold. His elegant three-piece suit was muddy and stained. He cradled a half-empty bottle of cheap wine to his chest.

"No thanks, I just had some," he murmured when Weaver shook him. Then, opening his eyes. "Ah, go chase a fire truck, Buck."

Buck did get the lawyer dried out for a week but he went back to the skids. From the beginning Rock had predicted it was a futile mission, but it did cross his mind that Buck had staged the thing partly for his benefit. Howard's own alcohol intake had increased alarmingly since his return from Alaska. Several friends had remarked on it.

Rock sent no money to his parents nor did he attempt to help his Aunt Mumangeena who was also on welfare. He did write his sister, Helen, offering to pay daughter Irene's way to Seattle and sponsor her education, but when Helen refused to let the 15-year-old go, Rock turned his back on his family.[2]

His net worth was about $50,000, he told Arthur Upicksoun when his old classmate came to visit in 1951,[3] and his major philanthropy appeared to be giving a nonstop round of parties. The charming little house he leased overlooking the water at Ferncliff was perfect for entertaining.

Rock no longer introduced himself as an artist but as a "novelty designer," so fellow members of the Legion were surprised and pleased when he volunteered to decorate the walls of their post with murals of Washington scenery.[4] Occasionally he painted portraits for friends. He did a bust of his father from memory, but most of his artistic energies were confined to the lucrative etching of ivory steak-knife handles and bracelet pieces.

In August of 1951 Howard got word that Sam Rock was dead and that Allen and his wife were taking his mother into Fairbanks to live with them. The thought of the free-spirited Emma cooped up in a city apartment away from friends and her small team of dogs caused Howard almost as much grief as his father's loss. Allen made it clear, though, that he was persona non grata, so Howard turned his attention to problems closer to home.

The Ferncliff parties had gotten out of hand. There were allegations of wife-swapping and two of Howard's friends left spouses to run off together. Gossip at the Legion became equally embarrassing. Someone painted out one of Rock's murals, apparently in anger over the Eskimo's attentions to his wife. Rock dropped out of the club.[5]

Mary Ellen Ashenfelter Horner Knott Gibson was looking good. She ordered Chivas. "Nothing but the best," she smiled, and her well-tailored suit lent credence to the boast. Her shoes and matching purse were handmade of expensive Italian leather, the outfit crowned with a fashionable hat. She didn't look white, but she didn't look Eskimo either. She was witty, well-read and she could talk on any subject.

"Looks like you've come a long way," Howard observed, admiringly. "Have you been back to White Mountain recently?"

"Back?" The thought truly stunned her. "Why would I do that? Only losers go back!"

It was Carl Morgan and his wife Beryl, White Mountain teachers, who first suggested that Mary Ellen might pass as a white woman and that was the route she had elected to take. Borrowing (never to return) a red wool suit and new blue coat from a trusting freshman named Kitty Evans, she traveled to Pasco, Washington, with the family in 1936. It quickly became obvious that passing for Caucasian would not be as simple as the Morgans had hoped, but Mary Ellen had been the fastest typist in her class and learned quickly.

She landed a job as a telephone operator and was on her way to establishing a career when she fell in love.[6] Sadly, George "Jack" Horner was the very thing she sought to escape. Part Cherokee Indian from the Oklahoma reservation with even less education than herself, Horner drifted from job to job and finally out of Mary Ellen's life, leaving her with a small daughter.[7]

Four years later, scraping by as a waitress in the Cascades Hotel, she met Lyle Knott, a Yakima mechanic, who married her and she bore him a son. It was in other respects a disastrous match and Mary Ellen started drinking. Gibson, her current husband, was a house painter who let her come and go as she pleased and he offered little resistance when she moved in with Rock.

Howard was enchanted to find a hometown girl who had become sophisticated enough to share his tastes. Determined to impress her, he purchased a honeymoon cottage near the beach in the West Blakely district of Bainbridge[8] and a new car which he proudly referred to as "My Little Chevy."[9] When winter came, he presented Mary Ellen with a fur coat and also contributed cheerfully to the upkeep of her wardrobe which included 50 pairs of shoes and almost as many hats.[10] She was a woman of considerable charm. She had class. Showing her off became the joy of his life.

"She's the finest cook I've ever seen," he boasted to his former housekeeper, Betsy, and her new husband, Lou Towne, an Alaskan riverboat man.[11]

"You could have gone all night and not mentioned that," Betsy winced, recalling some of the awful failures she'd foisted off on Rock before he taught her to cook. "But it's wonderful to see you so happy."

"You know, I really am," he marveled. "I don't know what my life would have been if I hadn't found Mary Ellen."

Considering the volatile romantic past of both parties, the match was remarkable in its tranquility. Howard showed no interest in other women. Mary Ellen gave scant cause for jealousy beyond her compulsive affection for alcohol. Although she had yet to divorce Gibson, Rock introduced her as "Mrs. Rock" and purchased his house in the name of husband and wife. He rejoined the Legion, became a solid citizen. When Eebrulik's girl, Dorothy Mazzola, came to visit her uncle in 1953, she found him living in pleasant domesticity. His home was neat and well-furnished. A bust and oil portrait of Sam Rock occupied places of honor in the living room. There was a well-mannered cat named Alice.[12]

Although Mary Ellen maintained ties with a number of Alaskans and enjoyed making rounds of Native bars, she detested anything that smacked of "Nativeness," and if outsiders inquired after her origin, she simply froze.

"Why are you ashamed of being what you are?" Howard asked her following a painful evening during which a well-meaning Bainbridge friend had asked about Eskimos. "There are no tougher people on the face of the earth,"

"Eighty percent of them can hardly speak English, let alone write it. They seem content to live in ignorance and poverty," she retorted. "I am appalled to have to admit I come from such a backward lot."

Another sore subject was children, for Mary Ellen had lost custody of her youngsters. She seldom spoke of them and Howard was surprised when they received a call from her daughter, Donna Jeanne Horner. Their first meeting was tense. Donna had suffered through too many of her mother's drinking bouts and been abused by a stepfather. She was a quiet, serious girl in her third year of high school, but much to Howard's delight, she was as anxious to learn about her Eskimo roots as Mary Ellen was to forget them.

Donna had been led to believe that Rock was her uncle. She needed a father figure and Howard came to think of the girl as his own. He remembered her birthday, gave her good advice and the Eskimo name of Punny-Chou-ook. He encouraged her in school, passed judgment on her beaux and delighted in her weekend visits. The girl's presence seemed to make little difference to her mother, though, for Mary Ellen was fast drifting into an isolated, alcoholic world of her own.[13]

Jimmy Houston and Rock were arguing about money. They'd done it for years with no personal ill will, but of late the quality of the Eskimo's work had become slipshod. Mary Ellen had been badgering Howard for more cash. He'd increased production at the expense of quality and his neck began giving him trouble because of long hours hunched over his work bench.

"You've gotten so money-hungry, Howard, you're just pushing the work out, not caring how it looks," Houston complained. "We've got stiff competition these days. Wilbur Wallock's doing some beautiful pieces. What we need are some new designs."

"Let me see what I can do," Howard acquiesced. "I've been feeling so damned rotten lately."

"Lay off the bottle, Rock," Houston said flatly. "If you don't, I'll have to fire you before you kill yourself."[14]

Howard had gotten into the habit of drinking his lunch at the Pike Place Market Cafeteria. Deke Brown often joined him and one day he brought along Ralph Perdue, an Athabascan who was setting himself up in the jewelry business in Fairbanks.[15]

"Maybe you should go back to Alaska, Howard," Deke suggested.

"I'd like to go back to painting but I wouldn't be able to make near as much money," Rock considered.

"What if you had a show or two and did jewelry on the side until you generate name recognition?"

"Do you think it's possible to make money up there?" Rock asked the Athabascan.

"Well, I intend to," Perdue said cheerfully.

When Howard suggested returning to Alaska, Mary Ellen laughed in his face. "Maybe you want to admit you're a loser but I'll be damned if I will," she said.[16] Their alcohol intake had became monumental and when Howard tried to cut down by switching from hard liquor to beer, she belittled his effort. He gave her an ultimatum: either taper off on drinking or get out. In mid-1956 she packed her many suitcases.

Howard was devastated. So was Donna Jeanne, for her mother took up with a seaman who had won $60,000 in an accident settlement and embarked on a non-stop binge.

"She loved you as much as she could love anything beyond that bottle," Donna Jeanne comforted. The girl was working a split shift for the phone company while she finished her final year of high school but she continued to take time from her crowded schedule to visit.

"Well, at least she left me Alice," he smiled as their spotted cat rubbed against his ankles.

"And a niece who needs you," Donna reminded him, for Howard was all the family she had left.

Somehow Rock held himself together for her, although it was painfully clear he was a beaten man. His shoulders became stooped; his looks, downcast. He still dressed neatly but his clothes were no longer new. Mary Ellen had exhausted most of his financial resources and he was burned out. He continued to drink to excess. And after several warnings, Houston finally fired him.

"Really, I'm doing you a favor, Howard," he said. "Get out of this business and try something new."

In vain, Howard tried Houston's competitors in search of similar employment. None had need of an engraver, but Herman Krupp, who headed Oceanic Trading Company, was always alert to new enterprise.[17]

"Say, don't you also paint?" he asked.

"Yes, sir, I studied art at the University of Washington for three years. I work well in oils."

"Bring by some canvases, then. Alaskan scenes. Maybe we can work out something."

At the age of 17, Herman Krupp had been dispatched to Siberia with $10,000 by his father who owned the Alaska Fur Company. The Russian Revolution had just ended, but Krupp did well trading and his territory was expanded to Japan and outlying islands. Also a talented musician, he had founded an orchestra, played for the Crown Prince of Japan, made recordings abroad and traveled freely. And when World War II was declared, the U.S. government allowed Krupp to maintain his trading business in Seattle in return for his help in mapping little-known Japanese coasts.

When the bottom fell out of the fur market, Krupp branched into ivory and souvenirs, supplying a large network of retail gift shops. He promised he would purchase all the 9-by-12-inch paintings Rock could turn out for $2.50 each, and pay slightly more for larger canvases. The paintings would retail from $12.50 to $30.

On his own, Howard found it difficult to market even his best work.[18] He was reduced to working part-time as a cement finisher and clerked at an art store to keep himself in supplies. Krupp's assignment was strictly mass production, but the trader had no objections to Rock's painting under an assumed name. So armed with two quarts of beer each night, Rock began to crank out hundreds of smiling Eskimo faces and adorable polar bears under the signature of Kunuk. It was a sad travesty of the career for which he had trained, but it kept him going.

When Donna Jeanne announced that she found a young man who wished to ask formally for her hand in marriage, Howard rose to the occasion, cooking up a remarkable dinner of curried lamb, interviewing the prospective bridegroom, and gravely giving his consent.[19] Occasionally Betsy and her husband, Lou Towne, would lure him to visit with promise of one of Lou's Chinese dinners, but most of his spare time was spent in Bainbridge bars[20] or in conversation with fellow night people like photographer Steve Wilson whose office lights often burned late.[21]

Rock first heard about C. Alan "Bud" Johnson and his wife, Suzanne, from Helen Springer with whom he had an occasional drink.[22] The Johnsons were talented artists who had been living on a shoestring with three kids. Their charming ceramic figures of Eskimos were selling well but they'd never been to the arctic and were determined to see it. "I think you can help them," she said.

The Johnsons invited Howard to supper and apparently their children had talked it up because as Rock approached their house, a neighbor's boy came running out from next door yelling, "Oh, there is the Eskimo!" Howard nearly collapsed laughing.

"Does that bother you?" Bud asked.

"No. Kids, I love," Howard said. And the Johnson youngsters took him at his word. Keith, 3, climbed into his lap right away, referring to him ever after as "Fouvver." Brian, 6, and Laurie, 8, listened breathlessly to his every pronouncement. Alaska was the focus of their lives. They asked a thousand questions.

Howard was shy at first but intrigued with the Johnson's dream. To their amazement, he'd been born in the village they'd selected to visit and they exhausted him with their enthusiasm. He left early, but he returned the next time they invited him.

"It's like taming a deer," Suzanne said to Bud.

"We don't want to crowd him," he reminded her.

"But we do want him to come back!"

At the time, the Johnsons were scouring the libraries for anything they could find on the arctic. Howard began reading along with them, engrossed in the accounts of the explorers in musty *National Geographics.* Historians declared his uncle, Attungowruk, was a scoundrel and a murderer. Rock argued nimbly in his defense. Soon he found himself telling the Johnsons of his childhood, discussing things of which he had never spoken before, such as his puzzlement and pain at being adopted out and his embarrassment in having an Eskimo name that was feminine. He spoke of his distress when his mother had made him prime her breast with his mouth to feed a younger brother. He recalled the day a walrus had been wounded on their beach, how its wailing mate tried to pull it back into the water. The whole village had turned out, he said. His mother wept. And when the animal died, the men began to butcher it, but all the while the other walrus kept calling and calling ...

The margin for survival in the arctic was a small one, and as Howard struggled to make them understand the ingenuity and courage with which his people dealt with it, he marveled anew at the great Eskimo traditions. The Johnsons were nondrinkers but Rock began visiting them often, discussing his Native heritage until sweat beaded his brow and he was forced to head for the nearest bar for his much-needed ration of beer.

Rock's favorite food was muktuk, the black skin and blubber of the bowhead whale, and that Christmas Bud and Suzanne went to considerable trouble to air freight some down for him. Their generous gift took him by surprise. His grin went from ear to ear and he began to giggle. "Muktuk!" It was the nicest thing that anyone had done for him in years.

Howard's youngest sister, Ruth, and her husband, Bernard Nash, had a new baby and four older children whose age range was close to the Johnson youngsters. At Howard's suggestion the two families began to correspond. His sister, Helen, and her husband were living in Kotzebue and agreed to rent the Johnsons their Point Hope house.

Both Rock's parents were dead now and Mumangeena was gone, too. Yet thoughts of returning to Point Hope grew increasingly appealing to him. The Johnsons lobbied enthusiastically. He promised to accompany them, but he still had doubts. Allen Rock had moved back to Point Hope to open a hunting lodge with his construction earnings. Howard wrote him trying to make amends but there was no response. With Allen against him, life in the village would be intolerable, not only for himself but for the Johnsons whom the villagers would associate with him.

Deeply troubled, Howard took the problem to his favorite bar and tried to solve it by drinking up the money he had saved for the trip. Unaware of his motives, already out on a limb because they'd purchased one-way tickets to Alaska for their whole family on a time-payment plan, the young couple volunteered to buy Howard a "fly now, pay later" ticket, too.

Rock's life in Seattle had fallen apart. Alcohol had become a real need. He had no dreams left, no future. At last he saw a way out and he accepted the Johnson's offer.

"It is so simple and so traditional, I wonder that I didn't think of it sooner," he told Donna Jeanne who was the one person in the world with whom he could speak in total frankness. "I will simply go home and make my peace with everyone and then go out on the ice to die. It's lovely there. A clean, quick death. It will look like an accident but my people will know that I've done an honorable thing."

Donna Jeanne nodded. She loved him but she also knew the full depth of his hurt. He did not want to go down with the derelicts on skid row and they both figured that was the direction in which he was headed. In a way, she envied him his solution.[23]

"That's a beautiful choice, if you must, Howard," she said simply. "But, oh, how I will miss you."

19

Home Again

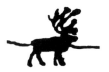

IT WAS THE END OF MAY, 1961, and winter had begun to loosen its hold on the arctic. The Chukchi Sea had torn its blanket of ice into a patchwork of floating slabs and sun burned through the graying, rotten snow to reveal bald hummocks of tundra. Still, Howard Rock shivered in his borrowed parka. The wind-bucking, twin-engined Beechcraft was not heated and 12 years of absence from home had destroyed his tolerance of cold.

His gaze was fixed on the yellowed plexiglass window. The barren coast passed below, unbroken since they'd left Kotzebue Sound save for the hump of Mulgrave Hills and a spongy blot on the landscape that represented the tiny village of Kivalina. Then, an hour out, he sighted the Ogotoruk Valley backed by the high bluff of Cape Thompson and the 20-mile curve of Tigara Spit.

Despite the lateness of the season, Rock was pleased to observe a broad hem of ice which still clung to the coast and he studied it carefully. There remained one high, jumbled pressure ridge where a man might lose himself, never to be found, and he fixed its location in his mind without any emotion save relief. There were three bottles of Jim Beam in his suitcase, enough to get him though the formalities of homecoming.

To a man, the villagers of Point Hope were aware of the estrangement between Allen Rock and his brother, Howard. Only the night before Allen had gotten drunk and reminded all who would listen of his sibling's ungodly penchant for white women and how he had turned his back on their people in pleasure-bent pursuit of an alien lifestyle. What was not clear to them was why Howard wished to return. It was rumored that the artist had become rich and successful. None would guess he had come home to die, a failure.

They waited in heavy silence as the mail plane rattled to a halt on the gravel strip. Allen stepped forward to meet the prodigal. For what seemed like a winter, the two brothers stood facing one another, expressionless. Allen was taller by a head but the similarity in their looks was striking and finally, as mirrored reflections, each extended a hand in friendship.[1]

"I have a place for you," Allen said, and Howard nodded, too shaken to speak.

The spring whaling season had begun badly with no strikes despite a heavy run. The village welcomed artists Suzanne and Bud Johnson and their family by staging a traditional dance but three days later, a white man in a small plane frightened off a sizeable group of bowheads. Although they were in no way responsible, the Johnsons felt a decided chill. Even the school newspaper blamed poor hunting on the presence of outsiders and a *Life* magazine photographer suspected of hexing the venture was summarily expelled from town.

"Eighty years we've been up here and in 24 hours outsiders blow the whole thing," lamented Keith Lawton, the Episcopal priest in residence.[2] Yet all was forgiven 24 hours later when Dan Lisbourne harpooned a whale and, shortly thereafter, Allen Rock landed the biggest bowhead on record—a 60-footer.[3] Expulsion of the photographer had apparently been the turning point, or Lawton's fervent praying, or maybe the Johnsons were responsible for the change in luck. Whatever the cause, Point Hope's meat caches were full for another season and Allen Rock could afford largesse even to a wayward brother.

Howard fell gratefully into the celebration of Nalukatuk, the time-honored tribute to a successful whaling season. American flags were raised over ancient feast grounds where a dozen or more weather-bleached bowhead bones had been planted upright in triumphal arches by legendary hunters of the past. Umiaks were turned on their sides and arranged in a large circle to shelter celebrants from fitful snow squalls. Everyone brought a plate.

The Rev. Lawton opened by giving thanks. As was customary for successful captains, Allen and Dan Lisbourne dispensed to one and all the choicest whale meats and muktuk, along with a fortune in store-bought candy and soda pop. A walrus-hide blanket rimmed with heavy rope was brought forth and manned by the strongest men in the village to serve as a trampoline on which youths tried to best one another in jumping high above the crowd.

Then heavy fog drifted in, shrouding the Nalukatuk area in ghostly gray-white mists. Outsiders headed home and four old men who had outwaited them rose in unison from the caribou skin-covered bench. Each carried a two-foot wooden hoop covered with tanned skin and a willow wand which served as the Eskimo's only musical instrument. Without a word, this chorus seated itself on bare ground before a gargantuan arch formed by the freshly planted jawbones of Allen's whale. Owktalik, the leader, commenced an eerie chant. Others joined in unison, slapping their drums lightly in expectation. Allen strode forward, unhesitant and proud. The tempo increased, booming like thunder as he danced, wailing the saga of his triumph to his deceased parents.

"Kakairnak ..."

Howard hadn't thought of his brother's Eskimo name in years but it came to him now and—enthralled—he recorded the event:

> The chanters reached a climactic point:
> A booming beat followed by a soft one
> Thence a steady crashing tempo.
> The chant issued louder, rhythmic with the drums ...
>
> Kakairnak danced ...
> 'Twas the dance of his life—his heart therein.
> What coursed through his mind, this man, my brother?
>
> Four old men, sage in the ways of Tigara
> Struck the last resounding beat
> Upon their whale-liver skin drums.
> The chant faded into the grounds of Kahkrook.
>
> Kakairnak walked slowly away from his dance.
> He sat down near my side,
> Rested his elbows on his knees.
> He gazed upon the grounds of the Nalukatuk.
> His head bowed slowly.
> The hands rose to bury his face therein—[4]

The 20th century was obscured by ancient ritual as the entire populace of 300 Eskimos reverted to their glorious past, and Howard—who was caught up in it—forgot the hurts of the world Outside. Village life was harsh, for his people still lived without modern amenities, yet he took renewed pride in the ingenious self-sufficiency of his race. The shore ice, on which he'd planned to die, drifted off without him and was soon followed by the rich promise of an arctic spring.

Rock had packed his oils and brushes but no canvases. Suddenly, painting became a compulsion and, begging some celotex from a construction crew, he began to work with a skill he'd thought was lost. Almost at once he hit his stride, his technique primitive but controlled by his long years of professional training. His letters to the Johnsons when they managed to work their way home, reflected new enthusiasm for life in general and painting in particular.

"The arctic is something very elusive to capture," he wrote. "When you capture some of that, you've got something that really stands out. It makes me think that if I could capture a huge hunk of it on canvas I would have a masterpiece."[5]

20

Eskimos Versus Edward Teller

Because he was focused on salvaging his career, Rock was slow to realize that all was not well with the village. Physically, little had changed since he was a child and a good whaling season always brought with it a sense of security. Yet he began noticing uncharacteristic flashes of fear which seemed to have something to do with a cadre of government men who were preparing some scientific test outside the village.

Allen laughed off the apprehension of their neighbors.

"It's good for business," he shrugged, and since his hunting "lodge"—a drafty shed tacked to the back of his residence—was the only place to stay in town, he did indeed prosper.[1]

Others, David Frankson, president of the village council, and hard-working Dan Lisbourne seemed worried, but Rock's command of Inupiaq proved too limited to query them. Neither would speak freely with him, anyway, for he had been gone so long they scarcely regarded him as an Eskimo. Finally he went to a visiting scientist, Don Foote, and asked what the problem was.

"Edward Teller, father of the hydrogen bomb, and the Atomic Energy boys," Foote declared angrily.

"I've heard they're planning a test out at Ogotoruk Creek. Seems like half the men I met in Kotzebue on the way home worked there last summer and made good money," Rock recalled. "Surely there's no danger..."

Foote's answer was bitter. In an attempt to win backing for Teller's project from the University of Alaska, the Atomic Energy Commission (AEC) had hired some of its faculty to do environmental studies of the test area. Foote's job was to document hunting patterns and he'd become completely caught up in the Eskimo lifestyle. Teller was out to destroy it, Foote insisted, and nothing was being done to stop him because the AEC was a sacred cow.

"You're the one Eskimo in this village who can read," he challenged. "Why don't you go over and take a look at some of the material Keith Lawton has been collecting? Then come back and tell me whether you think we'll ever see another whaling season."

Lawton—young, intense and intellectually curious—would ultimately give up his ministry for a teaching career, and he was a careful researcher.

"The blast is set for next spring. It is smaller than originally planned but it will still be 14 times more powerful than the explosion at Hiroshima, and Point Hope lies 30 miles north from the test site," he reported.[2] "We have reason to believe Teller's intent is to test the results of fallout on a remote people. There is no plan to move the Eskimos."[3]

Howard was flabbergasted. He had read nothing of these things in the Seattle papers but Lawton sounded certain.

"How do you know this?" he demanded.

"The National Academy of Science published a series of bulletins on atomic testing at different locations and that's what Don and I have been using. They pointed us in the right direction and Don has contacts all over the arctic—all over the world. His brother is working on a Point Hope article for *Harper's* but we're afraid it will come out too late to do any good."[4]

"Would you give me some things to read?"

"Of course," the weary preacher said. "We need all the help we can get."

The first inkling of intrusion had come to the isolated Eskimo community in the fall of 1958 when Dan Lisbourne went caribou hunting with his nephew and Peniluk Omnik and discovered a colony of tents at the mouth of Ogotoruk Creek. Jimmy Hawley, an Eskimo from Kivalina, was guiding the party of surveyors.[5] Dan was curious, but it is the Eskimo way to wait and see what happens. He hoped Geological Survey would issue a new map.

The bizarre nuclear experiment had been launched officially two years earlier when Dr. Herbert F. York, director of the University of California Radiation Laboratory, Livermore, proposed the AEC hold a symposium on the peaceful uses of nuclear explosions. Impetus came from Russian/American peace talks. A ban on nuclear testing was sure to follow, but investigation of industrial potential would keep the nation's nuclear war machinery intact. Sole objection to the ploy was voiced by Brig. Gen. Alfred D. Starbird, AEC's director of Military Applications, who worried that investigation of peaceful uses might "grow to such proportions as to divert effort from the weapons program."[6]

Although Dr. Edward Teller was an outspoken critic of the test ban, he opened the symposium in February, 1957, by promoting use of nuclear explosives for "landscaping." Creative suggestions included the blasting of a new canal between the Atlantic and Pacific oceans, but it became apparent that problems created by nuclear explosives might outweigh their promise. Hazards were discussed in a forthright manner. It was agreed that tests ought to be conducted in remote areas. Dr. Harold Brown, noted physicist who concluded the program, said that while he did not know "just how one dissipates the current backlog of public fear and lack of confidence" with respect to nuclear explosions, he did think that their industrial application "could provide a fine opportunity for people to obtain a more rational viewpoint."[7]

Excavation of a harbor would be the first practical test. Dr. Teller was to be technical advisor and, working from aerial photos, Cape Thompson, Alaska, was selected as suitably remote. The explosion as initially planned was to be the largest in the history of nuclear experiments—125 times more powerful than the bomb detonated at Hiroshima. It was to be one of the most ambitious projects ever launched by the AEC and man's first attempt to reshape the surface of the earth by means of nuclear power.

It wasn't until July of the next year—exactly two weeks after Congress had awarded Alaska statehood—that Teller and a small band of scientists arrived, unannounced, in the office of Gov. Mike Stepovich with the good news. Stepovich was out of town but, undaunted, Dr. Teller held an impromptu press conference to report the new state had been chosen for their test because it had "the fewest people and the most reasonable people."[8] The experiment would be controlled to a degree that he could "dig them a harbor in the shape of a polar bear" he promised, and about $5 million would be spent in the economically depressed area.

In Fairbanks, Teller met with city officials and University of Alaska faculty and introduced his plan as "Project Chariot." It was named in honor of a South American port that had been built to ship minerals of great value, he said.[9]

"We looked at the whole world—almost the whole world—and tried to pick a spot where we could most effectively demonstrate the use of this (atomic) energy. On the basis of preliminary study it looked like the excavation of a harbor in Alaska to open the area to possible great development should do the job," he said, adding that the selection of Cape Thompson was only tentative.

"We came here to be partners with you and because we want suggestions, but the blast will not be performed until it can be economically justified. It must stand on its own economic feet over a long-range period."

It would be weeks before university faculty learned that surveyors were already working at Ogotoruk Creek as Teller spoke and that the AEC had applied to the Bureau of Land Management to withdraw 1,600 square miles around the site. But they did show more resistance to the grandiose scheme than Teller had expected from such a remote university.

Teller assured his Fairbanks audience that fallout was as harmless as the dial of his glow-in-the-dark wrist watch. It had yet to be proven that fallout at Hiroshima caused cancer. But university staffers were abreast of the work of Linus Pauling and others who believed (soon to be confirmed) that even low-level radiation was potentially dangerous. There were studies that showed an unusually high incidence of leukemia in radiologists, they noted, and others which showed radiation caused mutations in fruit flies.[10]

Teller reminded them of the recent Sputnik launch. The Russians were ahead in the space race. It was vital that America learn as much as possible about nuclear power, he insisted.

"Actually the danger of such fallout, if any, is quite small compared to the obvious and imminent danger of Soviet power," he warned. "It is only by continued strength that we safeguard the peace."[11]

One month later, the AEC exhibited a film simulating a nuclear blast at Ogotoruk Creek at the Second International Conference on Peaceful Uses of Atomic Energy in Geneva.[12] Russians protested. AEC announced the project was being abandoned; then reversed itself and sold the whole package to Congress with a target date 1960.[13]

"The lack of a harbor between Cape Sepping and Cape Thompson hampers development of large-scale mineral deposits in the area, plus fishing has been impeded by the lack of a safe haven," Dr. Willard F. Libby, AEC chairman, told the Senate Foreign Relations Committee. A 2.5-megaton blast was planned. It would produce a harbor 2,000 yards long with a turning radius of 1,000 feet. Eskimos were to be temporarily evacuated, but Libby claimed radiation would be harmless within two weeks.[14]

Once again AEC public relations teams began stumping the state, winning the support of local chambers of commerce and the Alaska Legislature. Eskimos remained unapprised, but stubborn opposition came from the Alaska Conservation Society and a small corps of academics at the university.

"You say there's going to be no damage, but how do you know?" asked Albert Johnson, associate professor of botany who found himself Teller's partner at a university luncheon held in the physicist's honor. "You don't know and furthermore you're not going to find out."[15]

"But the blast will be in the winter time when there are no animals, so there won't be damage."

"There are herds of caribou out there."

"There can't be. What would they eat?" Teller snapped, and Johnson looked at him in disbelief. The shaggy-browed scientist had been working on the project four years and still did not know what any Alaskan school-child could tell him—that caribou grazed through the snows on wind-swept tundra.

To placate Johnson and his group, AEC scaled down the magnitude of the blast and initiated a $2 million environmental impact study involving 70 scientists. The research was a pioneering effort. Nothing like it had ever been done before and the local university was thrown a few juicy contracts which "they jumped at like prostitutes," Teller told a friend. Some of the researchers were located at Point Hope and, for the first time, Natives became aware that a nuclear test was planned.

Remote though they were, the Eskimos knew as much as most American citizens about the atomic bomb. One of the Weber boys had been sent with the Army to help clean up Japan after its annihilation and had returned to the village sick and sterile. Radio news broadcasts sometimes mentioned an atomic experiment in the Pacific called "Bikini" and testing in Nevada. Mark and Kitty Kineeveauk, who understood English better than most, heard that Indians there had lost their water and food sup-plies—even their homes because of it.[16]

Anxiously they discussed their concerns with the Rev. Lawton and with Don Foote who was growing increasingly disillusioned with the agency. Foote had previously worked for the government—some said with the CIA—in Norway. He was able to get classified information when others failed and he confirmed the Eskimos' worst fears.[17]

In November of 1959 the Point Hope village council wrote a formal—though somewhat grammatically incorrect—protest to the AEC[18] which went unheeded. The following January, three University of Alaska re-searchers complained that well-documented findings on possible dangers of the test were being withheld from AEC reports, and they were also ignored.[19] The university, which had been on the verge of folding a few years earlier, needed all the government contracts it could get, President William Wood pointed out. One protester was fired, another forced to resign and Dr. Teller was awarded an honorary doctorate.

Detailed studies had shown the building of a harbor at Cape Thompson economically unfeasible. The nearby coal deposit, which Point Hope Missionary Augustus Hoare dreamed of marketing at the turn of the century, was not of commercial quality. Harbor silting would make shipping impossible. Yet Teller, who toured the Ogotoruk Creek site with his wife en route to commencement, still spoke of its potential in glowing terms.

"If your mountain is not in the right place, just drop us a card," he quipped. "Nuclear explosives can be used to blast harbors in otherwise inaccessible coasts, to engage in the great art of what I want to call geographical engineering. To reshape the land to your pleasure ..."[20]

He spoke with a missionary zeal on the wonderful rewards that lay ahead for graduates in an atom-powered world: "a better life, a comfortable life ..."

He spoke, also, of atonement. "Please God, that by making harbors here in Alaska, perhaps near coal deposits, by exporting this coal cheaper to Japan, the Japanese might become the first beneficiaries of atomic energy, of the atomic explosions, as they have been the first victims."

And, in almost the same breath:

"We must be prepared for war and *then* war will not come."

Rock read Rev. Lawton's papers with increasing alarm. Teller's blatant lying was an outrage, but it was obvious the AEC had political as well as nuclear power. The village petition— "any informations you may have that we should know on this matter we are glad to hear them"—seemed pathetically inadequate in the face of the uncaring Goliath. Only Lawton's last folder held hope.

Alaska's U.S. Senator Bob Bartlett had become disillusioned by lack of coordination within Teller's agency and questioned irregularities in its operation. The Cape Thompson land withdrawal was to have been 40 square miles, yet the Bureau of Land Management leased Teller four times that amount of acreage without a public hearing.[21] No effort had been made to contact Eskimos who hunted the area until March of 1960 when, at the senator's insistence, AEC dispatched a team to Point Hope.

Russell Ball, in charge of general planning for Project Chariot, arrived in the village without notice, accompanied by Robert Rausch, chief of zoononic diseases for the Arctic Health Research Center in Anchorage, and Rod Southwick who supervised AEC publicity out of San Francisco. Keith Lawton had the presence of mind to record the meeting and Howard read his thick transcript with interest.[22]

The AEC representatives began by showing a film describing the test and Rock shook his head at the scientific jargon ... "an inline series of four equally placed 100 kiloton shots at a depth of 30 meters and a terminal shot of one megaton 50 meters deep. All shots of minimal fission yield ..."

He admired the way Lawton had dealt with the scientists, forcing them into some embarrassing admissions. Had they considered the 10-foot storm tides? They didn't know. What consistency would the radioactive debris be? A rather complex process, they answered.

Would the harbor actually be of use to anyone?

BALL: Ah ... there is not, at the present time, an economic need for such a harbor.... . It is now exclusively viewed as a very worthwhile experiment to help us learn how to dig craters.... . *(Ball sweated the answer but it was all lost on the Eskimos and no one spoke when Southwick asked if there were further questions. Briskly he moved to adjourn, but the transcript continued.)*

(Voice in Eskimo interrupting Southwick).

DAN LISBOURNE: Ah, the woman here, ah, mentioned, ah, said that all of these people here, ah, all of these people most of them are just silent right now and they have great fear in, ah, in this detonation. And, ah, the effects, and how, how the effects of it will be.

SOUTHWICK: Internationally?

LISBOURNE: No, *here!*

BALL: What? I don't, ah, quite under ... get what her question was ...

To Rock's surprise, the name of his old friend, Tommy Richards, appeared in the transcript. Richards had piloted the AEC's chartered plane and apparently could hold his tongue no longer.

TOMMY RICHARDS: She wants to know the effect of the *blast.*

LISBOURNE: The effect of the blast to the people.

BALL: On your own ... your own Eskimo people? (*Silence*) . Oh, well, ah, I believe we've covered that already, ah, I think we'll have to ... (turning to pilot Richards about the return flight).

RICHARDS: I don't think that's true. You haven't.

(Talk begins in Eskimo. Man's voice. Then a woman's voice, Dina Frankson.)

RICHARDS (*Translating*): Are you gonna go through with this thing when you know that Dina is afraid of the explosion?

(*Silence.*)

BALL: Oh! (*Silence.*) As we have said, eh, the Atomic Energy Commission is making very careful studies to make absolutely sure neither your nor any of your people will receive any harm from this experiment.... .

LISBOURNE: Ah, I think, Mr. Ball, that this ... the majority of us here, right now, have no understanding of what you have said previously having not known enough about the English language. And, ah, she was saying that, ah, she is a woman citizen of the United States and of Alaska and, ah, she's quite concerned about the, ah, the local hunters being ... going through all the time. And, ah, she also mentioned the springtime, like, ah, like in April, so they hunt seals on top of the ice in that area and here ...

(The dialogue continued with the AEC team professing amazement at the amount of game and birds eggs taken in what they'd presumed to be off-season and giving assurances that they would study the matter.)

DAVID FRANKSON (*who had for the most part been silent*): We council at the Point Hope that sent the protest letter to Atomic Energy Commission, stating that we don't want to see the blast down here. And *when we say it we mean it!*

(Finally one woman whose name was not given spoke at length in Inupiaq.)

RICHARDS (*Translating*): The more you talk the more scared she gets. (*Laughter from AEC people.*) The woman has a bad heart. What happens if she dies from a heart attack? Who will take care of her kids?

BALL: Heee. There will be nothing more than ah ... all you could do from here would be to perhaps hear the explosion, that's all. I don't think the noise would do her any harm. It would not be a very loud noise.

RICHARDS: Her question was what will you do if she *does* have a heart attack?

BALL: Damned if I know!

Rubbing his eyes, tired of reading by flickering oil lamp, Rock set the transcript aside. No one, as far as he knew, had ever beaten the AEC. What chance did they possibly have?

The coffee shop at Allen Rock's lodge was a popular gathering place and many villagers dropped by the back room to watch Howard paint. He was working on a large canvas which depicted the flukes of a harpooned bowhead flashing above a fragile umiak where men strained at their paddles. He'd caught the moment exactly. The colors were true. The excitement of the hunt blazed through and Dan Lisbourne got in the habit of studying the work.[23]

"It's good," he'd say after a long pause. And then, one evening he said, joking but not joking, "Howard, when the Lord comes and starts the big earthquake, I would like to be here to grab that painting. I don't want that picture left behind."

From a villager, it was enormous tribute. The first that Howard had ever received in his years as Point Hope's star misfit.

"Maybe so much of your brain was devoted to painting there wasn't room for the usual Eskimo instincts." Allen speculated. The crew that Howard elected to portray in the whale hunting scene was Allen's crew and he'd also done a portrait of Allen dancing at the whaling feast. The work not only flattered the gruff hunter, it amazed him with its perfection. And when he invited his brother along on a caribou hunt, he suggested the artist bring his sketch pad, instead of a rifle.[24]

They traveled up the Kukpuk River where Howard had stumped along as an eight-year-old with Aunt Mumangeena, and the trip brought back a memory of happiness made precious by its rarity.

The weather turned mild. Fuchsia moss flowers and sky-blue forget-me-nots brightened scars on the tundra. He had all but forgotten the joyous song of the longspurs and the comic antics of nesting ptarmigan. No wonder his work lost its soul in the city.

Pressing over the hills, the hunters found the Ogotoruk Valley carpeted with migrating animals—hundreds of them, traveling at a leisurely pace, grazing on the new growth that made spring welcome. The bucks were fat and sporting full velvet; sprightly fawns trailed plump does. Startled, probably by the scent of a wolf, they galloped into flight and the thunder of several thousand hoofs echoed along the muskeg-covered hills. It made one's adrenaline race to watch such a wild stampede. Then, as if nothing had happened, they grazed again.

They were mindless animals, but handsome. Howard hated to see them killed, but he was as tired of eating whale meat as the rest of the villagers. And he admired the dispatch with which the hunters carried out their mission.

On the homeward journey they passed the AEC site with its dozen or so Jamesway huts and startling array of heavy equipment. At the peak of activity the camp had housed 100 or more workmen. "Hot showers and the very best food and even their own airplane," one of the hunters recounted. "Quite an operation just to dig a batch of holes."[25]

Ogotoruk was a broad, deep valley and its Eskimo name translated to mean "poke" or "bag," no doubt because hunters seldom came away from the place empty-handed.[26] To the untrained eye it might seem a dull place, Howard realized, yet it was rich beyond measure. In this season the creekbed was always laced with caribou tracks; in the summer the valley would be bright with flowers. Ducks and swans massed here in fall; there would be berries. In winter men came here to trap and to fish through the ice. One could not expect a nuclear physicist to know these things. But the Ogotoruk Valley was well worth fighting for.

The village was preparing for a council meeting when they returned. Keith Lawton seemed excited.

"A representative from the Association on American Indian Affairs (AAIA) is coming to talk to us," he explained. "She's been working with Eskimos at Barrow and the council thinks she might be able to help us with the AEC."

Howard had heard of the AAIA—something about communist sympathizers, he recalled. Lawton said he'd heard that, too.

"What's the problem in Barrow?"

"Ducks!" Lawton chuckled. "The migratory bird treaty of 1916 forbids the shooting of eider ducks."

"But that's about all there is to eat in the spring before the whales come in, and there are millions of ducks."

"Exactly," Lawton said. "So two days after an over-zealous Fish and Wildlife agent jailed an Eskimo for shooting one, every hunter in Barrow—138 of them—armed himself with a dead duck and descended on the agent demanding to be arrested. The Fish and Wildlife man was just fit to be tied and had to let everybody go because he had no place to put them."[27]

The AAIA sent two representatives. Dr. Henry Stone Forbes, whose keen mind and vigor belied his 79 years, had come to observe as chairman of the agency's newly formed Alaska Policy Committee, but it was the short, plump, ultra-feminine blonde who accompanied him who did most of the talking. She looked as if she'd been outfitted for the arctic by Abercrombie and Fitch but once she opened her mouth, appearances were forgotten. La Verne Madigan was a Phi Beta Kappa graduate of New York University with an M.A. and a solid reputation as a classical scholar. She came equipped with a warm sense of humanity, a quick, perceptive mind and a mellow sense of humor. In traveling north she had bucked Oliver LaFarge, AAIA president and winner of a Pulitzer Prize in literature, who maintained that their organization was too over-extended to take on Alaskan problems. She was executive secretary of AAIA and she was determined to make herself useful.[28]

The meeting was run strictly by Roberts' Rules of Order and Howard was proud of the way slight, bespectacled David Frankson conducted it. Mrs. Madigan did not speak Eskimo but she spoke English slowly and plainly without talking down to anyone.

There was a rumor that the government might build modern housing for the Point Hope people in Nome, that there would be electricity and running water and many other things the bureaucrats assumed would better their lot. But the council made it clear that this solution was unacceptable. No one wanted to move and Mrs. Madigan did not seem surprised.

A peace movement was growing, she reported. There was a group called "Greater St. Louis Citizens Committee for Nuclear Information" and a man named Barry Commoner, a professor at Washington University, St. Louis, who might help. The Quakers were interested, and there were others who questioned the free rein Edward Teller had been given in the name of national security. Mrs. Madigan's main concern, though, seemed to be the land on which the AEC was holding the test. To whom did it belong, she asked? And Howard learned, to his surprise, that his father and other villagers had officially filed claim on their region in 1950.[29]

Anthropologists who dug on Tigara Spit believed Point Hope to be the oldest continually inhabited site in North America.[30] Eskimos had never signed any treaties or lost any wars to the United States, nor had they even considered selling their valuable hunting grounds, Frankson pointed out. It was his position that they owned the land and Mrs. Madigan agreed. If they could prove the Bureau of Land Management had no right to lease their property to the AEC, the test might have to be canceled, she said. If the village council would write a letter to the Secretary of Interior explaining their case, the AAIA would be able to hire lawyers and lobbyists to help them.

Rock had been listening quietly but it seemed to him the discussion was too narrow in scope. Perhaps they should send tape recordings of some of their discussions to other villages, he suggested. Surely Eskimos had many problems in common and there was strength in numbers. Dr. Forbes, who earlier had admired his paintings, nodded in agreement and David Frankson eyed Rock thoughtfully. At length, the council decided to follow his suggestion and they also elected him to draft the letter to the Secretary of Interior.

Hon. Stewart Udall
Secretary of Interior
Washington, D.C.
Mr. Secretary:
We, the members of the Village Council of Point Hope, Alaska, with considered reluctance, have decided to write to you concerning the problems

facing us since the start of the construction for Project Chariot.

As any reasonable and loyal citizens of the United States the people of Point Hope are not against experimentations of the peaceful uses of the nuclear explosions, but, due to the proximity of this Project we have found ourselves in the circumstances so potentially dangerous to our way of life that we are forced to make declarations in the face of this impending event. The site of this proposed explosion is such that it would greatly endanger our hunting and fishing areas that have sustained our survival through thousands of years. We know what unfavorable conditions can do to our economy and with this added threat and, certainly, its effects, if allowed to happen, our hunting grounds would surely be impaired. A situation like that can result in such dire conditions that might necessitate abandonment of our village. That is the last thing in the world we would want. We are deeply rooted here. Our forefathers have fought hard for our survival, as we are now doing, and they are buried here. To be forced to abandon such a heritage would be most disastrous for the village of Point Hope and its people. This is our home. In spite of its geographical locale we love it and want to live in it.

We are a self-sustaining race. To perpetuate this fact we need the surrounding hunting fields. Our traditional hunting areas cover some forty mile radius at least. In the land section of this space we hunt caribou, ground squirrels, foxes, ptarmigan, wolves, wolverines, geese, brants, lynx, porcupines, grizzly bear, arctic owl and many species of fresh water fish such as grayling, arctic char, Dolly Varden trout, and white fish. Cape Thompson itself has always been one of the sources of our fresh murre eggs. There are berries that are picked during summers. In the sea we are dependent on whales, belugas, walrus, oogruk, seal, polar bear, trout, salmon, crab and tomcod.

At this point, Mr. Secretary, we would like to pose a question that has been foremost in our minds. The clarification of this inquiry would be most enlightening to the people of Point Hope. Why was the Bureau of Land Management, which we understand is under the Department of Interior, given any right to allow the Cape Thompson area of land to be utilized by the Atomic Energy Commission for the explosion of Project Chariot? Under the Aboriginal Claims Act of 1884, we, the people of Point Hope, have a claim to this land and we consider your office, the Department of Interior, to be the protector of our rights. We are, of course, adhering to the provisions of this Act and will expect your office to continue to protect our rights until such time as the Congress of our United States Government, through your guidance, further defines, in a more detailed manner, the broad provisions of the Act of 1884, which has called for such long overdue definitive legislation.

Mr. Secretary, it seems to us very appalling that there has never been any serious effort in consultation of the people of Point Hope concerning the transfer of land by the Bureau of Land Management to the Atomic Energy

Commission for the Project Chariot. There was, also, a pronounced lack of orientation upon the probable adverse effects of the Project. If this undertaking is allowed to continue to its ultimate conclusions and if any degree of harm to our hunting grounds should result from the nuclear explosion at Cape Thompson, we will and must resort to legal channels to sue for our incalculable heritage and our age-old aboriginal rights to hunt on our land. It is saddening to us that such declarations have to be made but we feel deeply that our way of life in the village of Point Hope is being dangerously threatened.

Most sincerely,
Members of the
Village Council
Point Hope, Alaska[31]

The letter had taken more than a week to write for, although Rock was far better equipped than any of his peers to communicate with the outside world, he was a college dropout with no legal experience. He believed—they all believed—that the future of Point Hope might rest on his presentation. It was heavy responsibility.

21

Fresh Start

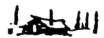

WITH A CHUCKLE Howard placed nine slightly bent cigarettes, his winnings from the Fourth of July celebration, on the battered chair that served as a night stand by his bunk in Allen's lodge and kicked off his shoes. No need to call on a Jim Beam nightcap to induce sleep. The day had been happily exhausting.

"Some people in high places should witness the Fourth here. They would clearly realize the unquestioned loyalty these, my people, have for their country," he wrote his friends the Johnsons.[1] It had been impressive for its patriotism and it had been fun.

Howard was recruited to play baseball with the winning team of older men where he and Dan Attungowruk distinguished themselves as the best on the field.

"The best in clumsiness, that is," he noted. "It was hilarious at times."

His sister, Ruth, proved a superb first baseman and the rest of her family also did well. Brother-in-law, Bernard, placed second in the two-mile foot race winning a mouton coat. Nephews, Sammy and Junior, came in first in their divisions, while nieces, Helen and Judy, ran third.

The evening was capped by Eskimo dancing, home movies of the whaling festival taken by a visitor named Lee Rayfeldt, and a patriotic prayer. Too patriotic, Howard reflected. Many of the villagers were so dedicated to their government, it was hard for them to imagine it might expose them to serious danger.[2] Only a far-sighted few, like Frankson and Dan Lisbourne, really understood the threat atomic testing posed to their lifestyle.

Don Foote, the University of Alaska graduate student researcher, had a newspaper clipping that said rays from the Hiroshima blast caused cancer, a discovery reported for the first time in print by the Atomic Bomb Casualty Commission's Medical Services.[3] Foote said their tundra was already blighted by radiation from previous testing. Scientists reported that although the level was generally low, Alaskan caribou, on which the Eskimos depended for meat, grazed on lichens in which the dosage was dangerously concentrated and the animals had about the same amount of strontium 90 in their bones as cattle raised in the Nevada test zone.[4]

Foote pointed out that the Kukpuk River, Point Hope's only summer water source, flowed within 10 miles of the AEC's site. And he predicted that the test would contaminate the sea water and snow.[5]

Lighting one of his prized cigarettes, Rock pondered his own future. He was not just broke, but in debt. Rayfeldt, the visitor, was much taken with the painting of Allen at the whaling festival, but couldn't make up his mind. Earlier, the local airline had expressed interest in buying some of his canvases but the high prices he demanded had frightened them off.[6]

He knew the work was good. What he needed was a show in Fairbanks. Ralph Perdue, the Athabascan jeweler he'd met through Deke Brown, was well-established there now and might help.

Word of Rock's work traveled and Otto Geist, Alaska's leading resident archaeologist, sought him out. Geist, 79, had fought in three wars and traveled far before immigrating from Bavaria in 1924. He was self-taught, widely read, with a fondness for poetry and art, and he found the Eskimo painter such good company that he extended his visit to Point Hope.[7]

Howard was working on a masterful picture of the old Revenue Cutter *Bear*.

"I sailed on her, too, you know," his guest observed, chewing with relish on an oily lump of seal meat. "It's a real historic craft. Ought to be in a museum."

"The ship?" Howard asked, glancing at Geist in amusement. The small, stocky scientist had lived with the Eskimos of St. Lawrence Island for several years and he loved Eskimo food.

"The painting, Rock. The painting should be in a museum. I've a mind to buy it for the University of Alaska."

Geist paid $200 for the *"Bear"* and a check for the same amount came in from Kotzebue for the portrait of Allen. Edith Bullock, a woman who ran a tug and barge company there, had purchased it after seeing Lee Rayfeldt's photo of the work.[8]

Delighted, Howard began working non-stop as he had in the days when he mass-produced etched ivory for Jimmy Houston, but this time his goal was perfection. He sketched another whaling scene which Allen and other hunters pronounced a "true representation." With careful brush strokes he captured a proud buck caribou against a moody arctic sky, and a lovely arctic swan.

Again the AEC intruded. Earlier in July, Rock discovered that the village council had incorrectly typed the letter he had drafted for the Secretary of Interior. Pointing out their mistakes, obtaining corrections from them, had been an awkward affair and when a second visit from AEC officials was announced, Rock moved quickly to make sure their reception was well-planned. Otto Geist, who was still in residence and well-liked by the Eskimos, proved a great help. Villagers, forewarned by David Frankson, turned out 300 strong and the Rev. Keith Lawton mustered with two tape recorders.

Commissioner Leland J. Haworth and John S. Kelly, chief of the AEC Peaceful Explosives Branch; James E. Reeves and R. L. Southwick, in charge of publicity of the organization, announced they could stay just three hours, but angry questions kept them well beyond their deadline.

"We will make sure that everything is safe before the detonation," Southwick insisted in the face of the carefully thought out protest. "Again we stress that nothing will be done to explode the Project until we know that everything is safe for all concerned."

"Why were the people of Point Hope not consulted or given orientation in the initial stages of Project Chariot?" Rock demanded, forgetting the low profile he intended to keep. "We do not want to wind up as guinea pigs!"

The exchange was so volatile that John S. Kelly admitted privately to the Rev. Lawton, "We have been stupid in not consulting these people."[9] And Howard returned to his brushes well pleased that the village had finally made a strong stand.[10]

In early fall the *North Star II*, a war-surplus Victory Ship converted by the Bureau of Indian Affairs to supply remote villages, swung on its hook off Point Hope, and Moe Cole rammed ashore in a landing barge. He was armed with about 30 pounds of candy which he dispersed to mobs of youngsters in generous handfuls, calling many by name, inquiring for their parents and grandparents. Moe was captain now, having worked his way up from mess boy, and everyone on the coast seemed to know and like him.

"Howard, you son-of-a-gun, I heard you were hiding out here!" he boomed at the sight of his old comrade. "Just happen to have a little something for you, too."

"You remind me of the Pied Piper," Howard grinned. "Do you always come so well-armed?"

"Hell, no one ever gave me candy when I was a kid. I'm just trying to make up for it. But I think you'll prefer the bottle of Jim Beam I have tucked under my coat."

The years had done little to change Cole. He was happy, content with his wife, his family and his life.

"What about you, Howard?" he asked, concerned.

Rock shrugged. "They tell me I'm not the best marriage material, but maybe that's just as well," he said turning to the dazzling row of paintings that lined his small quarters. Moe was impressed with the work.

"Anything you need?" his friend asked.

"Maybe some reading material ... "

"I thought of that," Moe said, producing a large paper bag full of periodicals. Rock reached in eagerly and came up with a stack of girlie magazines, the kind that would scandalize the average church-oriented Point Hoper.[11]

"Ah, Moe!"

Roaring with laughter, Moe dug in his big pocket and topped the pile with a worn *National Geographic.*

Archaeologist Dr. Helge Larson, who had worked with Howard's parents before the war, returned to the village, bringing with him a new book, *Ipiutak and the Arctic Whale Hunting Culture,* which Rock found fascinating. He spent off-hours in long conversations with the author and also explored his roots with the impressive colony of resident scientists that the AEC was sponsoring in the village. Don Foote was planning his thesis on arctic history. Dr. Burton Ostenson of the University of Puget Sound, who was paying $1.50 for seal snouts, offered a wealth of information from his hunting informants.[12] The Rev. Keith Lawton and his wife were bright, well-read, and welcomed the painter's company.

Rock was still not accepted among the majority of his peers, however. The point was brought home when they excluded him from the board of Eskimo delegates who met at Point Hope in preparation for an Association of American Indian Affairs (AAIA)-sponsored conference to be held in Barrow that winter. Their business was conducted in rapid-fire Eskimo which Howard could no longer understand. Point Hope's seat went to Dan Lisbourne. Guy Okakok of Barrow was made chairman and Frank Degnan of Unalakleet became secretary.

Degnan was clever, well-traveled, and had managed to get some education at a boarding school but his fluency was still in Eskimo. Okakok was a serious thinker but the column he wrote on Barrow news for the Fairbanks paper was an embarrassment of pidgin English. Howard shook his head as he read the minutes of the conference that Lisbourne sent to AAIA:

> Guy Okakok open the floor, and have started the meeting. He said, men you all know, why we are here to attend the meeting. "First", I would like each one of you to know, we Eskimos have been taking birds for food since time immemorial have not violated the migratory birds treaties. Right now lies the solution of the war or fight between we Eskimos and the Fish and Wildlife Agents. Yet we Eskimos have been living on ducks from generations to generations, taking the ducks with slings implements of our own devising before the white man ever lay his eyes on Alaska... .
>
> Mr. Degnan stood and said, Mr. Chairman, I Have heard lots about your Eskimos up at Barrow, its not only in your place Barrow but we have same problems like you have. Since then as you mention about migratory birds, I further more will say that this treaty between United States, Canada, and Mexico be changed right away ...

The minutes went on to include Lisbourne's plea for support against the AEC:

> They told me, the measurement what they to blast is 40 x 60 miles. That means our hunting ground will be destroyed. If they do where are we going to hunt the games, and how are we to find food for our families. Our people of Pt. Hope don't want to move or leave their ground.[13]

Considering what little formal education they had, they had done well. But, even with the help of AAIA, how could they hope to hold their own against the all-powerful AEC?

In October, the weekly mail plane brought exciting news. Ralph Perdue was enthusiastic about the whaling scene Rock had shipped him and agreed to pay the artist's fare to Fairbanks and back him in a show. Dr. Geist also promised to promote his work and Howard rushed to produce more paintings.[14]

The heavy rains of fall had ceased and snow was encroaching on distant hills when the artist collected his paints and struck out for one last visit to the grave site of his uncle, Attungowruk.[15] Originally the body of the illustrious chief had been entombed above ground on a platform of whale ribs. When the family converted to Christianity, they were required to bury their dead, but Attungowruk had been a powerful shaman. In life he had belittled the Christian teachings and so they interred his bones in the original location, a handsome span of open tundra, well apart from the Episcopal cemetery.

Deftly Rock sketched the grave markers, a dome of seven time-silvered whale ribs backed by a wide jawbone that stood double their height. Then he turned his attention to the terrain. In a way, the landscape of the arctic was much like modern art, he thought. At first the eye sees nothing, but gradually one comes to understand its subtle beauty and its worth.[16]

For hundreds of years before Attungowruk, this land had nurtured his Eskimo people. And it had sustained him. He might not subsist off it as a traditional hunter, but he was Eskimo, nonetheless, and he drew from it. He had turned to it when all else failed him. It had rejuvenated his spirit and he would not easily give it up.

Brushing in the sweeping grey of a wintering sky and the sleeping tundra, Rock's mind turned to a report the AAIA woman, Mrs. Madigan, had just written to the village council on their letter to the Secretary of Interior.

> Mr. Carver, (the assistant Secretary of Interior) telephoned in ... He had your letter in front of him and read it while we were talking. He said, "These people are asking what right the Bureau of Land Management has to give the Atomic Energy Commission land they claim before Congress has acted on Alaskan aboriginal rights." He thought a minute and then he said, "That's a damned good question."[17]

22

Inupiat Paitot

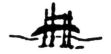

ATHABASCAN RALPH PERDUE was born in a tent on the banks of a Yukon River slough six miles above Koyukuk where children were expected to earn their keep. At age 10, when his heart was set on continuing school, his father announced he planned to educate him to a pick and shovel. Mr. and Mrs. E. E. Perdue, for whom the boy had been working at the trading post at Galena, agreed to sponsor him. He spent a year and a half at a Catholic mission in Skagway when the couple went on vacation outside the territory, then followed them to Kotzebue, Candle and Fairbanks, working at whatever jobs he could to get through high school.

Hoping to travel, he joined the service in 1952, only to fight the "Battle of Ladd Field," a local Army base, as the company clerk. Evenings he moonlighted in a jewelry store in Fairbanks and, on discharge, used his GI Bill to learn the jeweler's craft.

Perdue loved art and made it a point to learn from people who knew how to judge it. He had met Rock when the artist was earning from $75 to $150 per day etching ivory (while most were making $22) and he decided the Eskimo was still worth backing.[1]

Eebrulik Rock had returned to Point Hope after working the summer construction season in Fairbanks and, although he was not particularly close to his brother, he offered Howard rent-free use of a small house he kept in town. Eebrulik's daughter, Dorothy Mazzola, was also in residence with her family, so quarters were crowded and noisy but the price was right. With his show just six weeks off, Rock set up a borrowed easel in Eebrulik's living room and began working at a furious pace with Dorothy's little daughters at his side, gravely imitating the way he backed off to view his brush strokes, giggling at the stories he told them.

No one had much money. Howard had used most of his earnings from earlier painting sales to pay off Point Hope debts. His niece had little income. Perdue, who was struggling to build a house and raise a family, did janitor work at the Nordale Hotel to pay rent for his jewelry shop in the lobby. But the handsome Athabascan was personable and he knew everybody in town. He and his outgoing wife, Dorothy, made sure their protege was introduced to influential people and prospective buyers. And if the round of supper invitations lagged, they made a place for Howard at their own table.[2]

Although Fairbanks was a former gold rush town of fewer than 15,000, the nearby University of Alaska attracted many intelligent, articulate people, and archaeologist Otto Geist offered Rock valuable entrée. Claire Fejes, artist and writer, invited him to read his poetry to a group that met regularly to discuss philosophy and art.[3] Rusty Heurlin, a local painter who had earlier befriended Eebrulik, provided art supplies and encouragement.[4]

Stimulated by the creative atmosphere, Howard found himself doing his best work, but the mailman brought disquieting interruptions. Guy Okakok, organizer of the upcoming Eskimo meeting at Barrow, had chosen Herbert Konooyak over Rock as the Point Hope delegate, but La Verne Madigan, the representative from the Association on American Indian Affairs, kept insisting that Rock attend. She offered to pay expenses. She appealed to his conscience. Few of the delegates had more than a fourth-grade education, she reminded him.[5]

Timing couldn't have been worse. The Barrow conference was scheduled November 15-18, just two weeks before Rock's art exhibit was to open at Fairbanks's finest hotel. The show would make or break him and he was still struggling to complete needed canvases. Finally he took the problem to Perdue who had almost as much at stake as the artist, and found the decision made for him. Although Perdue's adopted parents and his wife were Caucasian, the Indian had seen more than his share of discrimination and was a strong advocate of Native rights. He had helped found the Fairbanks Native Association, and he was personally backing Nick Gray, former mayor of White Mountain, who was campaigning for equal rights in the southern part of the state.[6]

"Of course you'll go for the AAIA," Perdue said.

It had been almost 30 years since Rock had seen Barrow but it hadn't changed much. The old mission, Bureau of Indian Affairs school and a collection of scrap lumber shacks skewed by frost heaves were backed by a cheerless winter sky. He was housed with other delegates at the Top of the World Hotel, a derelict edifice featuring rooms the size of shower stalls. There was no plumbing and no central heating, but he brightened when Tom Snapp turned up as his roommate.

Snapp was the only newspaper man in the state who seemed to care about Native problems. If an Eskimo got drunk and killed someone or won a sled dog race, the local papers would cover it, but the subject of Native rights was seldom broached. Snapp was genuinely concerned and he'd been quick to notice that the reassuring statements of AEC scientists didn't jibe with the facts. A talented investigative reporter, he had produced a lively series on Project Chariot for the local Fairbanks paper and when Howard moved to town, Snapp made it a point to get to know him.[7]

"It's horrifying," Snapp was saying as he settled into their tiny room, organizing his books and pencils for the conference the *Fairbanks Daily News-Miner* had dispatched him to cover. "Alaska's Native people are treated worse than second-class citizens."

"I'm a little befuddled on some of the issues," Rock admitted.

"The Eskimos have a higher infant mortality rate than even India," Snapp informed him in his odd southern drawl. "Their average life expectancy is something like 27 years in some areas. Their medical care is a disgrace and so is their education system. You know how bad their housing is. There are no jobs. Fish and Wildlife and the big game guides ignore Eskimo hunting rights and they can't even own the land on which they have lived for hundreds and hundreds of years... ."

The rotund reporter had a disconcerting habit of shifting his weight from foot to foot, swaying back and forth when he got engrossed. Watching him was like being aboard ship, Howard thought, but Snapp was a mine of information and he admired him. On summer vacation from a University of Missouri School of Journalism graduate program, the southerner had ventured north to visit his sister and stayed on when the News-Miner begged him to fill in for a missing staffer. The job frustrated Snapp because he was seldom allowed to travel the bush or to cover Native problems in depth. This meeting would be a wonderful opportunity to play up the issues, he said.[8]

"If only we can grasp them," Howard worried.

A few doors down the hall La Verne Madigan voiced the same concern to Jim Hawkins, Alaskan director of the Bureau of Indian Affairs, and John Carver, newly appointed Assistant Secretary of Land Management. The hotel was so cold they'd taken to wearing their parkas indoors. Carver, who had traveled from Washington, D. C. to attend, was rubbing his hands together to restore circulation.

"I'm prepared to give the Natives strong support," he said.

"But it will only work if they can get themselves organized," Hawkins reminded him. "If they can't, we've gone about as far as we can go."[9]

Although he would play no official part in this meeting, Madigan knew Hawkins had staked his career on its outcome, for it was he who had asked the AAIA to launch its fight against the Atomic Energy Commission on behalf of the Eskimos. The AEC was at the height of its power. Anyone who opposed it was automatically in trouble, so Madigan had gone to great lengths to destroy Hawkins' correspondence and to distance herself from him during her Alaskan travels.[10] Alaska's U. S. Senator Ernest Gruening was already seeking his dismissal because the brash young Republican appointee had angered him on other matters. Unbeknownst to Hawkins, Madigan had obtained Carver's promise to leave him at his Alaska post until after this meeting, but he was soon to be transferred to the political backwater of Minneapolis.[11]

"We've done our homework, Jim," she said, reassuringly. But she was by no means certain.

With satisfaction, Martha Teeluk counted more than 200 Eskimos crowded into the old Barrow meeting hall. As far as she could tell she was the only student, and one of two women delegates, but there was a good representation of Yupik Eskimos from her remote Kuskokwim district. Although still a young woman, Teeluk had taught in village schools at Hooper Bay, Scammon and Emmonak, and already had a sound understanding of Native rights from her tenure on the Education Committee of the Fairbanks Native Association. Born at St. Marys of a Kotlik family, educated in the Catholic school there, she had enrolled at the University of Alaska after the Bureau of Indian Affairs questioned her teaching credentials. With five children to support, Teeluk was working her way and had little time to spare, but she realized this meeting was vital. Because her Yupik people were from the sub-arctic and spoke a different language from Inupiaq of the far north, she had been assigned the job of interpreter. There were only four whites in attendance; the AAIA woman, two government men and the reporter. Deftly she translated Mrs. Madigan's opening introductions and John Carver's reassurances for her delegation.[12]

Madigan eyed her anxiously. She had promised Hawkins she would intercede if the Natives had trouble establishing their own agenda, but she had no way of knowing if the interpreters were getting it all straight.[13]

Guy Okakok needed no prompting. He named the meeting "Inupiat Paitot" (the people's heritage) and gave each delegate his turn in a well-ordered fashion.

"Natives have been pushed too far," Jonah Tokienna from Wales declared, setting the tone in Inupiat. "It's about time to take action."

Hunting rights were a major problem in his village, he reported.

Simon Paneak, representing a migrant tribe of hunters from Anaktuvuk Pass, warned that outsiders generally made the mistake of thinking Eskimos lived like white men by gardening, with little comprehension of the hardships of living off the land. Federal game enforcement people were attempting to severely limit the number of caribou they could hunt. "We don't want to starve do we, men?" he rallied.

David Kagak of Point Hope reported that white trophy hunters, who competed with the Eskimos for game, took hides and heads but left carcasses to rot. Edward Penatac and Paul Tiulana spoke of the squalor in which federal officials had relocated his people from remote King Island to the slums of Nome. Others voiced concerns of health, education, welfare and the fact that federal officials were withdrawing from public domain large tracts of land which they depended on for hunting.

"I am 71 years old and I've seen everything that goes by, but I never thought that we from an outlying region had almost the same problems as you from the north," conceded Alexander Vaska who came from Yupik country where customs differed vastly from the Inupiat. "Now I know we have common problems, I say we must unite and take action. It's about time now, men, with the help of God!"[14]

Later, representatives divided into panels encouraging testimony from the floor. Again, statements were well thought out and Martha Teeluk suppressed a smile as she translated for a weathered Yupik hunter.

"Who owns the birds that fly in the air we hunt for food?" he challenged white government game wardens who had joined the crowd.

No one could answer.

"If you don't own them, you can't make laws against hunting them for food. God put them there for food and you have no right to put them in," he declared.[15]

Between meetings, citizens of Barrow entertained their visitors with a series of Eskimo dances and dinners in private homes and Howard was delighted to find himself a guest of Alice Perry Solomen, a fellow student at White Mountain, in the company of his former grade school teacher, Tony Joule.[16] Joule had been delegated to write Inupiat Paitot's policy statement and Howard wasted no time in lobbying for a newsletter to continue the dialogue of the convention. Joule was noncommittal but when his final report was submitted, detailing Native issues on land ownership, health, welfare and education, Rock was pleased to read the conclusion:

> We should be established. Truthfully, the Association on American
> Indian Affairs should not pay the expenses each time forever. It is suggested

that a self-supporting organization be recognized by this conference and pay small dues toward the cost of another conference. It is also suggested that a bulletin or newspaper be published and circulated every so often to villages about what is being done within the Inupiat organization. This organization should be well established, not to be allowed to die. All the native villages should be informed what has been accomplished for the good of these villages.[17]

Reporter Snapp, who was straining to catch a few English words in the closing discussion, was astonished to hear his own name mentioned with that of Howard Rock.

"You have been appointed to a committee to look into the possibility of starting a newspaper," delegates told him.

Snapp had discussed methods of communication with Rock, but they'd been thinking on a considerably smaller scale.

"You mean a newsletter, don't you?" he said.

"No, we want a newspaper!" the Eskimos insisted.[18]

23

Success

HOWARD STRAIGHTENED HIS NECKTIE as he peered at his painting of a polar bear. He'd worked on it most of the night. The paint was scarcely dry, but it would have to do. His show was opening today.

"Breakfast, Uncle Howard."

He winced at the thought of freeloading another meal, although his niece, Dorothy, had done her best to make him feel he was welcome.

"Maybe my show will produce a little grocery money."

"Don't worry," she said cheerfully. "Of course it's going to be all right."

But it wasn't. There was a fair turnout and many enthusiastic comments about the 10 paintings Ralph Perdue had artfully arranged in the elegant, wood-paneled showroom of the Travelers Inn, but no sales.

"It's the weather," Perdue insisted. "After all, it's 22 degrees below zero, Howard! But tomorrow's prediction is for 15 above. That will get us a good crowd."[1]

The following day, Rock arrived early on the off chance that hoped-for buyers might materialize and, with time on his hands, he began a letter of thanks to La Verne Madigan for backing the Barrow conference.

> It was a beautiful thing to experience, as the meeting took shape, when the participants began to realize that their problems were generally the same. They will be talked about in the home villages and the Natives in Alaska will have been much better informed of their rights. It was apparent that the final report at Point Barrow had a heartening and sobering effect on the population there. It is my wish that this impact be carried through and much more thoroughly through future meetings. It is very necessary and important that the Natives realize a cohesion so their voice can be heard through balloting. As you and I know, the number of votes is substantial and would be a nice morsel for anyone seeking a seat.

In Washington, D.C. a few days later, Madigan marveled at the letter. While the rank-and-file were still struggling with the concept of a united

front, Howard was already weighing its political clout. What a pity the
Eskimo leadership considered him an outsider. But then, Rock himself,
had other plans.[2] An enclosed clipping proclaimed his art exhibit a near
sellout.[3]

Dorothy Mazzola was delighted with her uncle's success. He'd awakened her after the show, as excited as a kid, waving what she thought was a
ten-dollar-bill under her nose.

"It's not a ten, Dorothy. It's a *one-hundred-dollar-bill.* All for groceries!"

He'd sold six paintings; the big whaling scene for $1000, the bear for
$750 and smaller works at $500 and $200.

"I think I can make a living at it," he told her, jubilantly. "I honestly
do."[4]

By the time he arrived in Anchorage three months later with nearly a
dozen canvases to enter in the Fur Rendezvous Art Show, his uncertainly
had returned. Anchorage was cosmopolitan by Fairbanks standards, a
much larger town and well-removed from the bush.

"Really, I have no idea how folks here will react to my work," he told
Erna Marcum, a school teacher who was exhibiting in the booth next to
his. Marcum owned a representative collection of Alaska's finest artists
including Sydney Laurence. Quizzically she studied the Eskimo's canvases.

"Primitive," she smiled approvingly.

"Maybe too primitive," Howard worried.

"No, your style is so controlled...disciplined. You've had real training."

He nodded. She singled out a wooded landscape featuring a rustic
storage cache on tall, stilt-like legs.

"Would you sell it to me? I mean after the show, of course."

"I'd be pleased. It might be my only sale!" Howard chuckled. Later,
when he sold out and was offered more for the work than the price he'd
quoted Marcum, he turned down the higher bid.

"You didn't have to," she said, although she'd fallen in love with the
painting.

"I'm a man of my word, ma'am," Rock insisted.[5]

On the success of the Anchorage show, Howard paid his debts and
moved from his cramped quarters to a comfortable room in the Nordale
Hotel. Perdue displayed his new works at the jewelry store and when sales
lagged, Howard paid off his hotel bill in paintings or Perdue, himself,
would buy them. Revenues increased as the artist's reputation grew and
Perdue was optimistic.

In March, the Governor's Advisory Committee on Economic Development proposed legislation to move the people of Point Hope, Kivalina

and Noatak to temporary housing in Nome during the AEC's test, recognizing that the project "would provide the United States with extremely valuable scientific information along the lines of peaceful application of nuclear energy," and that "such a nuclear explosion at this particular site would be of tremendous economic value to Alaska."[6]

Angered, Howard took time away from his easel to write the author of the resolution a three-page letter citing the dangers of the test, explaining the needs of the subsistence hunters who occupied the land and concluding:

> The idea the resolution poses is that the three villages be merged into one is an ill-considered one. The idea that they be forced to evacuate their traditional homesites, it seems to me, cruel and tragic. Why should they have to do it? There has never been any clear-cut presentation of economic benefits that the above villages would derive from the proposed explosion.... The resolution is a weird application of better housing for the natives. It sounds like a proposition to house the natives through laying waste to their traditional ways of making a living. It is, I feel, a device designed to pull the wool over their eyes.[7]

Radiation from previous atomic blasts already had people worried. Don Foote and his wife, Berit, who had check-ups after a brief stay in Point Hope, discovered they had body counts of Cessium 137 at 37 and 88 nu (respectively), as compared to a normal count of from 2.0 to 4.1 nu.[8]

Rock had no intention of becoming involved with leadership of the opposition. Guy Okakok, Frank Degnan and Paul Tiulana had that firmly in hand, but the Madigan woman kept writing him on the latest developments, asking for suggestions, and he was still working with Tom Snapp on the possibilities of starting a Native newspaper. During his research he met a group of young Native activists who were also students at University of Alaska, and Kay Hitchcock, an English professor who had founded the Alaska Native Rights Association with a group of fellow Quakers.[9] At the prompting of Ralph Perdue, Rock also joined the Fairbanks Native Association and Perdue, in turn, took an interest in the work of AAIA.[10]

The Land Office of the Bureau of Land Management had just dismissed the aboriginal rights protests filed the previous November by BIA Director James Hawkins on behalf of the Athabascan villages of Tanacross, Northway and Minto, whose hunting lands were being claimed by the state.[11] The Indians claimed about 5.8 million acres and the state had already filed patent for 1.7 million of them.[12] In response, Perdue's people were attempting to revive their traditional governing body, Tanana Chiefs, along the lines of the Eskimo's Inupiat Paitot. The NRA collected $800 door to door for the first Athabascan conference and AAIA agreed to donate $5,000 to the cause which coincided perfectly with its own long-range planning.[13]

In 1958, an AAIA lawyer, Arthur Lazarus, published an article titled "Native Land Claims in Alaska" citing the Congressional Act of May 17, 1884, as basis for aboriginal rights.

The heart of this legislation is a clause declaring Natives "shall not be disturbed in the possession of any lands actually in their use and occupation now claimed by them but the terms under which such persons may acquire title to such lands is reserved for future legislation by Congress."

Lazarus maintained that, in theory, possessory rights in Alaska remained as they were 75 years ago, "unconfirmed, yet unextinguished." But he noted that "in reality, native rights become increasingly vulnerable with the passage of time."[14]

In response, La Verne Madigan consulted a young lawyer named Ted Stevens who worked as solicitor for the Secretary of Interior, and decided that AAIA should wait to act until after Alaska became a state when it was presumed the Native people would have a better chance of getting a settlement. Section Four of the Statehood Act (passed in 1958) provided for preservation of Native claims—neither diminished nor enlarged—for Congress to settle later, but the newly formed state soon began selecting Eskimo and Indian hunting grounds and even long-settled village sites as part of the 104 million-acre "dowry" the federal government had granted it.[15]

Alarmed, Ted Stevens—now a private citizen in Alaska—contacted Madigan who, in turn, besieged Oliver LaFarge, president of AAIA, to take up the Alaskans' cause.

"Ted said that he thought all forces should join to get Alaska Native claims settled as quickly as possible," she reported. "He said he thought the Natives should receive land, not just money. He said no one in either party 'gives a damn about this'."[16]

When LaFarge demurred, Madigan went ahead on her own, using the AEC as her springboard, and she was gaining ground.

"Rye with just a splash of water."

Bar-owner Tommy Paskvan nodded. Rock always ordered the same drink and sat at the same out-of-the-way table in the shadow of the bar.

"How are the Eskimos doing with that AEC fellow, Teller?" Paskvan asked, proffering a stout glass.

"I think we may put him out of business," Howard answered with the hint of a smile. He felt at home in the Elbow Room. The quiet, well-mannered owner had studied mining at the University of Alaska and when he decided to stake his claim on Second Avenue, his bar just naturally attracted the college crowd. Natives weren't discouraged from drinking there but derelicts usually preferred the raucous atmosphere of cheaper bars down the street, which suited Howard just fine.[17]

Earlier in the year Joe Upicksoun arrived in town from a lucrative job on the DEW Line (the government's Distant Early Warning System) with a case of Jim Beam, and Howard had partied with his old enthusiasm. His work suffered. Perdue was disappointed in him, and since then he'd paced himself.[18] In fact, this was his first drink of the evening and it was 11:55 p.m. He and Guy Okakok had gotten so involved talking to La Verne they hadn't noticed the time.

La Verne had previewed the article on Project Chariot written by Joseph Foote, Don's brother, for *Harpers Magazine,* and was sure it would help swing public opinion in the Eskimos' favor. She seemed certain they could force the federal government to allow Barrow residents to heat their homes with natural gas from a nearby reserve. Already there was a bill in Congress. She spoke of Paul Tiulana's concern that Natives retain mineral rights along with surface title to their lands. Howard and Guy had come up with a dozen more good proposals.

Talking with La Verne, brainstorming, was exhilarating. It robbed Rock of valuable painting time, but he found it addictive.

Ensconced at the Nordale in a room still blue with cigarette smoke that lingered from their long discussions, La Verne pulled out a battered portable to type a letter to Henry Forbes, head of her Alaska Policy Committee.

> Howard Rock or Guy Okakok went off with my ball-point pen. It is midnight. The three of us sat here until 10 minutes ago, writing down proposals to be taken to the villages....
>
> I was surprised to find out how strong an impact the Pt. Barrow Conference had all over Alaska. Eskimos everywhere were informed about it, and waiting eagerly for the next development. Now that one group has spoken out clearly, the others are beginning to drop the fiction that they are people without a trouble in the world. The whites are just as much aware of the new Eskimo stirring. In Nome, strangers come up to me on the street to refer to the Barrow Conference and express opinion *pro* and *con.* The *con* people are really worried about what the Eskimo may do next!
>
> Howard and I are working out organizational plans. Tomorrow I shall meet with Mrs. Hitchcock and her group, and have a meeting with the "Fairbanks Eskimo Village." The following day Guy and I start for Barrow via Anaktuvuk Pass. From Barrow we shall make a round trip to Barter Island, stopping off at some village of which Guy knew and of which I never heard.

(Nikilik?) Then from Barrow we shall go west to Wainwright, Point Lay and other villages between there and Kotzebue. Guy has surpassed himself in making advance arrangements for the village meetings. He is taking along a tape recording of the Barrow Conference and 100 copies of our Inupiat Newsletter....

The Eskimos are so amazingly bright. I wish you could have seen Guy Okakok's and Howard Rock's faces light up when I mentioned the ecological reserve. They are passionate thinkers, as I once wrote you. Ideas—good ones—come tumbling out a mile a minute.[19]

On Madigan's return from the bush, Rock and Tom Snapp met with her to lay groundwork for a newspaper. Since foundations viewed the start-up as too risky, they asked Madigan for the names of AAIA's five richest members. Dr. Forbes headed the list and Howard, who was not at his best seeking handouts, wrote him a somewhat stilted letter, with little hope of a reply.[20]

The organizational meeting of Athabascans in Tanana the following June turned into an endurance test. Lodging for several plane loads of delegates was provided by the Rev. Thomas Cleveland, the Episcopal minister, who doubled up his four kids to provide room in his home and, in the absence of his wife, attempted to cook for all comers. Many subsisted on peanut butter. Most slept on the floor and Howard, who came in late, ended up bunking in the reverend's closet.[21]

Meetings were also a free-for-all because Ralph Perdue had grown suspicious of the AAIA and NRA, which some thought to be communist organizations and (even more unnerving) hell-bent on corralling Alaska Natives on reservations. Madigan denied it, but Perdue captured the floor to protest that outsiders were running things. Political candidates, including U.S. Senator Ernest Gruening, were expelled from the hall while delegates settled their differences and Fairbanks newspapers carried banner headlines on the debate.[22] Despite the furor, Tanana Chiefs soon formed a united front that unnerved whites who opposed them and racial tension flared.

"I am reminded of what Ted Stevens said a few years ago when he told me about Alaska," La Verne Madigan wrote her home office in the summer of 1962. "He said that the intimidation, economic and otherwise, of the Natives and their friends would be unimaginable to us in the lower '48, and he advised a sustained national public education program be applied. Rene d'Harnoncourt of our board agreed that courage would be needed by anyone working in Alaska—intellectual and possibly physical courage. With every day that passes I realize how honestly Stevens spoke and with how little exaggeration."[23]

Howard Rock emerged from his meeting with U.S. Senator Bob Bartlett, shaking his head. Bartlett had served as Alaska's Territorial delegate to Congress before statehood. He had thrown his considerable weight against the AEC after its spokesman had assured him the atomic blast at Point Hope would produce no more radiation than the luminescent dial of his wrist watch, and moved to curtail testing. But he showed little sympathy for Native land rights. La Verne had warned Rock that neither Bartlett nor Gruening would back a Native claims settlement. The claims bill that AAIA had asked them to present to Congress after statehood had been consigned to a dusty file at the Department of Interior.

"What did he tell you?" Tom Snapp asked anxiously. He'd been on the edge of his chair ever since the senator called requesting the interview.

"He assured me that the Eskimos and Indians had no historic or aboriginal rights. He based his statement on a Supreme Court decision; he thought it was the something called the Tee-Hit-Ton case,"[24] Howard shrugged. "I wanted to discuss it but he got suddenly called away."

"About what I expected," Snapp sighed. It was late summer and there hadn't been much good news lately. Dr. Forbes had never answered their request for financial backing, despite Mrs. Madigan's hunch that he might be receptive.[25]

Although Henry Stone Forbes was born into a long-established New England family of considerable wealth, he was keenly aware of the problems of poverty and the plight of unsophisticated aboriginal people faced with white intrusion. On graduation from Harvard in 1905, he spent a year in the Philippines living on remote islands, working odd jobs. Two years later, on a break from Harvard Medical School, he traveled the coast of Labrador to its northern tip. After witnessing real carnage during World War I, serving with the American Red Cross in Serbia and France, he settled into research and industrial medicine, but he continued to travel widely.[26]

Now in semi-retirement, Dr. Forbes devoted considerable time to helping Native Americans. When Oliver LaFarge appointed him to oversee work of AAIA in Alaska, the doctor visited remote villages and also Nome, where the government had relocated Eskimos from King Island when rock slides imperiled their traditional site. The squalor in which Forbes found the King Islanders horrified him.

"The government has put them in the red light district covered with bars," he told his wife, Hildegarde, who was also an active AAIA member. "Their school is sliding into the water and nobody seems to care."

Forbes didn't see eye-to-eye with Alaska's Senator Gruening with whom he had graduated from medical school, and AAIA's research showed the

Alaska Natives could expect little support from other congressmen and government officials. Forbes had attended the Point Hope meeting where Howard Rock suggested publication of a newsletter and realized it would be an excellent way to generate attention for the cause.[27] The idea of a full-blown newspaper had not occurred to him, and after Rock approached him for backing, Forbes consulted AAIA lawyer Art Lazarus, who was also a friend.

"Let me tell you a story about a man who made a pact with the devil," Lazarus smiled at the straight-backed old New Englander. "The devil promised to give this man a million dollars a year as long as he could spend it on something new. And when he ran out of new things to buy, the devil would take his soul. The man did fine at first, but after purchasing mansions and cars and yachts he was running out of ideas. The devil was sure he had him until the man bought a newspaper. Then, of course, he never ran out of new things to spend money on."

Forbes chuckled, but he had become increasingly fascinated by the fast-moving organization of Native groups in the north.[28]

"It's just like a murder mystery that comes out once a month," Oliver LaFarge agreed. "I can't wait for the next letter from Alaska." And Forbes made up his mind.

"I'm going to back it," he told his wife. "But only if Howard Rock will run it. He's intelligent and a good leader and I can't see anyone else for the job."[29]

In August, Rock received a terse letter from his would-be benefactor asking why the Natives wanted a newspaper and what the issues were. Howard left the reply to Snapp who responded with specifics that covered 48 pages, and Forbes phoned back almost immediately. He would fund their venture with $35,000 in its first year, he promised, provided they publish at once with Rock as editor and Snapp as his assistant.

Snapp had already started shipping his belongings back to Missouri for his final year of graduate school and he had no intentions of dropping out. Howard, whose total journalistic experience had been drawing covers and submitting an occasional story or poem to the White Mountain school yearbook, was desperate.

"You've got to stay until I get some experience, Tom," he pleaded. And Snapp, who had become nearly as caught up in the Native cause as his Eskimo friend, weakened.

"I'll stay for a year and one day. No longer," the newsman finally agreed.[30]

24

Tundra Times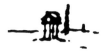

THERE WERE JUST A COUPLE OF WEEKS in which to organize if the newspaper was to be launched in time to capitalize on the upcoming statewide election. Tom Snapp's sister, Colleen, and her husband, Lloyd Redman, had volunteered their trailer home for an office while they were on vacation in Texas. There were no desks on which to work. Layout sheets and copy littered the floor.

Tom was washing a counter-top full of dirty coffee cups accumulated during the marathon three days he and Rock had just spent working without sleep.

"There he goes again," Howard warned, looking up from the ancient Underwood typewriter someone had donated, just in time to see the Redman's pet parakeet plunge head first into the soapy dishwater. Snapp fished the bird out, toweled him off and put him gingerly on the counter where the bedraggled creature set about preening soggy feathers.

"Really, Howard, we should put him back in the cage for his own good."

Rock looked pained. He couldn't bear to see the bird cooped up behind bars and Snapp sighed heavily. Usually it took months to start a newspaper and here he was with no notice whatsoever, under absolutely crazy conditions, trying to make an editor out of Eskimo artist.

"What should I write about?" Rock was asking. Guy Okakok had already turned in a column on his adventures working for the Hudson's Bay Company. Al Ketzler was reporting on his new Athabascan organization and Martha Teeluk had written a piece on Native activities statewide. They were planning to run a congratulatory letter from Bob Bennett who had just been appointed commissioner of the Bureau of Indian Affairs to replace Jim Hawkins. Tom was researching the lead story but there was still space to fill.

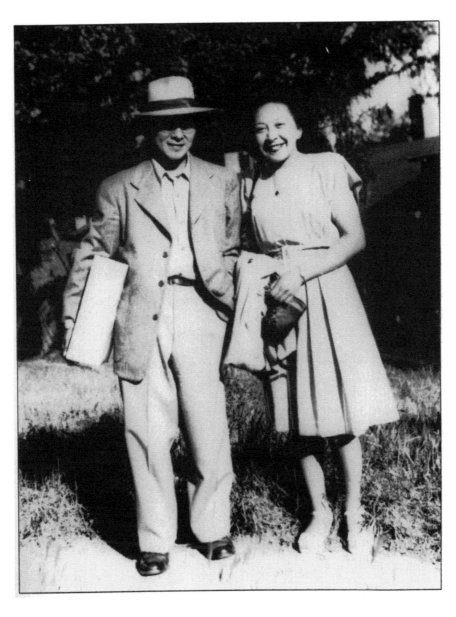

ROCK AND HIS HOUSEKEEPER   Betsy Peterson (Towne) served as Howard's
housekeeper when he moved to Bainbridge Island. Betsy and her husband, Lou, were
among very few Seattle friends Rock stayed in touch with after he returned to Alaska.
Photo Courtesy of Betsy Peterson Towne.

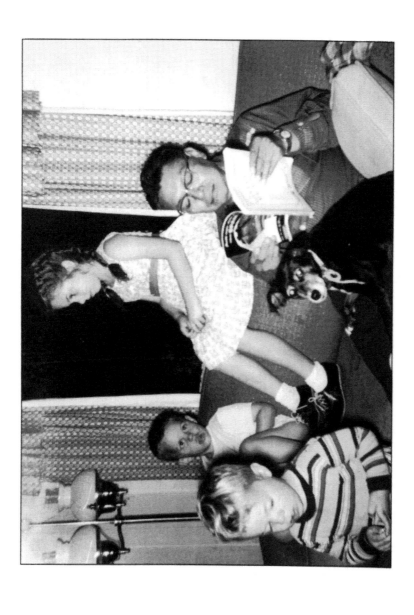

AT HOME WITH THE JOHNSONS   Artists C. Alan Johnson and his wife, Suzanne, met Rock in 1960 when they were preparing for a trip to Point Hope and he adopted their family. Here he spends a comfortable evening with the Johnson youngsters: Keith, 3; Brian, 6; and Laurie, 8. *Photo Courtesy of Suzanne and C. Alan Johnson.*

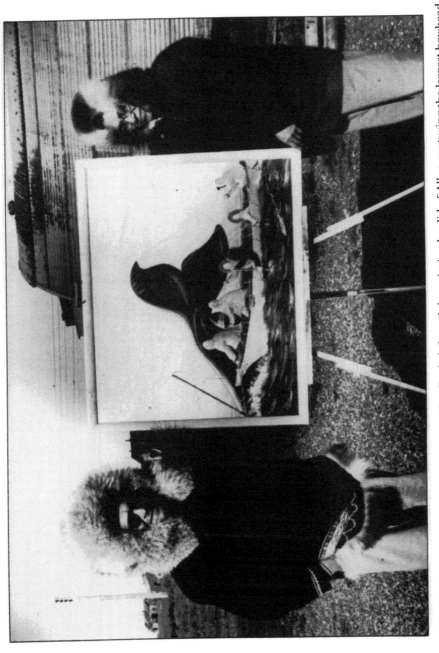

WHALER AND ARTIST Howard poses with his brother, Allen Rock, left, and the painting he did of Allen capturing the largest bowhead whale ever recorded at Point Hope. *Photo courtesy of Hildegarde Forbes.*

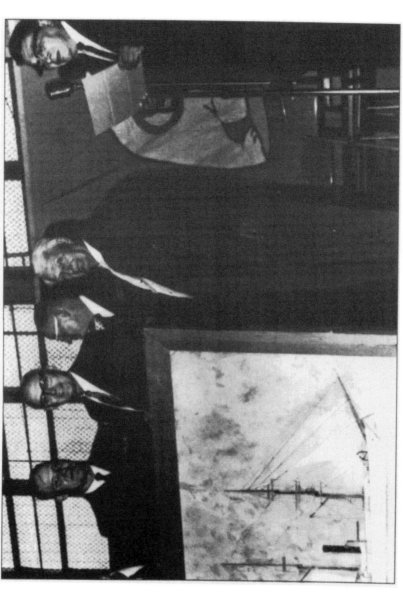

FIRST BIG SALE Rock presents his painting of the famous Revenue Cutter *Bear* to the University of Alaska. The canvas was purchased for the college by archaeologist Otto Geist, fourth from left. Dr. William Wood, university president, is second from the left. *Photo courtesy of University of Alaska Fairbanks.*

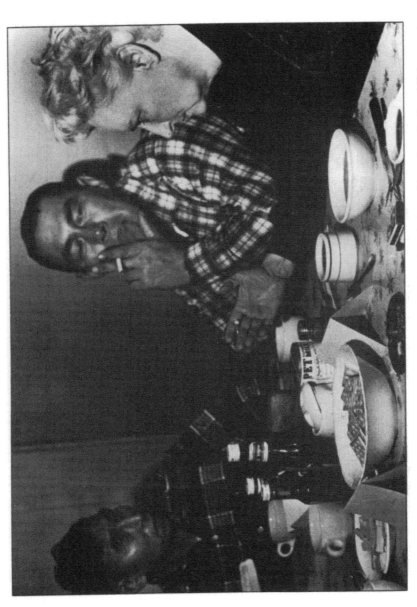

PLANNING INUPIAT PAITOT La Verne Madigan, executive director of the Association of American Indian Affairs, spent many smoke-filled evenings talking Eskimo politics. Here she plans a regional meeting with Guy Okakok of Barrow, left, and Dan Lisbourne of Point Hope. *Photo courtesy of the* Tundra Times.

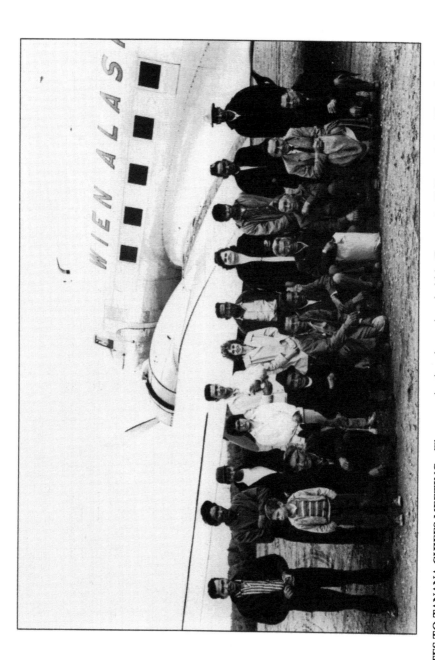

DELEGATES TO TANANA CHIEFS MEETING   The organizational meeting, held in Tanana in 1961, made headlines for days.   *Photo courtesy of Theodore Brinton Hetzel.*

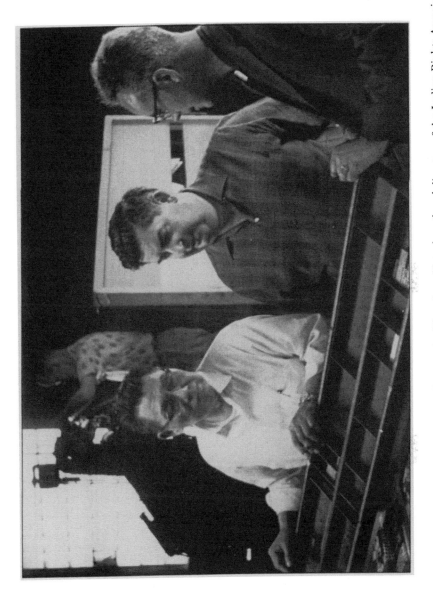

LAUNCHING *TUNDRA TIMES* Howard Rock and Tom Snapp give Theodore Hetzel, national director of the Indian Rights Association, a tour of the printing plant at *Jessen's Weekly* where early issues of the *Tundra Times* were printed. Hetzel took the photo himself.

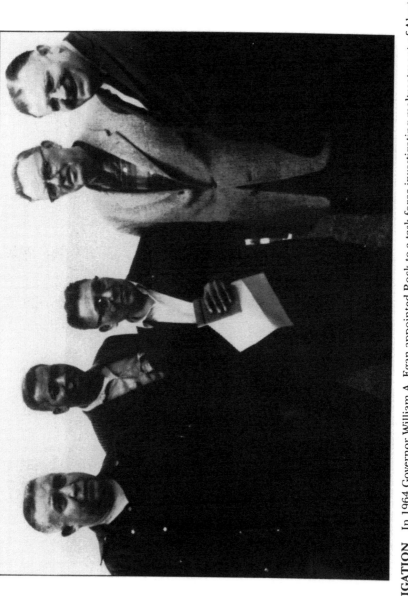

PRIBILOF INVESTIGATION In 1964 Governor William A. Egan appointed Rock to a task force investigating maltreatment of Aleuts on the Pribilofs by the U. S. Department of Fish and Wildlife. Members pictured from the left were Roy Peratrovich, tribal operations officer for the Bureau of Indian Affairs; Willard Bowman, executive director of the Human Rights Commission; Rock; Hugh Wade, Secretary of State; and James C. Rettie, senior economist from the office of the Secretary of Interior. *Courtesy of* Tundra Times.

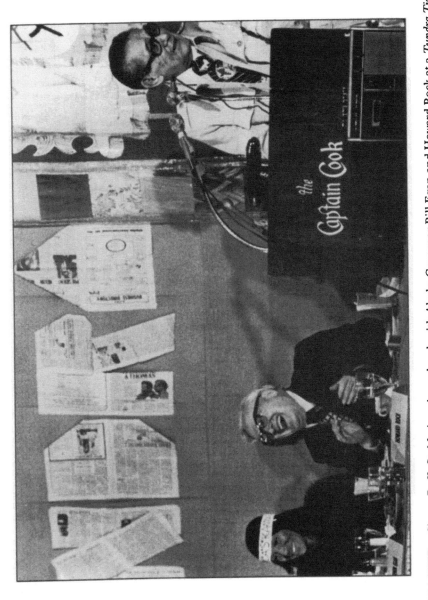

CELEBRITY BACKER Singer Buffy St. Marie enjoys a laugh with Alaska Governor Bill Egan and Howard Rock at a *Tundra Times* banquet. Other celebrities followed. *Photo courtesy of Jimmy Bedford.*

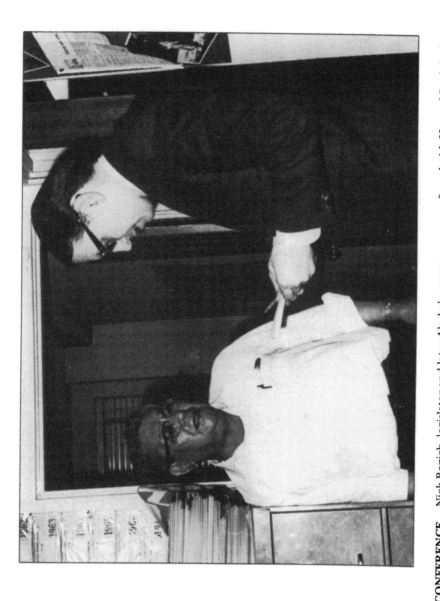

POLITICAL CONFERENCE   Nick Begich, legislator and later Alaska's congressman, conferred with Howard Rock in the summer of 1971. Like many elected public officials Begich dropped into the office routinely whenever he was in Fairbanks. *Photo by Lael Morgan.*

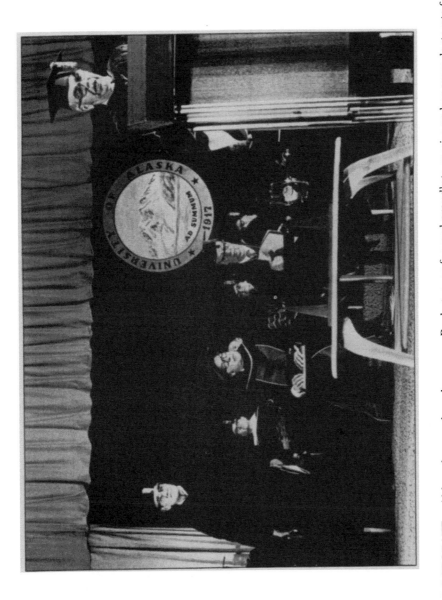

AN HONORARY DOCTORATE   Although worn down by cancer, Rock steppec forward proudly to receive an honorary doctorate from the University of Alaska in 1974. The award caught him by surprise and he was absolutely delighted by it. *Photo by Jimmy Bedford.*

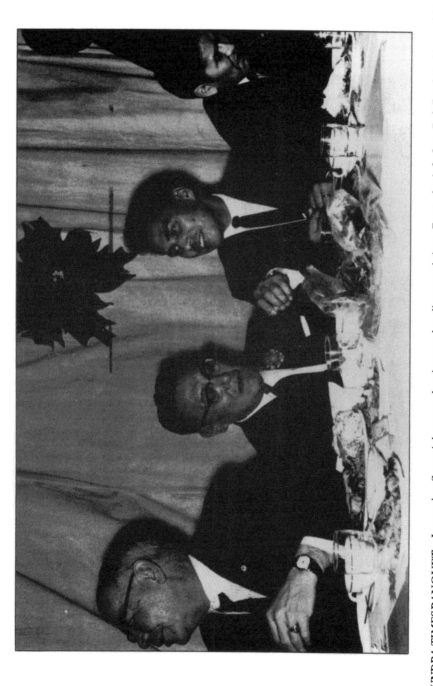

FIRST *TUNDRA TIMES* BANQUET   It wasn't a financial success but it was a howling good time. From the left, Sen. Bob Bartlett, Howard Rock, Tyonek Chief Albert Kaloa and Ralph Perdue share a joke. *Courtesy of* Tundra Times.

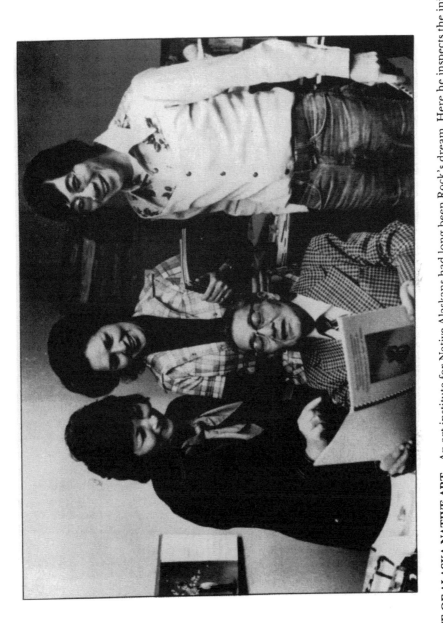

INSTITUTE OF ALASKA NATIVE ART   An art institute for Native Alaskans had long been Rock's dream. Here he inspects the initial proposal which brought it into being with Laura Bergt, Mary Jane Fate and Tom Richards Jr. *Photo by Sue Gamache.*

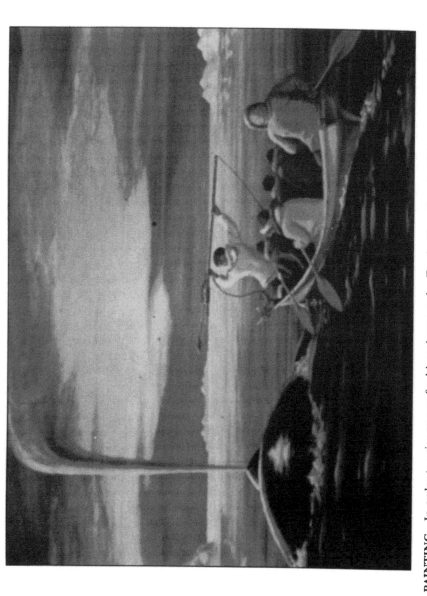

ROCK'S FINAL PAINTING In order to raise money for his retirement the *Tundra Times* Board of Directors suggested Rock do an oil painting that could be auctioned off at a banquet in his honor. This whaling scene was the result. *Courtesy of Arctic Slope Regional Corporation*

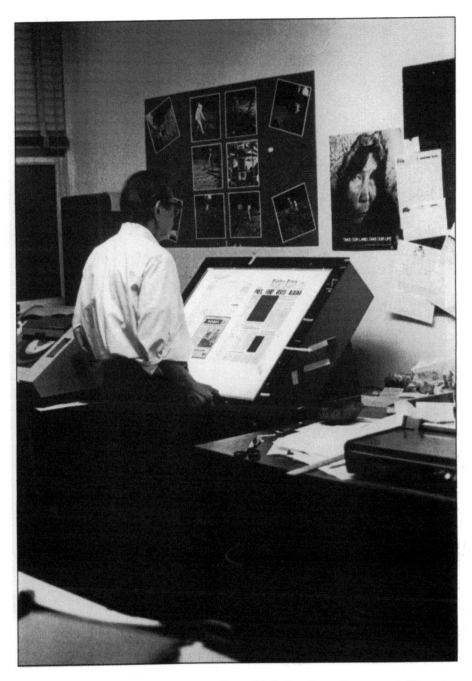

AT THE LAYOUT TABLE   Rock worked over his light table to the very end. He met the deadline for the April 21, 1976, issue of *Tundra Times* before checking into the hospital for a final bout with the cancer and died less than a week later. *Photo courtesy of Sue Gamache.*

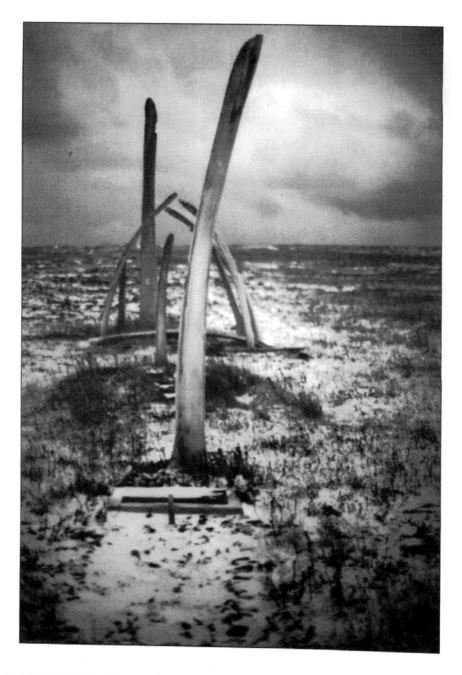

PLACE OF HONOR   Howard Rock was buried next to his great uncle, Chief Attungowruk, at a remote tundra site apart from the Christian cemetery. The whale rib that backs his conventional tombstone is a traditional mark of honor in Point Hope.

"Write about what you know, Howard," the newsman counseled. "All that fantastic stuff you've been telling me about how your people survived in the arctic. It will make a great series."

Rock nodded and began to type.

"Arctic Survival—Hair Seal—The Big Little Animal," Snapp read with approval. "Nachik, as it is called by Eskimos, is the hair seal. It doesn't mean much to many people but to Eskimos this little animal has much significance. Nachik, in many ancient Eskimo songs, takes the star billing...."

They stopped briefly for supper, accidentally spilling peanut butter and jelly on a couple of layout sheets. The print shop would not be pleased, Snapp reflected, but that was the least of their worries.

Their efforts to organize had been met with hostility from businessmen and bureaucrats who had reason to fear a united Native front would undermine their power base. After a couple of burly whites threatened to give Rock a beating and Snapp was bitterly assailed by Natives who believed *News-Miner* editorials that the AAIA was trying to move them to reservations, the two men decided to solicit advertising as a team. Safety in numbers.[1]

Painter Rusty Heurlin, long supportive, had spoken vehemently against them because he had heard AAIA was both communist and reservation-oriented. Howard quietly packed the paints and easel the artist had loaned him so Heurlin could reclaim them. It hurt to lose a friendship over charges that would prove untrue, and it would also be impossible to replace the painting supplies on short notice in Fairbanks.[2] But it had become clear that Rock could no longer afford time to paint or the luxury of friends who were alien to the Native cause.

Naming the paper was another stumbling block. They had intended to call it "Inupiat Oqaqtut," meaning "The People Speak" in Eskimo.

"What about the Athabascans?" asked Al Ketzler, whose people were trying to work with the Inupiat. There were also the Aleuts and the Indians of Southeastern to consider.

"And what if we have a non-Eskimo for a secretary? She would have the darnedest time trying to put 'Inupiat Oqaqtut' over the phone."

Sandy Jensen, a grey-haired member of the Native Rights Association who had taken on the assignment as secretary to the new paper, listened thoughtfully.

"How about 'Tundra Times'?" she suggested. Tundra, the basic ground cover of Alaska, proved a perfect compromise.[3] Using the fine-line style he had long employed in etching ivory, Rock designed a masthead incorporating Eskimo, Indian and Aleut scenes, flanking them with "Inupiat

Paitot" (the people's heritage) in Eskimo and "Dena Nena Henash" (the land speaks) in Athabascan. Then he and Tom hammered out an editorial policy.

> There are two main reasons for the appearance of the *Tundra Times*.
> First: It will be the medium to air the views of the Native organizations. It will reflect their policies and purposes as they work for the betterment of the Native peoples of Alaska. It will also reflect their aims ... their hopes. It will strive to aid them in their struggle for just determination and settlement of their enormous problems.
> Second: It will strive to keep informed on matters of interest to all Natives of Alaska, whether they be Eskimos of the arctic, the Athabascans of the interior, and other Indians and Aleuts of the Aleutian Islands.
> We have also realized that an unbiased presentation of issues that directly concern the Native is needed. In presenting these things that most affect Natives, we will make every effort to be truthful and objective.[4]

In addition, they privately made the decision to correct grammar and spelling mistakes on copy that came from Native reporters who had little formal education. The pidgin English of bush correspondents with which the *News-Miner* entertained its readers would do little to further *Tundra Times'* image and they wanted the paper to be readable.[5]

Members of the Fairbanks Native Association, the Native Rights Association, friends and family began selling $5 subscriptions door-to-door. Footsore but well-pleased, Rock and Snapp drew up ads for the First National Bank of Fairbanks, Sears and Roebuck, S. F. Saario Furs and nine politicians.

The Atomic Energy Commission announced deferment of testing at Cape Thompson just in time to make their deadline. The brief story was relegated to the back page with the promise to report the reasons behind Natives' opposition in the next issue.

It was everything they'd hoped for with the bitter exception of an obituary:

> On July 20, 1962, Miss La Verne Madigan, executive director of the Association on American Indian Affairs, met with a sudden accident and passed away. She was, perhaps, the greatest champion of the Natives and fearless fighter for their rights.
> The news of her death was a shock and a numbing blow to her friends among the Natives as well as non-Natives. The sense of loss of a great student of Native matters was most keen. The immediateness of this feeling left in some of us a great void.

Madigan had been thrown from a horse while vacationing in Vermont. The paper's editorial page tribute credited her with helping uncover the "true facts" on Project Chariot, for her initial research on Native land rights and for making possible conferences that enabled the Natives to organize. And, lest enemies hope that the cause she had pioneered would end with her death, the writers concluded:

> It has often been said that when one recognizes his problems, half the battle is won. In our conferences and in this paper we hope to bring out our problems even more and work toward their solution.
>
> The channeling of her (Madigan's) knowledge and the application of it in conferences is a firm foundation that she left to her friends, the Natives of Alaska. This seed of necessity to which she so greatly contributed will be a constant reminder in our struggle to attain just recognition and final settlement of our historic rights and claims.[6]

La Verne's passing was particularly painful for Howard, who had come to rely on her keen advice. However he had also developed strong rapport with Dr. Forbes, who had impressed him during their brief meeting in Point Hope and whose frequent letters took on a warm fatherly tone, almost from the beginning. Howard enjoyed corresponding with him and—squishing together yet another peanut butter and jelly sandwich, pouring another cup of coffee— he sat down to type an update.

> Please excuse our delay in writing for the last few days. We have been extremely busy getting ready for the first publication of the *Tundra Times.* We noted with pleasure your advice about taking occasional walks. Tom and I did a lot of that looking for advertisement. In fact, Tom wore a blister on his heel. Fortunately we are still having nice weather and have not had any sore throats. However we would appreciate your advice on a good tranquilizer for "shattered nerves."
>
> Secretary of Interior Stuart Udall was here in Fairbanks this week and we were fortunate in getting a fine interview with him which we used for the banner story of our first issue. We questioned him at length at a news conference at which five *News-Miner* reporters were present. They heard the many strong statements he made concerning our problems but the *News-Miner* did not print these.
>
> The *Tundra Times* will be off the press tomorrow about 4 p.m. We will rush airmail copies to you.
>
> P.S. I am very happy to tell you that *Tundra Times* staff writer, Tom Snapp, has been awarded the top press award in Alaska for 1961 (best coverage of an individual in radio, newspaper or TV).[7]

Irene Reed would always remember the night of October 14, 1962, not just for the excitement of playing midwife to an important newspaper, but for the sheer drudgery involved in folding, strapping and addressing the tabloid for mailing. Reed was a friend and classmate of Martha Teeluk, heavily involved in the Yupik language studies at University of Alaska. She'd worked with Teeluk on her first article for the publishing venture, and was anxious to be of further help.

Although it was late, the Redman's trailer was packed with volunteers, many working on the floor for lack of table space. The parakeet chirped nervously, occasionally rattling the door of its cage. Reed glanced at the headline. "Interior Secretary Udall Visits Alaska; Historic Rights and Claims Settlement is Number One Problem Declares Official." The paper was well laid out, neat and concise.[8]

"Congratulations," she called to Tom Snapp who appeared weary but was strapping and folding with the best of them. "There's going to be plenty of excitement when this hits the streets."

Howard reviewed the first edition with mixed emotions. It had taken far more time to produce than he could ever have imagined. With experience, he would get faster at the job of writing and pasting up. He could still paint on the side, between phone calls, he told himself. But in his heart he knew his art career had ended when he drew the masthead.[9]

25

The Search For Leadership

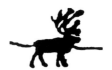

AAIA PRESIDENT OLIVER LAFARGE sent a letter of praise, calling the new paper "interesting and professional."[1] Also encouraging was a review in *Harper's Magazine:*

> An eight-page biweekly, it (the *Tundra Times*) provides unique coverage of such news as the prospects for polar bear hunters (poor), the best way to cope with hair seal intestines, the protection of Native rights from encroachment by the government or white settlers, and the culture of the Eskimos, Aleuts and Athabascan Indians. While its reporting is not quite so professional as that of the *New York Times*, it has a lot of charm. Witness the dispatch from Charlie Tuckfield, staff correspondent in Point Hope, who recorded the killing of six bowhead whales. As a result, he noted happily, "Most all ice cellars are pretty well supplied with muktuk now.... . We have a lot of visitors from Noatak and Kivalina by dog team.... . Eskimo life is real good. Most all people here are real friendly. Everybody is welcome in our village.[2]

Garbed in an Army surplus jacket and a stout tan cap, Dr. Forbes arrived in person to congratulate his staff and was surprised to find them less than confident.[3]

"Some of my former colleagues at the *News-Miner* sent word over that they'd give us just six weeks,"[4] Tom Snapp explained, en route from the airport.

Because of the high cost of living, local printers were charging almost $1,200 an issue when the going rate outside the state was $900. The municipal utility company had demanded an outrageous deposit because none of the newspaper's incorporators—Rock, Martha Teeluk or Al Ketzler—had a credit rating.

"The other day I got on the phone and made a call that cost more than $100," Snapp recounted. "The operator waited until I hung up and then called back to say we had to come down and pay the bill at once. I didn't like it at all."[5]

Spirits brightened when they showed Forbes the second edition, which Howard had just gotten off the press. Prominently placed among the amusing features and a heartening number of campaign ads, was the text of a talk given by James Officer, assistant commissioner of the Bureau of Indian Affairs, at the June meeting in Tanana.

> I hope you all vote in your state election, and I hope you vote for the people who promise to do the things for you that you feel you need, and against those who either don't promise to do these things or who have demonstrated that while they may promise them, they won't deliver those promises.... .
>
> You have a unique opportunity I think in Alaska that not all of the Indian tribes have had. You do have an established citizenship right; you haven't in every case already lost your land; there are still other avenues you can use to obtain title to some of it, perhaps even to all of it in some cases.
>
> I feel that the Bureau of Indian Affairs has been very negligent ... We have abdicated what I think is our responsibility to one of our sister agencies, the Bureau of Land Management, and we are finding out, not so gradually, that we can't always depend on the BLM to look at the problem the same way we do.[6]

By printing Officer's speech they had clearly set stride for the political mission ahead. "It's a fine edition," Dr. Forbes told them sincerely. "You deserve a lot of credit."[7]

Next day, together with AAIA lawyer Art Lazarus, they flew to Kotzebue, traditional trading center and minor port just south of the Arctic Circle, to attend the Second Annual Inupiat Conference which attracted delegates from as far away as Barter Island and Norton Sound. It was a three-day meeting and, while Lazarus and Snapp helped the Natives work out their by-laws, Forbes toured the waterfront, pondering the future.

Young ice was forming, rattling against gravelly shores in a slushy mass. With interest, the doctor watched two Eskimo hunters push through a skiff to land two big bearded seals and three small, spotted ones.[8] Many Kotzebue Natives worked for wages and enjoyed such amenities as electricity, heating oil and a few staples from the store, yet it was obvious from a large number of meat-drying racks that they still depended largely on hunting. The goal of white educators had always been total acculturation, but Howard maintained that Natives should preserve the good things in their culture, enjoying the best of both worlds. He broached the idea in *Tundra Times'* second issue:

With the introduction of some good things of civilization such as flour, sugar, tea, coffee, beds and fuel, the people of the arctic have worked out a system of economy that is a blend of their culture and that of civilization.

The combination of the two cultures is compatible, and with a little boost of learned help it could be made more successful with a good economy. The people of Point Hope, as well as those of other villages, will not readily give up certain good and proven parts of their way of life. These include the dance, hunting, dog teams, language, and one of great importance, the annual event of whale hunting.[9]

Such thinking reaffirmed Forbes' faith in Rock's leadership potential and he was relieved that Inupiat Paitot had finally voted the artist into office as executive secretary. Guy Okakok had been re-elected president after deprecating his own abilities and asking assembled delegates to elect a new person. Okakok's political activities had cost him his column in the *News-Miner* and endangered his job with the trading post in Barrow. Forbes knew Okakok was having difficulty feeding his large family, as was Paul Tiulana. Others must soon take their places.[10]

Howard, Snapp and Tony Joule, the quiet, bright, retired schoolteacher, were still hard at it with Lazarus when Dr. Forbes returned from his constitutional and he stopped to listen to their heated discussion. He thought of them privately as "the brain trust." They had things well in hand.[11]

Shortly after Forbes' departure, the Redman family returned to claim their trailer, so Snapp and Rock went out in search of office space. Rents were astronomical. They'd hoped for something impressive but they settled for the dank, cold anteroom of a dirty little building on the main street. Previously it had served as Gruening's campaign headquarters. One of the senator's posters flapped in the draft on a battered wall.[12]

"It's ... er, pretty basic, all right," observed Haverford College professor Ted Hedzel, whom they'd met earlier at meetings of the Tanana Chiefs. In addition to being national director of the Indian Rights Association, Hedzel was an excellent cameraman, and he'd volunteered to photograph the newspapermen in their new location. "How about a tour of the plant?" he suggested gamely.

Rock looked at Snapp and then back at their guest with a faint smile. The door that visitors assumed led to the inner office dead-ended in a small, junk-filled closet.

"Well, the place comes equipped with a stove and a refrigerator, neither of which work," Rock began. "So that's where we keep our papers."

"It saves having to buy a file cabinet," Snapp added.[13]

But the location was right. Richard Frank noticed the *Tundra Times* sign and walked in off the street one afternoon to introduce himself as chief of the Minto people. Although his village school had gone only to third grade, the plain-speaking Athabascan was keen-minded and well-traveled. He had lied about his age to work on the river boats at 14, joined the Army to serve in the South Pacific during World War II, emerged as a qualified mechanic with his high school equivalency and returned to his village to replace his father as traditional chief.[14]

A month earlier Frank had appeared at a meeting of the Alaska Conservation Society which was considering the state's plan to build a recreation area at Minto Lakes, complete with a road from Fairbanks which would attract sportsmen to the heart of his village's hunting grounds. Without use of the lakes, Minto's people and their children would go hungry, the chief told members.

"Nothing is so sorrowful as for a hunter, empty-handed, to be greeted by hungry children," Frank pleaded. There had been absolute silence when he spoke, but no one rose to Minto's defense.[15]

"Everyone knows that this is our land," the Indian told Rock, desperately. "My people started blanket claims in the '30s. We've always used our land for hunting and trapping and we're trying to get title.

"I've been going to the meetings since I was a kid and I'll never forget when all the people of Minto voted for a reservation under the Indian Service Program. That was a lot of land. But then it was explained that we'd have to have permits to go off the reservation. We're a free people. They voted against it."

"We should work together," the Eskimo suggested.

They talked until late afternoon. Frank was well aware of the distrust his Indian constituents felt towards Eskimos who had traditionally been enemies. But he liked the solid, thoughtful editor who shared his concern for their aboriginal inheritance.

"You have the same ideas as I do," he marveled. "Only I don't have the tools."

According to Frank, the Minto people had twice filed land claims with the Bureau of Land Management (BLM). However BLM insisted it had no record of the transactions. All the papers were mysteriously missing.[16] Of hundreds of Native claims filed, only 101 Native allotments of 160 acres or less had been granted in all of Alaska since 1906 because BLM rejected hunting and fishing activities as proof of use and occupancy.[17]

The *Tundra Times* demanded an accounting and spoke passionately for preservation of the Native land base:

Land that has been kind to one's ancestors and the same land that is kind to their descendents today is hard to leave, let alone give up. Yet that is what the state is doing nowadays, trying to make Native folks give up their lands... .

We Natives should realize we are in transition from one economy to the other. We have moved from a strictly hunting economy to a semi-cash economy. And we are moving more and more toward a cash economy. In order to do so, we have to learn to use and develop our land and its resources in other ways besides hunting, trapping and fishing.

We Natives should realize that we will not be able to compete fully with big business for a long time yet. Since we cannot do that now, we should try to hold on to our lands because that is the greatest insurance we can have for the well-being of Native children that will come after us. Without land we can become the poorest people in the world.[18]

Tom Snapp was expert at ferreting out records and he discovered the missing claims were buried in government archives in Juneau and Washington D. C. Five oil companies had filed leases between the Native villages of Nenana and Minto. Private businessmen were following suit and the state, having gotten word of oil activity, was stepping up its own selection.[19]

"What we need is a lawyer," Howard said.

"But we don't know who to trust," Snapp shook his head. "You can't tell who is your friend."

Bill Byler, La Verne Madigan's replacement at AAIA recommended Ted Stevens, but Rock was dubious. Stevens had run (and lost) on the Republican ticket against Democrat Gruening in the recent battle for U.S. Senate and, although Gruening showed no interest in Native land rights, he had passed the first antidiscrimination law in the nation during his tenure as Alaska's territorial governor. Traditionally, Natives were Democrats. There was no way AAIA could tell Rock and Snapp of Steven's early work on their behest without sinking him with his own party. Finally Stevens sold himself. He had spoken out for settlement of Native land claims during his campaign and he promised the newspapermen he'd work for free.[20]

In the 1930s the Tlingits and Haidas of Southeastern Alaska had gone to U.S. Court of Claims to collect for valuable timber lands taken from them by the government. The case was still pending with no verdict in sight, and the court had no power to award land title, only money. No one wanted to go that route.[21]

"What alternatives do we have?" asked Nenana's Al Ketzler who had discovered the state had designated his village lands as a mental health selection.[22]

"File a protest," Stevens advised.
"But they'll just dismiss it," Snapp argued.
"Then we can appeal. Get it on the record."
"We'll need to document the land use," Rock said, thinking ahead.

It was a real mess. Various groups had filed on the same general areas at different times using different boundaries. Many of the maps were too crude to submit. There was nothing to do but start over. While Stevens worked with Minto, Snapp and Rock descended on Nenana armed with huge topographical maps and elaborate overlays of plastic.[23] When they ran out of money, they dipped into their own pockets. It was time-consuming, painstaking work but eventually they documented subsistence usage of the entire Tanana Chiefs region and, by the first week of March, Ketzler had collected 980 signatures on a protest petition to send to Secretary of Interior Stuart Udall and President John F. Kennedy. It asked that Udall impose a "land freeze" to stop all transfers of land ownership for the areas surrounding their villages until Native rights could be confirmed.[24]

Ketzler, whose Athabascan mother had never had a chance to learn to read, was married to the daughter of a white activist who was heavily involved in the Native Rights Association.[25] He had been among the first to propose a congressional land settlement, appearing as a guest of honor at the second meeting of Inupiat Paitot. "Your grandfathers and mine left this land to us in the only kind of deed they knew ... by word of mouth and our continued possession," he told them. "Until recent years, a man's honor was the only deed necessary. Now, things have changed. We need legal title to our land if we are to hold it." [26]

Although educated in local schools and untraveled beyond Alaska, Ketzler impressed AAIA leaders who invited him to lobby in Washington for his villages. Delighted, Ketzler got together with Sears Roebuck to purchase a suit and was busy packing when the Federal Aviation Agency, where he worked as a mechanic, gave him verbal warning to stay out of politics or give up his job. Ketzler, who had five kids to support, got his boss to back down on the grounds that AAIA was a private organization. Then he decided to postpone the trip in order to cover for Rock and Snapp who, under deadline, were trying to wade through the report of a BIA fact-finding task force that had interviewed representatives from 100 Native villages and taken testimony at meetings of Tanana Chiefs and Inupiat Paitot.[27]

Results were not encouraging. Temporary use, not permanent ownership of land, was recommended, along with withdrawal of "small acreages" for village growth and grants of up to 160 acres to individuals for home, fishing and hunting sites. Chairman of the three-man committee was W. W. Keeler who, although an American Indian, was also head of Phillips Petroleum Company. Working with him was Hugh Wade, Secretary of State to Alaska Governor William A. Egan who turned a deaf ear to any mention of a claims settlement. Together they had out-voted BIA representative James Officer.

In an editorial, Rock and Snapp expressed agreement with "about 70 percent" of the report which dealt with inadequate educational and economic privilege, but voiced strong opposition on the commission's land stance, the lack of provision for cash payment for lands lost, and for mineral rights for lands on which they would receive title:

> We take sharpest disagreement with suggested proposal of land claimed by Natives on the basis of historical occupancy, use and need. Although the Task Force agrees with Natives in recognizing the guarantee of aboriginal rights in the Organic Act of 1884, the Statehood Act of 1958 and various other acts and court decisions, it stops short of recommending full recognition of Native land claims. ... Natives have steadfastly maintained they need large areas of land for hunting, fishing and trapping now and for development of resources later as their economy changes.[28]

Nobody appeared to be listening. Roscoe Bell, head of the Alaska's Division of Lands, suggested the state select and patent Indian lands, then work out a mutual-use plan or sell them back to the Natives.[29] The federal government was proposing to dam and flood land encompassing several Indian villages to produce electric power and create a recreation area. Senator Bob Bartlett pushed for continued state land selection. Gruening was backing a monetary settlement through the U.S. Court of Claims and Ralph Rivers, Alaska's only congressman, opposed any land grants to Native claimants. "What would they do with it?" he asked. "They wouldn't use it. It would just lie there."[30]

Land rights were by no means the only issue that the *Tundra Times* had to focus on. The median income of village Natives in 1963 was $1,204 and one in three had no cash income.[31]

Twice as many Natives babies died in infancy as white babies. Ten times as many Natives as whites died of influenza and pneumonia, three times as many died of accidents and twice as many killed themselves.[32] Natives had little chance of schooling beyond eighth grade unless they traveled thousands of miles to attend BIA boarding schools which ranked far below normal educational standards.

Some were even denied the personal freedom that U.S. citizenship was supposed to guarantee. After seeing the first edition of the paper, the Rev.

Deacon Smile V. Gromoff, president of the Aleut community of St. Paul Island in the Pribilofs, had written protesting a wage plan the U.S. Fish and Wildlife Service was forcing his people to accept because the agency had complete control of their island and its economy. It was rumored that Pribilof Aleuts were not allowed to travel freely to and from their villages and Tom made a note to check it out.[33]

Howard stopped answering the letters of friends from Seattle. There was too much else to do. He and Tom usually worked through the night before each deadline, often arguing over the editorials. Tom tended to overreact, overstate. Howard understated which proved more effective. Snapp said the artist had a natural knack for writing. Rock enjoyed doing pieces about his Eskimo heritage, but he couldn't come to grips with the mechanics of a news story. He bested Snapp on lay-out and paste-up but he wasn't much good as a salesmen.[34] Martha Teeluk hinted, more than once, that he wasn't much of a boss, either, so he left that to Tom. And he worried about the newsman's impending departure.[35]

"Quitting time, Uncle Howard!" Mae Shroyer was back from selling *Tundra Times*, door-to-door, with a fist full of cash.

"You always amaze me," he told her honestly. "I don't see how you do it."

"Charm and good looks," she giggled, quite unaware of how right she was. "Come on, let's go to Tommy's."

Mae had moved to Fairbanks with her two young children and landed a good job working for Fred Crane, a lawyer. Howard was her staunchest backer and she had gotten into the habit of dropping by the office at closing time, making sure he remembered to eat.

"It's not good, your camping in that old hotel."

"I saw a nice house for rent down on First Avenue over the weekend," he considered. "What would you say to renting it together? I'd buy the groceries ..."

"That would sure help with the budget," she agreed.

They got along splendidly. Mae was a great cook and Howard doted on the children. He started dating a woman in town, making new friends. Things got easier at the paper.[36]

In April, Rock was named top newspaper columnist in the state by the Alaska Press Club,[37] and, by the time Tom Snapp headed south, the Eskimo had mastered everything except basic news writing. Terry Brady, an able young reporter who had also worked for the Bureau of Land Management as a firefighter and knew the bush, took over in Tom's stead and the paper continued to dig at issues. Although the circulation was tiny—fluctuating between 1,500 and 3,300—the *Tundra Times* was read avidly by many powerful people in government and also by other members of the press who followed up on its headlines.[38] When Rock broke the news the AEC had filed a new withdrawal application near Point Hope for "biological investigations,"[39] other media gave the story good play. The test was abandoned two months later[40] and Point Hope gave Rock an award for outstanding service to his village.[41]

With an air of triumph, the travel-weary editor pulled an unopened can of beer from his overcoat pocket and set it in a place of honor in his cramped office. He had obtained it in the Pribilofs despite federal government restrictions that banned private citizens from possession. It symbolized an act of defiance by the Aleuts who had presented it to him and, also, the amazing effectiveness of the *Tundra Times*.

"It's the first time I've realized we have real power," he told Tom Snapp, who had manned the office while Howard visited the islands.

Tom nodded, thoughtfully. "We sure have been stepping on some awfully big toes," he said.

Snapp had returned to Fairbanks with his master's degree in journalism and learned that the U.S. Fish and Wildlife Service had barred a political candidate from the villages of St. Paul and St. George on the Pribilofs. The government agency, which made big money off the islands' fur seals, controlled the personal lives of the resident Aleuts needed to run its operation, and Snapp launched a damning expose against it.[42]

PRIBILOFS IN SERVITUDE
People Arbitrarily Moved; Times Writer Threatened,
Political Candidate Barred

Most people think slavery in the United States was abolished with the Civil War and the Emancipation Proclamation. Yet today in the Far North, in Alaska, slavery still exists, in milder form perhaps than expected in the deep South, but slavery nonetheless... .[43]

In response to the paper's demand for a probe, Governor Egan named Rock to a special investigative commission along with Hugh Wade, his Secretary of State; Willard Bowman, executive director of his newly formed Human Rights Commission; Roy Peratrovich, tribal operations officer for the Bureau of Indian Affairs, and James C. Rettie, senior economist in the office of Secretary of Interior Udall. Senator Bob Bartlett scheduled congressional hearings and legislation was being introduced into Congress that would institute a major reform.[44]

The paper also moved to aid Andrew Isaac, the sage old chief of Tanacross village, who had filed land claims with BLM in the early 1950s. The agency made no response for almost a decade when, inexplicably, Isaac's paperwork showed up at its Fairbanks office and was rejected. By 1964 the state had selected not only Tanacross hunting grounds but land surrounding the village itself. Then, in 1965, Isaac discovered the state planned to sell lots around the village fishing ground, George Lake, at Alaska's booth at the New York World's Fair. Roscoe Bell, director of the Division of Lands, said he knew of no claims around the lake and the man in his Fairbanks office who had leaked information of the pending sale, was fired without explanation.[45]

"We are not a chess game. We are human beings and right now a very upset and disturbed people," Chief Isaac declared angrily.[46] *Tundra Times* bannered the scandal and again, government agencies snapped to attention. But where, Rock wondered, was the Native leadership they needed to force Congress to move on the whole land issue?

Although there were many strong regional leaders, no one was well-recognized statewide except Nick Gray who was dying of cancer. Tlingit lawyer William Paul, who had pioneered Native rights since the early 1920s, influencing Gray and many other Native spokesmen, was up in years and not universally trusted. Twice, without success, Rock had attempted to rouse interest in a permanent statewide organization, but no one moved to take the initiative.[47] Even Inupiat Paitot languished, inactive.

26

Victory In View

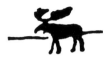

In 1952 the government limited commercial fishing on Cook Inlet to just two days a week, which pretty much ruined any chance the Tyonek Indians had of making a decent living. They turned to coal mining without success and, by 1955, the village of 200 Athabascans was so near starvation that citizens of neighboring Anchorage collected 2,500 pounds of food to see them through the winter.

When oil prospectors arrived, the tribe sought advice from Stanley McCutcheon, an Anchorage lawyer who had hunted and fished with them as a boy. McCutcheon took their case as a favor, knowing they had no money for a retainer. His colleagues scoffed but, despite a lot of wrangling, McCutcheon established the right of the Tyoneks to manage their own reservation free of Bureau of Indian Affairs interference and, in 1963, he helped the tribe negotiate $11,671,675 in oil lease revenues.

The Tyoneks were generous with their windfall, loaning seed money to help fund Native rights organizations, and the example they set was even more valuable. Deciding against a per-capita dole, Tyonek villagers worked together with Albert Kaloa, their clever young chief, building a modern village to replace their random sampling of shacks and tattered log cabins. Instead of hiring the job out, they did the work themselves under the direction of a contractor, acquiring vocational skills as they built. They also established an educational scholarship program for any Tyonek who expressed interest in further self-improvement.

After an unnerving run of would-be investment counselors, carpetbaggers and encyclopedia salesmen, they closed their airport to all but invited guests and took out an ad to salesmen in the Anchorage paper which read: "Don't call us. We'll call you. The scalp you save may be your own."

In business, the Tyoneks made a point of favoring those who had been kind to them in the lean years. They purchased an airline and investment property. They built a monumentally handsome office building in Anchorage which they leased to their old nemesis, the Bureau of Indian Affairs.

Neighbors, who'd long regarded Tyoneks as the proverbial drunken Indians, were amazed when villagers who had been considered hopeless alcoholics voluntarily went on the wagon.[1]

"If the Tyoneks can do it, any Native can do it!" people were saying.

The Supreme Court ruling of one-man, one-vote had just brought reapportionment to the Alaska Legislature which cost the Native minority some seats, yet they were gaining in power.[2] Although they constituted only one-fifth of the population, Alaska Natives had become so politically aware that they carried one-fourth of the vote. Mike Gravel, speaker of the House, was among the first to notice. Married to a former Miss Alaska, well-educated, ambitious and personable, the Anchorage-based Democrat had his sights set on the U.S. Congress and he figured that if he could garner the "bush" vote, he could afford to lose in major cities throughout the state. To explore the issues and gain high profile, he initiated rural Legislative Council hearings and in Barrow he encountered Charlie Edwardson, a 22- year-old Eskimo who was passionately articulate despite an agonizing stutter.[3]

Edwardson was a product of BIA schools, had worked with scientists at the Naval Arctic Research Lab, picked up some courses at University of Alaska and technical training at the RCA Institute in New Jersey. He made friends with the Alaska congressional delegation in 1963, enlisting its help protesting the ghetto-like conditions under which RCA housed Alaskans they lured outside the state for training.[4] He could be militant and rude and he sometimes appeared unkempt, but there was charm in Edwardson's sincerity and he was intelligent. He quickly got Gravel up to speed on the inequities of bush housing, education and health care and, in late 1965, Gravel invited him to Juneau to serve as a page in the House. The Eskimo would be of help in planning his upcoming campaign for Congress, Gravel realized.[5]

Howard Rock was encouraged. President Lyndon Johnson had backed a number of anti-poverty measures that would supply Alaska Natives with much-needed funding. His domestic Peace Corps had dispatched its first group of Vista Volunteers to remote villages. Senator Bartlett was lobbying Congress for improved village housing and Gravel had come out for locally controlled regional high schools to replace distant BIA facilities in Sitka and Oregon.

Despite his illness, Nick Gray was successfully organizing Natives along the Kuskokwim, leaving the operation of Cook Inlet Native Association to a dedicated young Athabascan named Emil Notti who actually had a degree in engineering.[6] Hugh Nicholls, an outspoken Barrow man, was shaking up the bureaucracy there and some young Turks—Lester Suvlu, James Nageak, Able Akpik and the Edwardson kid—were making waves with the Barrow Improvement Board.[7]

"It's like people in the bush are waking up," Rock told Dick Jones whom he'd hired as controller for the *Tundra Times*.

"They'd better wake up. The legal beagles have sure undercut them in legislature. Pretty much melted the Ice Block," Jones reminded him, referring to the bush coalition that the reapportionment had all but destroyed. "It will take some real deal-making to put it all back together again."

Jones had been struggling to reconcile accounts with a monstrous heap of unpaid bills. He was an overly well-upholstered man who owned his own business service. Many of his clients were Native people and Howard felt comfortable with him.

"What if we got them all together?" Howard suggested. "You know, throw a cocktail party or maybe a banquet ..."

"You mean for all the politicians?"

"The politicians and our leadership."

"I think it's a darned fine idea," Jones said. "Maybe we could sell 'em some stock."

The *Tundra Times* had announced it would become a publicly held corporation.[8] Twenty-thousand shares of stock were issued: 7,000 to Howard, 7,000 to Dr. Forbes and 5,000 shares to be sold to insure survival of the newspaper so that Forbes, who was now 83, could cease funding.[9] Unfortunately, the first *Tundra Times* banquet, held in early December of 1965, did little to improve cash flow. The Barrow delegation, which had reserved 60 seats, failed to show and only $1,825 worth of stock was sold. However, the event was an unequivocal social success.[10] Two hundred turned out, including Alaska's governor, congressional delegates, a large number of political hopefuls and Native leaders from throughout the state. Master of Ceremonies Al Ketzler set an informal tone for the evening by telling a series of howlingly funny, off-color jokes. Governor Bill Egan, who emerged weak from laughing with the happy crowd, thumped Rock on the back in hearty congratulations.

"Great party!" he chuckled.

"And the first time that we could really identify with the Native community," Mike Gravel pointed out.

It had been Rock's busiest year. Promising to work part time for *Tundra Times*, Tom Snapp had taken a better paying job as editor of *Jessen's Weekly*. Mike Bradner, a liberal-minded University of Alaska alumnus, became the paper's capitol correspondent in Juneau. Judy Brady, wife of Terry Brady, Rock's first reporter, took over local news for a while and there were other volunteers, but there were always gaps to cover. Rock traveled the state frequently, pursuing stories, working on committee assignments. He had moved the *Tundra Times* to new offices in the Chena building. Forbes guaranteed the paper $25,000 to provide equipment and a smooth transition to weekly publication on an offset press.[11] The details of going public—selecting a board of directors and selling stock—took endless hours. And Howard had also taken time for romance.

She was young, pretty and idealistic. She worked for a state agency in Juneau and shared Rock's concerns for Native welfare. She was divorced and had a child with whom he got along well. She impressed his nieces when she came to Fairbanks for the *Tundra Times* banquet. He gave her a wolfskin parka. She showered him with handknit sweaters and said she loved him. After considerable thought and a delightful courtship he asked her to be his wife and she turned him down.

"I'm terribly independent," she wrote, suggesting they continue their relationship on the same happy, informal basis they had been enjoying. "Let me age a bit. I'm still trying to find my wings ..."

He would settle for nothing less than marriage and he gave vent to his jealousy.

"Dear Howard, I love you—I can make your life happy and full and comfortable," she pleaded. "How I miss your letters."[12]

He saved her letters but he wrote no more and looked no further. It had been three years since he'd had any kind of a break and he found himself emotionally drained. Finally he ran an article in the paper titled "Editor Needs a Vacation," asking for a volunteer to sit in for him.[13]

A bear of a man sporting a handlebar mustache answered the plea. Jimmy Bedford, head of the Journalism Department at the University of Alaska, had worked on newspapers in Missouri, Kansas, England and Afghanistan and once served as United Press International's correspondent in Kabul. Howard trusted him immediately, and gratefully packed his bags.

For three weeks Rock wandered Southeastern Alaska as a tourist, indulging in sketching the awesome scenery, meeting new people. A letter from Merv Mullins, Bedford's student editor, caught up with him in Juneau. "Where is the aspirin bottle?" Mullins wanted to know.

"The policy of the *Tundra Times* is that any man who takes the place of this editor shall be supplied with 25 cents worth of aspirin for the duration of three weeks labor," Howard replied. "In the event the substitute uses up the supply before the end of three weeks, he will have to endure the additional headaches to the best of his ability and consider this discomfort as a contribution to the cause of the *Tundra Times.*"[13]

Three weeks came and went. Bedford put his own ad in the *Tundra Times* seeking an editor. "Only Howard Rock need apply," he specified.[14] Rock returned smiling and retaliated by putting Bedford on the *Tundra Times* board of directors.

Controller Dick Jones, 36, died suddenly, leaving Rock with a book-keeping tangle to sort out, and the paper suddenly became more than a full-time job.[15] New leadership was emerging, eager young Natives from all over the state who had been raised traditionally but managed to glean enough education and polish to move comfortably in the white man's world.

The Arctic Slope Native Association filed the largest blanket land claim in the history of America. Native groups from Kotzebue and Nome followed suit and the Aleuts were organizing. The office of Economic Opportunity, headed by Al Fothergill, was providing travel money and had instituted a grass-roots program to make rural residents aware of their rights.[16] But without a statewide organization, the only way to coordinate these varied efforts was through the paper and the Eskimo publisher began working 18-hour days. His table at Tommy's Elbow Room became his after-hours office and sooner or later, everyone dropped by.

Fresh from pre-law studies at George Washington University, Willie Hensley was running for the Alaska House of Representatives from the Kotzebue district on the Democratic ticket and Howard found him an impressive candidate. The handsome, 24-year-old Eskimo had been quick to take on Senator Gruening who had complained about the Bureau of Indian Affairs helping Natives with their land protests and was insisting on a cash settlement.[17] Tonight, Hensley had brought Howard a research paper on the land claims he'd written for a course in constitutional law at the University of Alaska. Since the Natives had never signed any treaties or lost at war with the white man, the law student figured they had a pretty good case.

"If I can just get into the legislature, I think I can argue it well," he said earnestly. "I don't have much of a campaign chest, but people know me."

Raised with nomadic grandparents in the Kotzebue region, active in starting the Northwest Alaska Native Association there, Hensley was indeed well-known.

"I'll do what I can," Howard promised.

"He might win," Laura Bergt said brightly, slipping into an empty chair. She, too, was from Kotzebue and was the niece of Eskimo William Beltz who'd served with distinction in the Alaska Senate. Howard had hired her as his secretary, despite the fact that she was an outspoken Republican who served on the National Committee, and he had come to admire her. The wife of a local bush pilot with four youngsters to raise, she managed tô serve the paper well. She was also the Eskimo blanket-toss champion and had just taken over staging the Eskimo Olympics—a competition of traditional Native games—for the Fairbanks Chamber of Commerce.[18]

"That event could turn a profit," she insisted. "The tourists love it! And it's a great chance for our people to enjoy their traditional sports. The *Tundra Times* should sponsor it, Howard."

"Where would we get the time?" he shrugged. Sometimes she nagged him like a wife.

"I'd help, dummy," she said fondly. "And so will Willie."

Howard had long worried about the future of the *Tundra Times* for it had become evident that advertising and subscription sales would never carry it. Even with Forbes' help they often went in debt. The Fairbanks News-Miner, which now printed the paper for them, was patient about late payment but keeping the presses rolling was a struggle. Yet there was something close to magic in the way things always seemed to work out. When one good reporter quit, another would appear out of the blue to take his place. When there wasn't money enough to pay postage, an unexpected check would arrive in the mail. There was a newly created board of directors, strong backers like Jimmy Bedford; Daphne Gustafson, a lovely Athabascan who worked for Wien Airlines; Dorothy Perdue; his old friend, Tommy Richards; and Mary Jane Fate, a highly articulate Athabascan who, with husband, Dr. Hugh Fate, had pioneered the Fairbanks Native Association.

Dr. Forbes sometimes spoke of "good fortune" in connection with the Tundra Times' success and Howard began to entertain an eerie feeling that there were forces at work he could not easily comprehend. Weeks earlier in Kotzebue an old woman had spoken to him knowingly about the shaman's prediction of his greatness. Fascinated, he asked her what she had heard of his great uncle, Attungowruk, and she stared at him strangely.

"Attungowruk is not dead!" she said in a hoarse whisper. "He lives. His magic is strong."[19] Drinking Jim Beam in the modern ambiance of Tommy's Elbow Room, listening to Laura and Willie banter about politics over mellow music from the juke box, the idea seemed far-fetched, but Howard could no longer discount the spirits of his Eskimo ancestors.

In July, under the headline "Life Ebbing, Gray Pleads Cause," the *Tundra Times* featured a guest editorial by Nick Gray, who had less than four months to live.

> The myriad of problems which we will demand to be resolved by the State of Alaska and the U.S. Federal Government are extremely confusing and complex. But with careful selection of leaders among our people to represent each area—meeting delegates and representatives from all sections of Alaska so that we pool our efforts and then speak one voice.
> Such a voice representing 50,000 Natives—voters all, will impose upon our duly elected representatives in Juneau a thorough and complete survey.
> We must resist and forever detest the attitude of paternalism which government and state actions incur. Our hereditary claims can hardly be denied, since they extend far into the dark ages of history, far out-dating the beginnings of most currently established nations... .[20]

Bob Bennett, area commissioner of Bureau of Indian Affairs in Juneau, had been appointed national head of his agency and his confirmation hearings were set for the following January. In preparation, Bennett made a report to Congress saying, among other things, that the BIA was drawing up a "final solution" to the land problem in Alaska. Emil Notti, who had taken on Gray's assignment as president of the Cook Inlet Native Association in Anchorage, thought Alaskans should have something to say about it. In July of 1966 he wrote Native leaders around the state, hoping 14 or 15 of them could get together and talk about what they might be able to do about the problem. Rock learned about the letter in August and publicity-shy Notti was astonished to find it bannered in the *Tundra Times.*

"A statewide meeting of Alaska Native leaders may be coming soon—to coordinate actions of different Native organizations and to discuss vital issues facing the Alaskan Eskimo and Indians today," Rock reported. *Tundra Times* continued to promote the event for the next month and on October 18 about 300 Native delegates showed up in Anchorage, ready to join forces.[21]

It was the peak of the election campaign. Gravel had come within a hairbreadth of toppling Rivers in the primary, demonstrating the increased strength of the Native vote. Governor Bill Egan was fighting a losing battle for support against contender Walter Hickel in the face of a dispute with Natives over control of the Office of Economic Opportunity. Candidates hosted delegates to an endless succession of luncheons, cocktail parties and dinners.

"One thing about this conference is that you don't have to spend much money for meals," Notti noted. "I've never seen anything like it."

Outsiders predicted the Natives would never be able to organize because they came from vastly different sections of the state, with different languages and customs. But in the early 1950s and '60s the Bureau of Indian Affairs had sent hundreds of Native youths to high schools in Mt. Edgecumbe and Wrangell. Many of the delegates were former classmates, or at least had experience with Natives from other cultures, and they shared many common needs.[22] It would take a year for the Alaska Federation of Natives (AFN) to become fully established, but foundations had been laid and when Rock fired up his headline machine for the next edition, the banner read, "STATEWIDE NATIVE UNITY ACHIEVED AT CONFERENCE."[23]

The second *Tundra Times* banquet, which followed the AFN meeting, attracted 500 and proved a money-making sellout. Guest speaker Secretary of Interior Stewart Udall traded barbs with newly elected Governor Walter Hickel and gave a complicated speech that sounded important, but no one was sure what it meant. Rock and Notti wrestled with the text after the crowd had gone.

"I think he's announced some sort of a land freeze," Howard was saying. "Homesteaders won't be able to get title until our claims are settled...."

"Let's go over it one more time," Notti suggested anxiously. "A moratorium on the process of patenting state land selections in order to preserve status of Alaskan lands until Native Claims can be settled.... . That's got to be it."

"I think we're in business, Emil," Rock said.[24]

Since *Tundra Times*' founding, Howard had shared his hopes and fears with Dr. Forbes in a nearly unbroken series of weekly letters and by late 1967 he could write in triumph. Governor Walter Hickel had been swayed from his vehement opposition to the claims movement by a solid "bush" coalition spearheaded by newly elected Representative Willie Hensley, with prodding by Athabascan Representative John Sackett, a 21-year-old Republican freshman from Galena. Rock was being considered for appointment to a land claims task force the governor was creating because Udall's land freeze had managed to stymie building of a trans-Alaska pipeline to recent oil discoveries on the Arctic Slope.

John Schaeffer, Frank Ferguson, Oliver Leavitt, Al Adams, Robert Newlin and Howard's old friend, Joe Upicksoun, had joined the ranks of Inupiat leaders. Tlingits Byron Mallott, John Borbridge, Irene Rowan, Roger Lang and Sam Kito moved to the fore. Don and Jules Wright, Morris Thompson, Ruby Tansy, Robert Marshall and Tim Wallace ably represented the Athabascans. Ray Christianson and Phillip Guy helped organize the Kuskokwim. Aleuts Flore Lekanof, Carl Moses, Lillie McGarvy and Mike Swetzof were active on the Aleutian Chain; Harry Carter and Jack Wick in Kodiak; Blance Palen, Harvey Samuelsen and Nels Anderson in Bristol Bay region; Cecil Barnes in Chugach, Larry Meculief and Agafon Krukoff in the Pribilofs. Jerome Trigg and Tom Drake spoke for Nome. Roy Huhndorf, an Eskimo raised in Athabascan country, and Ralph (Andy) Johnson worked with urban Natives in Anchorage, George Miller in Kenai. And there were dozens more, well-educated, articulate in English, yet at home, too, with traditional tribal elders. The Native movement had real power at last and Rock gave much of the credit to Forbes who, over the years, had quietly expended about $100,000 on the *Tundra Times*[25] with no strings attached:

> I find myself thinking how amazing it has been and the short time it took for the Native leaders to emerge into the prominence they have achieved. I think the *Tundra Times* has a great deal to do with this happy situation. When we came off the press for the first time over five years ago, there was no real leader among the Native people of Southeastern Alaska. The Native people were dead spiritually, it seemed, because no news media would publicize their tragic situations and their problems. The *Tundra Times*, more than anything else, I think, has awakened the fervor to do something and help to bring out the potential in leadership among our people. I remember calling the leaders (back about four years ago) "LETHARGIC," and "do-nothing leaders" in my editorials.
>
> It's a wonder nobody punched me in the nose for saying such things. For some time, I felt that I was getting nowhere but all of a sudden there it was. Our people began to speak out and their voices were heard through the *Tundra Times*. The first meeting of the Eskimo people at Barrow which your AAIA organized and financed, could also be classed as the real beginning of the awakening of our people in Northern Alaska.... I can say that your generosity has been a great factor in the new Native situation now developing.[26]

Failing in health, Dr. Forbes had been thinking a lot about Rock's selfless dedication to the paper. The Eskimo editor had steadfastly refused raises until the *Tundra Times* got on sounder financial basis. Forbes knew Rock had been able to put nothing aside for the future on his meager salary and for Christmas he transferred a $5,000 bond to the Eskimo's personal account.

Howard was sorting through the morning mail when he came on a letter from his bank notifying him of the transfer and stared at it in astonishment. Betty, his secretary, thought he might be choking because he made some odd little noises.

"No, it's all right," he told her. "Much better than all right."

He'd save the money, of course, for that rainy day that was always around the corner. But he really ought to do some little thing to celebrate. His first thought was to take his niece, Mae, to dinner, but she'd just moved to Kotzebue where she'd landed a good job with the welfare department. There was a Kentucky Fried Chicken franchise in town and Mae loved fried chicken. He decided to send her a great, big bucket of assorted pieces. It would be a wonderful surprise if the airline didn't get weathered out too long.[27]

Check in hand, he pushed back his squeaky old desk chair and pondered the curious course his life had taken. Had he stayed with his promising art career, he surely would have rebuilt his finances and fallen back into the comfortable life style he had enjoyed in Seattle. But he reminded himself that, given the threat to his Eskimo heritage, there really had been no choice.

With a chuckle he thought of his brother, Allen, who had visited the *Tundra Times* office just before the last whaling season, bent on preserving the honor of their clan.

"You are the only man in our family who hasn't caught a whale," the hunter began. "I tell you what, Howard. Why don't you take over my crew this spring? I'll furnish everything, equipment, crew and food. All you have to do is be captain for the season."

Fleetingly, Howard considered his own roundish midriff and shortness of breath in comparison with Allen's physique which, despite middle age, was still without an ounce of fat.

"You're very kind to offer that, Allen," he said, hesitantly. "But you know I'm a busy man running the paper and it is quite a responsibility."

"I know that, brother," Allen answered putting an arm around Howard's shoulders. "But do you know what it's like to catch a whale—a great, big agvik? The sense of achievement of getting a whale is one of the greatest feelings a man can ever get. The striking of the whale might be a nervous moment. Nervous or not, you do it. You are doing it for your people—your family. When the big whale begins to turn over (turn turtle) you say to yourself, 'I caught a whale—this is my whale—mine, and I did it. It will feed many people for a long time—I did it—my whale!'"

Allen was a stubborn man of tradition, certain he was right. It was not the first time he had tried to convince his brother that he should catch a bowhead, and in the beginning Howard had felt confused, thinking that catching a bowhead and editing a newspaper were poles apart. Now he knew better.

"Yes, Allen, I think I know exactly how thrilling catching your own whale can be," he replied with assurance.[28]

The death of Henry Forbes in August of 1968 was a wrenching loss to Rock, not so much from a financial point of view—for the *Tundra Times* was almost self-supporting—but because the doctor was his friend, his sounding board and the only person with whom he kept close counsel. Others saw pieces of the puzzle but Forbes had been an astute, experienced observer who understood the total picture. He had taught Rock well but it would be lonesome without him.

To the public, the Alaska Federation of Natives presented a united front, but hammering out a compromise land claims settlement proposal between wildly varying factions required a deft referee. Rock provided a calm, objective voice that steadied them and finally won the ear of Congress.

The Sydney Laurence Auditorium in Anchorage was packed when the Senate Committee on Interior and Insular Affairs visited Alaska to hold hearings on Native land claims in late 1968. Some of the testimony was in Eskimo, Indian and Aleut. Some was in broken English. Standing tall, wearing a neat flannel shirt, Chief Andrew Isaac, age 70, told the Senators:

> I saw my first white man in 1904. He was a preacher. During the course of the years I saw more white men. In the early 1940s a highway was built near Tanacross, and the white men have come to our land more and more... .
> We made our claim in 1963 because the state came in and selected our land—everything, even our village and graveyard. This is not fair. We own our land—the white man does not.[29]

Athabascan trapper Peter John talked in terms of muskrats and beavers. Tlingit attorney William Paul Sr., spoke eloquently in the language of law. Girlish Martha Nick Cooke, a Yupik from Bethel, said it simply: "Take our land, take our life."

Having met his deadline with the story, Howard retired to his table at Tommy's and reviewed the week with Laura Bergt who had fallen into the habit of joining him at the end of a hard day. They both realized the Anchorage hearing would be just the first in a long series and the beginning of a seemingly impossible fight for national recognition. Rock looked tired. He had been working too hard, Laura thought, but he was fiercely committed.

"Do you really think we can win?" she asked gently.

"We must," he said.

Epilogue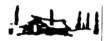

The Alaska Native Claims Settlement Act was signed into law by President Richard Nixon on December 18, 1971.* Won without racial violence, it was the largest Indian settlement in history, giving Alaska's indigenous people clear title to 40 million acres (equal roughly to two percent of all the land in the United States) and a cash award of $962.5 million. Had Natives formed to become a single business entity, it would have numbered among the 10 largest corporations in the country, but the law required that 13 regional corporations invest and manage the windfall.

The legislation had been a compromise. No one was completely happy with it but, considering the alternatives, it was a remarkable victory. In the *Tundra Times* Howard Rock hailed it as "the beginning of a great era for the Native people of Alaska," but he realized that managing it would be a heavy burden.

"Let us recognize the task that will fall on our shoulders. It will test the strength of our leaders as well as the rest of our people," he warned. "We have proven that we can handle highly complex problems, such as the Alaska Native land claims. We must not do less in the future. We must meet it with confidence and then do more for the good of our people and those of tomorrow."[1]

Rock stayed on as editor of the *Tundra Times* to monitor the process until August of 1973 when he was diagnosed as having terminal cancer. Doctors gave him only a few months and after surgery it appeared he would not have strength to continue his work. Since he had spent Dr.

---

* The Native lobby was so effective that this legislation passed the U.S. House by a vote of 307-16 and was unanimously voted by the Senate.

Forbes' "rainy day" money to keep the paper going, the *Tundra Times'* board decided to throw a fund-raising banquet and asked Rock to do an oil painting that could be auctioned off in his behalf. Howard had not touched a brush for over a decade but the idea pleased him and he turned out a magnificent canvas of a whale hunt. With a pencil rendition, the painting brought in about $6,000 for what everyone tactfully referred to as a "little vacation." Accompanied by long time friend Tom Richards Sr., Howard flew to Hawaii leaving Richards' son, Tom Jr., 24, in charge of the paper. There, against all medical odds, Rock began a remarkable recovery.

By March of 1974, Howard was back at his desk. Tom Richards Jr., whom Rock had come to love like a son, was a good writer and a gifted photographer but was new to the business world, and the *Tundra Times* had gone heavily in debt under his management. Rock whipped it back into shape and soon began putting money in the bank.[2]

In May of 1974, the Eskimo editor was surprised and utterly delighted to receive an honorary Doctor of Humane Letters degree from the University of Alaska for "friendly persuasion rather than militancy (that) has marked his journalistic efforts and won for him high honors and great respect." Congratulations from President Richard Nixon followed. In February of 1975, out of the blue, the *Tundra Times* was nominated for a Pulitzer, and in October of that year Rock shared Alaska's Man of the Year award with Ted Stevens, now a U.S. Senator.

Cancer continued to dog him and chemotherapy made him frail, but Howard still held court at Tommy's Elbow Room every evening after a full day's work. He also traveled widely as a member of the Indian Arts and Crafts Board of the U.S. Department of Interior, enjoying the company of celebrities like Vincent Price, Shirley Temple Black, astrologer Jean Dixon and Buffy St. Marie, whom he talked into a guest appearance at the *Tundra Times* banquet.

Working with Mary Jane Fate, Laura Bergt and Tom Richards Jr., Rock won federal funding for an Institute of Alaska Native Arts, realizing a long-time dream. And he also landed a Ford Foundation Grant for the *Tundra Times.*

But time was running out. On April 2, 1976, Howard left an uncharacteristic note on the composing machine of Lee Alder, secretary and close friend:

> Lee, the way I feel now I don't think I will be much help getting the paper together. Three doctors looked me over and put me under some sort

of observation. Nothing too serious, I think, but whatever else ails me has weakened me further. So I can't make the trip to San Francisco (for the Arts and Crafts Board) DARN IT!

I'll try to put the front page together and whatever else I can do I'll try it. TUM-DEM. Rock, the Editor.

Those who saw him the next week noticed nothing unusual although he delegated most of his work to Sue Gamache, a University of Alaska student whom he was grooming to be editor. On the following Monday, the day before deadline, he appeared in the office early with scarcely enough strength to speak. He didn't want to go home and he refused to go to the hospital until the paper was out. Next morning, impeccably dressed but dangerously weak, he appeared for his regular appointment at Bassett Army Hospital and was not allowed to leave. When staffers phoned to ask if there was anything he wanted, he dispatched a nurse with the message:

"The only thing Mr. Rock says he wants is out!"

Death came quietly at 11:40 p.m. on April 20. Rock's niece, Mary Dirks, and Tom Richards Jr., who were by his bed, saw him draw two incredibly long breaths and let them out slowly and peacefully. Then there were no more.

It was the beginning of spring whaling season, and three hours after Howard's body arrived back for burial in the village of his birth, hunters captured their first bowhead. Villagers took it as a favorable sign.

"He has brought us joy instead of sadness," Eskimo Reverend Donald Oktollik, a former reindeer herder, said at the beginning of the Episcopal funeral service in the church where Rock had worshiped as a boy.[3]

At his own request, Howard Rock was buried apart from the Christian cemetery on a lonesome stretch of tundra next to the body of his Great Uncle Attungowruk at the original village site of Point Hope.[4] The grave is marked with a contemporary granite headstone bearing both his English and Eskimo names, and the rib of a giant bowhead, Tigara's traditional homage to a mighty hunter.

Notes

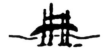

CHAPTER 1

1 Sam Rock, letter to the Rev. A. R. Hoare, *The Alaska Churchman*, Aug. 1914.

2 James Arthur Allen, *A Whaler and Trader in the Arctic*, Alaska Northwest Publishing Company, Anchorage, Alaska, 1978. p. 55.

3 Dinah Frankson interviewed at Point Hope, Alaska, 1981.

4 *The Shaman Aningatchaq*, told by Jimmie Killigivuk and translated by Carol Omnik and Tom Lowenstein, Cambridge Free Press, Cambridge, England, 1981, Footnote 6.

5 Dinah Frankson interviewed at Point Hope, Alaska, 1981.

6 This prediction was first mentioned to the author by the late Phyllis Parry, historian for the Episcopal Church, Fairbanks, Alaska, who said she'd noticed it several years earlier in church records. In 1982 she was unable to locate the original source (thought to have been the diary of the Rev. Frederick W. Goodman). However, Rock's sister, Helen, confirmed the story and several of Rock's close friends reported he knew about the prediction and pondered it at some length.

7 Basil King, unpublished biography of Augustus R. Hoare, Episcopal Diocese of Alaska, University of Alaska, File #81-62.

CHAPTER 2

1 Froelich Rainey, *The Whale Hunters of Tigara*, Anthropological Papers of the American Museum of Natural History, 1947.

2 Howard Rock, unpublished manuscript, 1975.

3 James W. Vanstone, *Point Hope, an Eskimo Village in Transition*, University of Washington Press, 1962. Introduction.

4 According to Beechey's log: "We ascended Cape Thompson and discovered low land jutting out from the coast to the west and northwest as far as the eye could reach. At this point (Tigara) has never been placed on our charts. I named it Point Hope in compliment to Sir William Johnstone Hope. On nearing it we perceived a forest of stakes driven into the ground for the purpose of keeping the property of Natives off the ground and beneath them, several hillocks, which we afterwards found to be Esquiamaux yourts or underground winter

habitations." *Narrative of a Voyage to the Pacific and Bering's Strait to Cooperate with the Polar Expeditions; Performed in His Majesty's Ship Blossom, Under the Command of Capt. F. W. Beechey * * * in the Years 1825, 26, 27, 28*, London, H. Colburn and R. Bentley, Vol. 1.

5 Alexander Kashevarov, 1838, Papers of Don Foote, rough draft of thesis, "Exploration and Resource Utilization in Northwestern Alaska," Don Foote Collection, Box 46, University of Alaska Archives, Fairbanks, Alaska.

6 *English-Eskimo and Eskimo-English Vocabularies compiled by the Ensign Roger Wells, USN. and Interpreter John W. Kelly*, Ethnographical Memoranda Concerning Arctic Eskimos of Alaska and Siberia, U.S. Government Printing Office, 1898, p. 7.

7 Ibid.

8 J. A. Cook, *Pursuing the Whale: A Quarter of a Century of Whaling in the Arctic*, Houghton Mifflin, 1926, p. 3.

9 James Arthur Allen, *A Whaler and Trader in the Arctic*, Alaska Northwest Publishing Company, Anchorage, Alaska, 1978, p. 158-61.

10 Mary Cox, *John Driggs Among the Eskimos*, National Council of Churches, New York, 1956.

11 Letter from George T. Turner, nephew of John Driggs, 403 Welden Rd., Shellburne, Wilmington, Del., to Don Foote, Aug. 17, 1963, Don Foote Collection, Box 24, University of Alaska Archives, Fairbanks, Alaska.

CHAPTER 3

1 John Beach Driggs, *Short Sketches from Oldest America*, G. W. Jacobs & Company, Philadelphia, 1905.

2 Sam Rock and Eebrulik Rock in interviews with Froelich Rainey, Froelich Rainey Collection, folder titled "Point Hope Stories and Legends," University of Alaska Archives, Fairbanks, Alaska.

3 James Arthur Allen, *A Whaler and Trader in the Arctic*, Alaska Northwest Publishing Company, Anchorage, Alaska, 1978, p. 156.

4 Ruth Rock Nash in an interview at Point Hope, 1972.

5 Sam and Eebrulik Rock in interviews with Froelich Rainey, Froelich Rainey Collection, folder titled "Point Hope Stories and Legends," University of Alaska Archives, Fairbanks, Alaska.

6 Ibid.

7 Howard Rock, "Whale Hunt Ended in Tragedy; Boys Were Saved by Clothing," *Tundra Times*, Dec. 2, 1963.

8 John Driggs, *Short Sketches from Oldest America*, G. W. Jacobs & Co., Philadelphia, 1905.

CHAPTER 4

1 *The Alaska Churchman*, August 1914, page 120, "Letter from Sam Rock to Rev. A. R. Hoare." In an accompanying note, Hoare explains: "Sam Rock ... presents, in his most interesting personality, one of the future possibilities of the Mission work ... The villages of these people are so scattered that separate Missions and Missionaries are impossible for each village, and when the Missionary at Tigara is alone, he cannot be leaving the Mission to travel among the Native villages, so that the hope of the future lies in the provision of Native Deacons ... Rock is one such worker whom the Reverend Mr. Hoare hopes to be able to train as such a helper."

2 Howard Rock, "Out of the Past," unpublished manuscript.

3 Howard Rock, "Nikka, the Leader Met Violent Death from Young Dogs," *Tundra Times*, Jan. 20, 1964.

4 Howard Rock, "Important Milestones," *Tundra Times*, Feb.3, 1961.

5 Walter Harper and Hudson Stuck, *Ascent of Denali*, Appendix G1, The Mountaineers, Seattle, 1977.

6 Howard Rock, "Tiny Tot Recites 'Little Jack Horner'; Deeply Impressed by Applause," *Tundra Times*, Feb. 5, 1975.

7 Howard Rock, "Samaroona, 'Sage of Tigara,' Master Storyteller," *Tundra Times*, March 2, 1964.

8 Howard Rock, "Important Milestones," *Tundra Times*, Feb. 3, 1964.

9 Howard Rock, "Out of the Past," unpublished manuscript.

10 C. Alan Johnson and Suzanne C. Johnson interview, Rollingbay, Washington, 1981.

11 Howard Rock, "Out of the Past," unpublished manuscript.

12 Eebrulik Rock interview, Fairbanks, Alaska, 1981.

CHAPTER 5

1 Basil King, unpublished biography of Augustus R. Hoare, Episcopal Diocese of Alaska, File 81-62, University of Alaska Archives, Fairbanks, Alaska.

2 Letter from teacher Fred Sickles to *The Alaska Churchman*, May, 1915.

3 Howard Rock in an interview, Fairbanks, Alaska, 1975.

4 During Alaska's Territorial days, "Outside," referred to the United States and usage is popular in discussing the "South 48" contiguous states.

5 David Frankson in an interview at Point Hope, Alaska, 1981.

6 Howard Rock, "Big Ship Impresses Eskimo Boy; He Impresses Sailors," *Tundra Times*, 10/18/65, and "Eskimo Boy Finds New World in Luscious Goodness of his First Orange," *Tundra Times*, Oct. 4, 1965.

7 David Frankson in an interview at Point Hope, Alaska, 1981.

8 Howard Rock in an interview at Fairbanks, Alaska, 1975.

CHAPTER 6

1 Description from Rock's articles on his family printed in the *Tundra Times*, "Training Huskies Is Not For a Lazy Man," June 17, 1963, "Boy Caught Grayling to Mumangeena's Delight," June 8, 1964, "The Shy Eskimo Who Heroically Killed the Great Polar Bear," May 5, 1963, "Uncle Nayukuk, Casual Man—Angered Auntie," Sept. 3, 1963.

2 Howard Rock, "Aunt Mumangeena Always Bragged of Mother's Prowess," *Tundra Times*, Nov. 18, 1963.

3 Howard Rock, "Shy Eskimo Who Heroically Killed the Giant Polar Bear," *Tundra Times*, May 20, 1963.

4 Howard Rock, "Training Huskies Is Not For a Lazy Man," *Tundra Times*, July 17, 1963.

5 National Archives, Group 75, Bureau of Indian Affairs, Alaska Division, Box 101, Northwestern District, General File, Reports of the Superintendent.

6 Howard Rock, "Diseases Swept the Arctic, Wiping Out Population, Shattering Traditions," *Tundra Times*, Oct. 26, 1964.

7 "North Star Award," *Tundra Times*, Jan. 6, 1964.

8 Howard Rock, "Samaroona, 'Sage of Tigara,' Master Story Teller," *Tundra Times*, March 2, 1964.

9 Howard Rock, "Saw Missing Son Riding Sea Slush in Moonlight," *Tundra Times*, Feb. 17, 1964.

10 Howard Rock, "Samaroona, 'Sage of Tigara,' Master Story Teller," *Tundra Times*, March 2, 1964.

11 David Frankson in interview, Point Hope, Alaska, 1981.

12 Walter Shields, District Superintendent, in letter to Dr. William Hamilton, Acting Chief, Alaska Division, Washington, D.C., 10/25/1915. National Archives, Group 75, Bureau of Indian Affairs, Alaska Division, Box 73, Northwestern District. Letter from Shields to W.T. Lopp, Feb. 13, 1916.

13 Arthur James Allen, *A Whaler and Trader in the Arctic*, Alaska Northwest Publishing Company, Anchorage, Alaska, 1978, p. 193-199.

14 *The Alaska Churchman*, Nenana, Alaska, Vol. 8, July 1920.

15 Howard Rock, "Out of the Past," unpublished manuscript.

16 Howard Rock, "Aunt Mumangeena Always Bragged of 'Mother's' Prowess," *Tundra Times*, Nov. 11, 1963

CHAPTER 7

1 Howard Rock, "Nikka, the Leader Met Violent Death from Young Dogs," *Tundra Times,* Jan. 20, 1964.

2 Howard Rock, "Training Huskies Is Not For a Lazy Man," *Tundra Times,* July 17, 1963.

3 Howard Rock, "Uncle Nayukuk Had Talent for Hunting When Needed," *Tundra Times,* Dec. 12, 1963.

4 Howard Rock, "The Shy Eskimo Who Heroically Killed the Giant Polar Bear," *Tundra Times,* May 20, 1963.

5 Howard Rock, "Popcorn Proves To Be a Delicacy, Mincemeat a Mystery," *Tundra Times,* Feb. 3, 1964.

6 Howard Rock, "Hunter Who Got a White Arctic Fox with a Little White Ball as Bait," *Tundra Times,* March 18, 1963.

7 Howard Rock, "Eskimo Boy Amazes Parents with 'Jack and the Beanstalk' Fairy Tale," *Tundra Times,* Aug. 24, 1964.

8 Howard Rock, "Pronouncing Rumplestiltskin Tickles Uncle Nayukuk's Funny Bone," *Tundra Times,* Sept.8, 1964.

9 Howard Rock, "Out of the Past," unpublished manuscript.

10 Howard Rock, "The Giant Whale Caused Eskimo Helmsman to Steer Umiak in the Air," *Tundra Times,* April 1, 1963.

11 Eebrulik Rock in interview at Fairbanks, Alaska, 1981.

12 Howard Rock, "Tiny Tot Recites Little Jack Horner Deeply Impressed by Applause," *Tundra Times,* Aug. 9, 1965.

13 North Star Award, *Tundra Times,* July 1, 1963.

14 David Frankson in interview, Point Hope, Alaska, 1981.

15 Howard Rock in interview, Fairbanks, Alaska, 1975.

CHAPTER 8

1 Missionaries met and divided up the territory. According to mutual agreement the Baptists got Kodiak and Cook Inlet; Episcopalians took the Yukon and lower arctic coast; Methodists got the Aleutians; Moravians moved to the Kuskokwim; Quakers to Kotzebue Sound; Congregationalists settled at Cape Prince of Wales and the Presbyterians got Southeastern Alaska and the northern arctic. Tay Thomas, *Cry in the Wilderness,* Alaska Council of Churches, Anchorage, Alaska, 1967.

2 H. Dewey Anderson and Walter C. Eells, *Alaska Natives: A Survey,* Stanford University, Stanford, California, 1935.

3 T.P. McCollester in a letter to Jonathan H. Wagner, 11/10/1924. National Archives, Group 75, Bureau of Indian Affairs, Alaska Division, Box 144, Seward Peninsula folder.

4 Jonathan Wagner in a letter to Commissioner of Education, Washington, D.C., 1/1/1925. National Archives, Group 75, Bureau of Indian Affairs, Alaska Division, Box 144, Seward Peninsula folder.

5 Jonathan Wagner in a letter to Dr. John J. Tigert, Commissioner of Education, Washington, D.C., 11/10/1927. National Archives, Group 75, Bureau of Indian Affairs, Alaska Division, Box 172, Seattle General File.

6 Undated press release from *Seattle Times*, National Archives, Group 75, Bureau of Indian Affairs, Alaska Division, Box 172, Outside Relations folder.

7 *Nasevik Yearbook*, White Mountain Industrial School, U.S. Department of Interior, White Mountain, Alaska, 1934, p. 31.

8 Alex Ashenfelter of White Mountain in interview, Anchorage, Alaska 1981.

9 *Nasevik Yearbook*, White Mountain Industrial School, U. S. Department of Interior, White Mountain, Alaska, 1932, p. 17.

10 Jonathan Wagner in a letter to Dr. John J. Tigert, Commissioner of Education, Washington, D.C., 11/10/1927. National Archives, Group 75, Bureau of Indian Affairs, Alaska Division, Box 172, Seattle General File.

11 Gertrude Fergus Baker in interview, Clallam Bay, Washington, 1983.

12 Esther Apodruk Nugleen in interview, Anchorage, Alaska, 1983.

13 Jennie Newlin Sours in interview, Kotzebue, Alaska, 1981.

14 Flora Dexter Peterson in interview, Anchorage, Alaska, 1983.

15 Ethel Smith Mills in interview, Kotzebue, Alaska, 1981.

16 Sophie Amaruk Lieb in interview, Anchorage, Alaska, 1981.

17 Arthur Upicksoun in interview, Anchorage, Alaska, 1981.

18 Esther Apodruk Nugleen in interview, Anchorage, Alaska, 1983.

19 Grace Downie Ekvall in interview at Calabasas, Calif., 1983.

20 Gertrude Fergus Baker, Alaska Nurses Association Papers, 1907-1978, University of Alaska Archives, Letters and Recollections File, 1921-1975, #12.

21 Ethel Smith Mills in interview, Kotzebue, Alaska, 1981.

CHAPTER 9

1 Eugene Sours in interview, Kotzebue, Alaska, 1983.

2 Gertrude Fergus Baker, Alaska Nurses Association Papers, 1907- 1978, University of Alaska Archives, Letters and Recollections File, 1921 to 1917, #12.

3 Arthur Upicksoun in interview, Anchorage, Alaska, 1981.

4 Howard Rock, "Out of The Past," unpublished manuscript.

5 Howard Rock, *Nasevik Yearbook*, White Mountain Industrial School, U.S. Department of Interior, White Mountain, Alaska, 1930, p. 3.

6 Jonathan Wagner in a letter to Dr. John J. Tigert, Commissioner of Education, Washington, D.C., 11/10/1927. National Archives, Group 75, Bureau of Indian Affairs, Alaska Division, Box 172, Seattle General File.

7 Eugene Sours in interview, Kotzebue, Alaska, 1983.

8 H. Dewey Anderson and Walter C. Eells, *Alaska Natives: A Survey*, Stanford University, Stanford, California, 1935.

9 Arthur Upicksoun in interview, Anchorage, Alaska, 1983.

CHAPTER 10

1 Rene Jaussaud, National Archives, Legislative and Natural Resources Branch, Washington, D.C., in phone conversation after researching White Mountain School records, 1983.

2 Frank and Mamie Pickett in interview, Sun City, Arizona, 1981.

3 Ibid. Mamie Pickett, in interview, Sun City, Arizona 1983.

4 Ethel Smith Mills in interview at Kotzebue, Alaska, 1983.

5 *Nasevik Yearbook*, White Mountain Industrial School, U.S. Department of Interior, White Mountain, Alaska, 1930.

6 Ibid, p. 2.

7 Frank Pickett in interview, Sun City, Arizona, 1981.

8 Ethel Smith Mills in interview, Kotzebue, Alaska, 1983.

CHAPTER 11

1 Ruby Dingee interviewed at Des Moines, Washington, 1980.

2 Frank and Mamie Pickett interviewed at Sun City, Arizona, 1981.

3 Alex Ashenfelter interviewed at Anchorage, Alaska, 1981.

4 Lilly Nash Walker interviewed at Nome, Alaska, 1981.

5 *Nasevik Yearbook*, White Mountain Industrial School, U.S. Department of Interior, White Mountain, Alaska, 1931, p. 5-7.

6 Frank and Mamie Pickett interviewed at Sun City, Arizona, 1981.

7 Grace Downie Ekvall interviewed at Calabasas, California, 1983.

8 Frank and Mamie Pickett interviewed at Sun City, Arizona, 1983.

9 Wilma Neeley Gale interviewed at Olympia, Washington, 1981.

10 *Nasevik Yearbook*, White Mountain Industrial School, U.S. Department of Interior, White Mountain, Alaska, 1932, p. 2.

11. Ibid. p. 23.

12 Ibid. p. 26.

13 Dr. Dorothy Jean Ray interviewed at Port Townsend, Washington, 1983.

14 Wilma Neeley Gale interviewed at Olympia, Washington, 1981.

15 Grace Downie Ekvall interviewed at Calabasas, California, 1983.

16 Frank and Mamie Pickett, Sun City, Arizona, 1983.

17 *Nasevik Yearbook*, White Mountain Industrial School, U.S. Department of Interior, White Mountain, Alaska, 1932. p. 11.

18 Clint Gray interviewed in Anchorage, Alaska, 1981.

19 Eebrulik Rock interviewed at Fairbanks, Alaska, 1982.

20 Ruby Dingee interviewed at Des Moines, Washington, 1982.

21 Ruth and Virgil Farrell interviewed at Sun City West, Arizona, 1983.

22 H. Dewey Anderson and Walter C. Eells, *Alaska Natives: A Survey*, Stanford University, Stanford, California, 1935.

23 Charles Wesley Hawkesworth letter to William Neeley, July 25, 1934, National Archives, Group 75, Bureau of Indian Affairs, Alaska Division, Box 254, Misc. Correspondence Folder, 1934-35.

24 Lilly Nash Walker interviewed at Nome, Alaska, 1981 and 1983.

25 Mamie Pickett interviewed at Sun City, Arizona, 1981.

26 Harry Apodruk interviewed in Seattle, Washington, in 1981.

27 Grace Downie Ekvall interviewed in Calabasas, California, 1983.

CHAPTER 12

1 Clint Gray interviewed at Anchorage, Alaska, 1981.

2 Harrison Carroll, "Eskimo Dandy is Feared Killed on Homeward Trip," copyright 1934. Newspaper clipping without date or name of publication from scrapbook of Mala, courtesy of Ted Mala, Anchorage, Alaska.

3 Howard Rock recollections in Fairbanks, Alaska, 1972.

4 Ibid.

5 Zelma Hawkesworth Herlihy, Newburyport, Massachusetts. Family papers.

6 C. L. Andrews, "Constructive Educator, Victim Odorous Politics," *Alaska Weekly*, April 1, 1932.

7 Mary Lopp Konquist interview at Laguna Beach, California, 1983.

8 Jeanne Engerman, excerpts and assessment of letters of Ellen "Nelly" Lopp, unpublished paper, Washington State Historical Society, 1983.

9 Howard Rock interview, Fairbanks, Alaska, 1975.

10 Gladys M. Tuttle in interviews at Trail, Oregon, and Niland, California, 1981. Mrs. Tuttle was a close personal friend of Max Siemes and took care of him in his last years.

11 Charles Wall in interview at Siemes' Homestead in Trail, Oregon, 1981.

12 Tom E. Clark, "Sikvoan Weyahok, My Eskimo Buddy," April 23, 1983. Unpublished manuscript.

13 Gladys Tuttle in interview at Trail, Oregon, 1981.

14 Tony Woolsey, a former student of Max Siemes, interviewed at Trail, Oregon, 1981.

15 Viola Houston used to work at the Rogue Elk Lodge. She was interviewed at her home nearby in Shady Cove, Oregon, 1981.

16 Ruby Dingee interviewed at Des Moines, Washington, in 1982.

17 Gladys Tuttle interviewed at Shady Cove, Oregon, 1983.

18 Howard Rock interviewed on his career as an artist in 1974.

CHAPTER 13

1 Ruby Dingee interviewed at Des Moines, Washington, 1983.

2 Zelma Hawkesworth Herlihy, Newburyport, Massachusetts. Family papers.

3 Seattle Times, May 2, 1941. Sen. Homer T. Bine introduced a bill to pay the Duwamish Indian tribe $4,158,000 and the Snoqualmie another $5,365,585. On May 11, 1941 the Snoqualmie withdrew a $9 million claim.

4 Clint Gray interviewed at Anchorage, Alaska, 1981.

5 Church Records, Point Hope, Alaska.

6 Clint Gray interviewed at Anchorage, Alaska, 1981.

7 C. L. Andrews, "Constructive Educator, Victim Odorous Politics," *Alaska Weekly*, April 1, 1932.

8 Ann Wilson, "Eskimo Artist Anxious to Start at University," *Star*, Seattle, Washington, Dec.26, 1936.

9 Katherine Lopp Johnson, daughter of W. T. Lopp, interviewed at Seattle, Washington, 1981.

10 Weyana Lopp Schaal, daughter of W. T. Lopp, interviewed at Seattle, Washington, 1981.

11 Alice Lopp Harby, daughter of W. T. Lopp, interviewed at Seattle, Washington, 1981.

12 Jeanne Engerman, excerpts and assessment of letters of Ellen "Nelly" Lopp, unpublished paper, Washington State Historical Society, 1983.

13 Professor Ruth Pennington, retired from University of Washington faculty, interviewed in Seattle, Washington, 1981.

14 Alice Lopp Harby interviewed in Seattle, Washington, 1981.

15 Weyana Lopp Schaal interviewed in Seattle, Washington, 1981.

16 Ibid.

17 Alice Lopp Harby interviewed in Seattle, Washington, 1981.

18 "Native Artist Will Exhibit Painting at Blue Shop Two Days," *Seward Gateway.* Clipping undated mailed by Rock to Ruby Dingee in letter of 1/2/38. Letter Walter Blue, Oct. 29, 1983

19 "Eskimo Artist Returning to Campus Classes," *Daily Alaska Press,* Juneau, Alaska, Dec. 10, 1937.

20 "Eskimo Puts His People on Canvas," *Christian Science Monitor,* March 14, 1938.

21 Kay Kennedy, "Alaska in Person," "The Brush for Him," *Alaska Life,* undated. Circa 1938.

22 Mary Lopp Konquist interviewed at Laguna Beach, Calif. 1983.

23 Jeanne Houston, member of the University Congregational Church, interviewed in Seattle, Washington, 1983.

24 Tom E. Clark, "Sikvoan Weyahok, My Eskimo Buddy," April 23, 1983. Unpublished manuscript and interview, Seattle, Washington.

25 "Eskimo Tutors 'Lingo': Arctic Students," *University of Washington Daily,* 2/24/1938.

26 Dr. Erna Gunther in interview at Fairbanks, Alaska, 1966.

27 Irwin Caplan, classmate of Howard Rock, in interview at Seattle, Washington, 1981.

28 Tom E. Clark, "Sikvoan Weyahok, My Eskimo Buddy," April 23, 1983. Unpublished manuscript and interview, Seattle, Washington.

29 Marion B. Appleton, Frank McCaffy, *Who's Who in Northwest Art,* 1941.

30 Prof. Fred Anderson, University of Washington Art Department faculty and former classmate of Howard Rock, in interview in Seattle, 1981.

31 "Artist's Scrap Book," Seattle Public Library, undated clipping.

32 Irwin Caplan, classmate of Howard Rock, in interview at Seattle, Washington, 1981.

CHAPTER 14

1 Cecil V. "Moe" Cole interviewed in Seattle, Washington, 1982.

2 Irwin Caplan, classmate of Howard Rock, interviewed in Seattle, Washington, 1981.

3 Prof. Fred Anderson, University of Washington Art Department faculty and former classmate of Howard Rock, in interview in Seattle, Washington, 1981.

4 Alice Lopp Harby, daughter of W. T. Lopp, interviewed in Seattle, Washington, 1981.

5 Howard Rock interviewed on art in Fairbanks, Alaska, 1974.

6 Cecil V. "Moe" Cole interviewed in Seattle, Washington, 1981.

7 Weyana Lopp Schaal, daughter of W. T. Lopp, interviewed at Seattle, Washington, 1981.

8 Index to Central Classified Files, Bureau of Indian Affairs, National Archives, Group 75, Alaska Division, Files #1907-52 and #49440.

9 Howard Rock interviewed in Fairbanks, Alaska, 1975.

10 Jeanne Thomas Houston, daughter of Dell Thomas, interviewed in Seattle, Washington, 1981 and 1983.

11 Sherry Johnson Arwine, daughter of H.K.L. Johnson, interviewed in Seattle, Washington, 1981.

12 Shirley Houston, wife of James Houston, interviewed in Seattle, Washington, 1982.

13 James L. Houston interviewed in Seattle, Washington, 1981.

14 Jeanne Thomas Houston interviewed in Seattle, Washington, 1983.

15 James L. Houston interviewed in Seattle, Washington, 1981.

16 Howard Rock interviewed in Fairbanks, Alaska, 1975.

17 Herbert Carlson, classmate of Howard Rock, interviewed in Seattle, 1981.

18 Cecil V. "Moe" Cole interviewed in Seattle, Washington, 1981. Bob and Sherry Johnson Arwine interviewed in Seattle, Washington, 1981. Several other sources also mentioned this event.

19 Prof. Fred Anderson, University of Washington faculty and classmate of Howard Rock, interviewed in Seattle, Washington, 1981.

20 Gladys Tuttle interviewed in Trail, Oregon, 1981.

21 Prof. Fred Anderson, University of Washington faculty and classmate of Howard Rock, interviewed in Seattle, Washington, 1981.

22 R.S."Deke" Brown interviewed in Chula Vista, California, 1981.

CHAPTER 15

1 Howard Rock interviewed in Fairbanks, Alaska, 1975.

2 R.S. "Deke" Brown interviewed in Chula Vista, California, 1981.

3 Howard Rock interviewed in Fairbanks, Alaska, 1975.

4 Charles Brooker interviewed in Vero Beach, Florida, 1983.

5 Howard Rock, interviewed in Fairbanks, Alaska, 1975.

6 Charles Brooker interviewed in Vero Beach, Florida, 1983.

7 Howard Rock interviewed in Fairbanks, Alaska, 1975.

8 Charles Lieb, artist and veteran who served in Tunisia at the same time as Rock's unit was there. Comparing notes one night in the late '60s at Tommy's Elbow Room in Fairbanks, Alaska, they discovered that they both knew Madelaine.

Lieb mentioned that the base commander had set his cap for her and Rock made no comment. The conversation was overheard by several in Rock's company including Fred Brown.

9 Patrick Faulcon interviewed in Paris, France, 1982.

10 Howard Rock interviewed in Fairbanks, Alaska, 1975.

11 Priscilla Faulcon Girardot of Paris, interviewed in New York City, 1982.

12 Howard Rock interviewed in Fairbanks, Alaska, 1975. Rock was extremely reticent to discuss his private affairs and feelings. Madelaine Faulcon was the single exception. He spoke of her often to friends and spent the major part of two interviews discussing their relationship.

13 Priscilla Faulcon Girardot of Paris, interviewed in New York City, 1982.

14 Patrick Faulcon interviewed in Paris, France, 1982.

15 R.S. "Deke" Brown interviewed at Chula Vista, California, 1981.

16 Howard Rock interviewed in Fairbanks, Alaska, 1975.

CHAPTER 16

1 Charles Brooker interviewed in Vero Beach, Florida, 1983.

2 Howard Rock interviewed in Fairbanks, Alaska, 1975.

CHAPTER 17

1 Howard Rock, interviewed in Fairbanks, Alaska, 1975.

2 Harry Apodruk interviewed in Seattle, Washington, 1981.

3 Washington State Department of Health, Division of Vital Statistics, certificate of Death #278, Sept. 7, 1945.

4 James Houston interviewed in Seattle, Washington, 1981.

5 Howard Rock interviewed in Fairbanks, Alaska, 1975.

6 Mrs. Ruth Wallace, classmate of Delores Broe at Eklutna School, interviewed in Fairbanks, Alaska, 1981.

7 Mrs. Esther Laughlin, a close friend of the Delores Broe and her mother, interviewed in Anchorage, Alaska, 1981. Confirmed by Danise Van Sickle, daughter of Delores Broe, Sedro Woolley, Washington, 1981.

8 Delores Broe accounted for her marriage and divorce in correspondence with Fortuna Hunter Odell, Bruce Hunter's sister. Danise Van Sickle interviewed Mrs. Odell on the subject in Juneau, Alaska, 1981.

9 Mrs. Esther Laughlin in interview in Anchorage, Alaska, 1981.

10 Norma Whitney Hurley in interview in Seattle, Washington, 1981. Marriage license, King County, Washington, #129818.

11 Delores Broe in correspondence with Fortuna Hunter Odell of Juneau, Alaska, 1947. Black eye confirmed by report of James Houston in Seattle, Washington, 1981.

12 Rock vs. Rock, #381996, King County, Seattle, Washington, May 3, 1947.

13 Betsy Peterson Towne interviewed in Seattle, Washington, 1981.

14 Eddie Rollins, Commander of Colin Hyde Post #172, American Legion, Bainbridge Island, 1952-1953 and records searches by Lee Rosenbaum of the same post. Rumors of scandal come from several island sources, none of whom wish to be identified. Sources are wildly varied but in agreement.

15 Florence Cragerude in interview on Bainbridge Island, Washington, 1981.

16 Angelia Thatch interviewed in Seattle, Washington, 1982.

17 Tom Richards Sr. interviewed in Anchorage, Alaska, 1981.

18 Howard Rock, "Out of the Past," an unpublished manuscript.

19 Mae Tuzroyluk Jacobson in interview in Kotzebue, Alaska, 1981.

20 Economic Report, Point Hope Store, Manager ANICA to Juneau ANS Feb. 9, 1949. Don Foote Collection, Box 4, Point Hope, BIA File, University of Alaska, Fairbanks, Alaska.

21 Irene Tuzroyluk Tooyak interviewed at Point Hope, Alaska, 1981.

22 Mae Tuzroyluk Jacobson interviewed at Kotzebue, Alaska, 1981.

23 Mamie and Frank Pickett interviewed at Sun City, Arizona, 1981.

24 Frances Rock interviewed at Fairbanks, Alaska, 1981.

CHAPTER 18

1 Angela D. Weaver, widow of Ed Weaver, interviewed at Seattle, Washington, 1982.

2 Irene Tuzroyluk Tooyak interviewed at Point Hope, Alaska, 1981.

3 Arthur Upicksoun interviewed at Anchorage, Alaska, 1981.

4 Eddie Rollins, Colin Hyde Post #172, interviewed on Bainbridge Island, Washington, 1981.

5 James Houston interviewed in Seattle, Washington, 1981.

6 Kitty Evans Harwood interviewed in Fairbanks, Alaska, 1981.

7 Donna Hopson, daughter of Mary Ellen Ashenfelter, interviewed in Anchorage, Alaska, 1981.

8 Deed and Purchaser's Assignment of Real Estate, Vol 569, page 523, Recorder's Office, Bremerton, Washington.

9 Betty Peterson Towne interviewed in Seattle, Washington, 1982.

10 Harry Apodruk interviewed in Seattle, Washington, 1981.

11 Betsy Peterson Towne interviewed in Seattle, Washington, 1981.

12 Dorothy Rock Mazzola interviewed in Anchorage, Alaska, 1981.

13 Donna Jeanne Horner Hopson interviewed in Anchorage, Alaska, 1981.

14 James Houston interviewed in Seattle, Washington, 1981.

15 R. S. "Deke" Brown interviewed in Chula Vista, California, 1981.

16 Donna Jeanne Horner Hopson interviewed in Anchorage, Alaska, 1981.

17 Herman Krupp interviewed in Seattle, Washington, 1981 and 1983.

18 Irwin Caplan interviewed in Seattle, Washington, 1981 and Eddie Rollins, interviewed in Bainbridge Island, 1981.

19 Donna Jeanne Horner Hopson interviewed in Anchorage, Alaska, 1981.

20 Betsy Peterson Towne interviewed in Seattle, Washington, 1983.

21 Steve Wilson interviewed in Bainbridge Island, Washington, 1982.

22 Suzanne and C. Alan Johnson interviewed in Bainbridge Island, Washington, 1980, 1981 and 1983.

23 Donna Jeanne Horner Hopson interviewed in Anchorage, Alaska, 1981.

CHAPTER 19

1 Suzanne and C. Alan Johnson interviewed at Rolling Bay, Washington, 1980.

2 J. Keith Lawton interviewed in Kotzebue, Alaska, 1981.

3 Suzanne and C. Alan Johnson Interviewed in Rolling Bay, Washington, 1988.

4 Howard Rock in letter to Suzanne Johnson July 8, 1961, Collection of Suzanne and C. Alan Johnson, Rolling Bay, Washington interviewed at Rolling Bay, Washington.

5 Howard Rock interviewed in Fairbanks, Alaska, 1973.

CHAPTER 20

1 Allen Rock interviewed by the *New York Times*, "Underground Atom Blast in Arctic Called Safe," by Lawrence E. Davies, Aug. 17, 1960, shrugged off worries of fellow villagers and said, "As far as I'm concerned, they can shoot it off any time."

2 Joseph Foote and Paul Brooks, "Report from Tigara," manuscript, Don Foote Collection, Box 10, AEC Project Chariot History, University of Alaska, Fairbanks, Alaska. The article was featured in *Harper's* as "Disturbing Story of Project Chariot," April 1962, pp. 60-62.

3 J. Keith Lawton interviewed in Kotzebue, Alaska, 1981.

4 Ibid.

5 Don Foote Collection, unpublished manuscript, Box 11, AEC Project Chariot History, Notes A, University of Alaska Archives, Fairbanks, Alaska.

6 Atomic Energy Commission, Conference on Peaceful Uses of Atomic Energy, Notes by Secretary, Nov. 26, 1956, AEC 811/4 copy no. 36, p. 1, US Archives, AEC Secretariat, Box 1264, Folder MRA- 9-1 Vol. 1, Historian's Office, U.S. Department of Energy, Washington, D.C

7 Joseph Foote and Paul Brooks, "Report from Tigara," manuscript, pp. 8–9, Don Foote Collection, Box 10, AEC Project Chariot History, University of Alaska, Fairbanks, Alaska.

8 Ibid., p. 3.

9 *Fairbanks New-Miner*, July 14, 1958.

10 Albert Johnson in correspondence with Prof. Dahl, Feb. 21, 1961, Don Foote Collection, Box 22, Albert Johnson file, University of Alaska Archives, Fairbanks, Alaska.

11 Edward Teller used this as a continuing theme. He was quoted as saying the same thing in the *New York Times*, Nov. 12, 1961.

12 *New York Times*, Sept. 4, 1958.

13 *New York Times*, Sept. 13, 1958.

14 Don Foote, "Chariot Major Policy Shifts," manuscript, p. 1, Don Foote Collection, Box 10, AEC Project Chariot, University of Alaska Archives, Fairbanks, Alaska.

15 Dr. Albert Johnson interviewed at San Diego State College, San Diego, California, 1983.

16 Transcript, March 14, 1960, Don Foote Collection, Box 12, University of Alaska Archives, Fairbanks, Alaska.

17 J. Keith Lawton interviewed in Anchorage, Alaska, 1982. Joseph Foote interviewed in Washington, D.C. 1982.

18 Point Hope Alaska Petition, Nov. 30, 1959, (Copy), Don Foote Collection, Box 20, AEC Project Chariot, University of Alaska Archives, Fairbanks, Alaska. The files of the Village of Point Hope were lost in a fire.

19 A. W. Johnson, William O. Pruitt Jr., L. Gerard Swartz and Leslie A. Viereck letter to Committee on Environmental Studies, Project Chariot, Jan. 7, 1960. Collection of Leslie Viereck, Fairbanks, Alaska.

20 Excerpts from tape of Teller's Speech to Graduating Class, University of Alaska, 1959, Don C. Foote Collection, Box 12, University Of Alaska Archives, Fairbanks, Alaska.

21 Joseph Foote and Paul Brooks, "Report from Tigara," manuscript. Don Foote Collection, Box 10, University of Alaska Archives, Fairbanks, Alaska.

22 Transcript, March 14, 1960, Don Foote Collection, Box 12, University of Alaska Archives, Fairbanks, Alaska.

23 Howard Rock in letter to Suzanne Johnson, July 8, 1960. Collection of Suzanne and C. Alan Johnson, Rolling Bay, Washington.

24 Ibid.

25 Dr. Albert Johnson interviewed at San Diego State University, San Diego, California, 1983.

26 *Dictionary of Alaska Place Names*, Geological Survey Professional Paper 567, p. 716, United Stages Government Printing Office, Washington, 1967.

27 Howard Rock, *Tundra Times*, May 20, 1961; Dec. 3, 1962; Jan. 7, 1963; May 6, 1963.

28 Sylvia Heurlin, secretary, Association on American Indian Affairs, interviewed in New York City, New York, 1981. "La Verne Madigan," *Indian Affairs Newsletter*, No. 48, October 1962, AAIA, New York.

29 Roy Vincent, President of the Village of Point Hope in correspondence with Secretary of Interior, February 1950, Don Foote Collection, Box 4, Point Hope, BIA Files, University of Alaska Archives, Fairbanks, Alaska.

30 James W. VanStone, *Point Hope, an Eskimo Village in Transition*, University of Washington Press, 1962. Introduction.

31 Point Hope Village Council in correspondence with Stuart Udall, July 25, 1961, Dr. Henry Forbes Papers, Special File on Alaska, Princeton Collections of Western Americana, Princeton University Library, Princeton, New Jersey, Box 2.

CHAPTER 21

1 Howard Rock in a letter to C. Alan and Suzanne Johnson, July 8, 1961.

2 Oliver La Farge in a letter to Stuart Udall, March 28, 1961. Dr. Henry S. Forbes Papers, Special File on Alaska, Princeton Collections of Western Americana, Princeton University, Princeton, New Jersey,   Box 2.

3 Earl Ubell, "Cancer Is Blamed on Rays of Hiroshima Atom Blast," *New York Herald Tribune*, Sept. 26, 1960. University of Alaska, Don Foote Collection, Box 10, Atomic Energy Commission File, Atomic Energy, Project Chariot, *AEC Newspaper.*

4 "Caribou's Fondness for Lichens May Bar Alaska Atomic Blasts: Study of Harbor Project Shows Food Chain Produces a Concentration of Strontium in Eskimos' Bones," *New York Times*, June 4, 1961, Leslie Viereck Collection, Fairbanks.

5 Oliver La Farge in a letter to Stewart Udall, March 28, 1961. Dr. Henry S. Forbes papers, Special File on Alaska, Princeton Collections of Western Americana, Princeton University Library, Princeton, New Jersey, Box 2.

6 Howard Rock in a letter to C. Alan and Suzanne Johnson, July 8, 1961.

7 Howard Rock in a letter to C. Alan and Suzanne Johnson, August 2, 1961.

8 Ibid.

9 Howard Rock in a letter to La Verne Madigan, Aug. 12, 1961. Dr. Henry S. Forbes Papers, Special File on Alaska, Princeton Collections of Western Americana, Princeton University Library, Princeton, New Jersey, Box 2.

10 Howard Rock in a letter to C. Alan and Suzanne Johnson, Aug. 2, 1961.

11 Howard Rock in a letter to C. Alan and Suzanne Johnson, Sept. 27, 1961.

12 Interview with Dr. Burton Ostenson, Tacoma, Washington, 1981.

13 Daniel Lisbourne in a memorandum to the village councils of Kivalina, Noatak, Kotzebue, Noorvik, Kiana, Shungnak, Kobuk, Buckland, Deering, Selawik, Shishmaref and Point Hope, October 30, 1961. Dr. Henry S. Forbes Papers, Special File on Alaska, Princeton Collections of Western Americana, Princeton University Library, Princeton, New Jersey, Box 2.

14 Interview with Ralph and Dorothy Perdue, Fairbanks, Alaska, 1981.

15 Howard Rock in a letter to C. Alan and Suzanne Johnson, Sept. 27, 1961.

16 Interview with Howard Rock, 1971.

17 La Verne Madigan in a letter to David Frankson, village council, Aug. 10, 1961. Dr. Henry S. Forbes Papers, Special File on Alaska, Princeton Collections on Western Americana, Princeton University Library, Princeton, New Jersey, Box 2.

CHAPTER 22

1 Interview with Ralph Perdue in Fairbanks, Alaska, 1981.

2 Interview with Howard Rock, Fairbanks, Alaska, 1975.

3 Interview with Claire Fejes, Fairbanks, Alaska, 1981.

4 Interview with Rusty Heurlin, Fairbanks, Alaska, 1981.

5 Interview with Howard Rock, Fairbanks, Alaska, 1975.

6 Ibid.

7 Ibid.

8 Interview with Tom Snapp and Howard Rock, Fairbanks, Alaska, 1972.

9 Interview with James Hawkins, Washington, D.C., 1981.

10 Ibid.

11 La Verne Madigan, Executive Director's Report, Association of American Indian Affairs, New York, Dec. 11, 1961. Dr. Henry S. Forbes Papers, Special File on Alaska, Princeton Collections of Western Americana, Princeton University Library, Princeton, New Jersey, Box 3.

12 Interview with Martha Teeluk, Anchorage, Alaska, 1981.

13 Interview with James Hawkins, Washington, D.C., 1981.

14 Guy Okakok, "Point Barrow News," *Fairbanks Daily News-Miner,* Dec. 1, 1961, p. 6.

15 Interview with Martha Teeluk, Anchorage, Alaska, 1981.

16 Interview with Alice Perry Solomen, Barrow, Alaska, 1981.

17 "The Eskimos Speak," *Indian Affairs Newsletter*, New York, Dec. 1961.

18 Interview with Howard Rock and Tom Snapp, 1972.

CHAPTER 23

1 Interview with Howard Rock, Fairbanks, Alaska, 1971.

2 A letter from Howard Rock to La Verne Madigan, Nov. 28, 1961. Dr. Henry S. Forbes Papers, Special File on Alaska, Princeton Collections of Western Americana, Princeton University Library, Princeton, New Jersey, Box 3.

3 "Point Hope Eskimo Art Exhibit Success, Nearly Sells Out," *Fairbanks Daily News-Miner*, Dec. 5, 1961.

4 Dorothy Rock Mazzola in interview at Mountain View, Alaska, 1981.

5 Erna Marcum of San Rafael, California, in letter March 21, 1977.

6 Letter from Frances P. Walker, member-at-large, Governor's Advisory Committee on Economic Development, to Dan Lisbourne, Point Hope Council President, March 13, 1962. Dr. Henry S. Forbes papers, Special File on Alaska, Princeton Collections of Western American, Princeton University Library, Princeton, New Jersey, Box 2.

7 Letter from Howard Rock to Frances P. Walker, March 19, 1962 Dr. Henry S. Forbes Papers, Special File on Alaska, Princeton Collections of Western Americana, Princeton University Library, Princeton, New Jersey, Box 2.

8 Letter from Don Foote to Joe Foote, University of Alaska Archives, Don Foote Collection, Box 19.

9 Letter from Tom Snapp to Dr. Henry Forbes, Aug. 27, 1962. Dr. Henry S. Forbes Papers, Special File on Alaska, Princeton Collections of Western Americana, Princeton University Library, Princeton, New Jersey, Box 3.

10 Interview with Ralph Perdue, Fairbanks, Alaska, 1981 and 1988.

11 "Aboriginal Rights Protest of Native Villages Denied," *Fairbanks Daily News-Miner*, February 28, 1962.

12 Letter from Tom Snapp to Dr. Henry Forbes, Aug. 27, 1962. Dr. Henry S. Forbes Papers, Special File on Alaska, Princeton Collections of Western Americana, Princeton University Library, Princeton, New Jersey, Box 3.

13 Mary Clay Berry, *The Alaska Pipeline: The Politics of Oil and Native Land Claims*, University of Indiana Press, Bloomington, 1975, p. 33.

14 Arthur Lazarus, "Native Land Claims in Alaska," *The American Indian*, Vol. VIII, #1, 1958.

15 Interview with Ted Stevens, Anchorage, Alaska, 1981.

16 Letter from La Verne Madigan to Dr. Henry Forbes, Nov. 14, 1960. Dr. Henry

S. Forbes Papers, Special File on Alaska, Princeton Collections of Western Americana, Princeton University Library, Princeton, New Jersey, Box #1.

17 Interview with Tommy Paskvan, Fairbanks, Alaska, 1981.

18 Interview with Joe Upicksoun, Fairbanks, Alaska, 1981.

19 Letter from La Verne Madigan to Dr. Henry Forbes, March 27, 1962. Dr. Henry S. Forbes Papers, Special File on Alaska, Princeton Collections of Western Americana, Princeton University Library, Princeton, New Jersey, Box 4.

20 Interview with Howard Rock, Fairbanks, Alaska, 1971.

21 Interview with Thomas G. Cleveland, Milton, Massachusetts, 1981.

22 "Verbal Debate over 'Running' of Chief Meeting," *Fairbanks Daily News-Miner,* June 27, 1961.

23 La Verne Madigan, report to executive directors, July 16, 1962. Dr. Henry S. Forbes Papers, Special File on Alaska, Princeton Collections of Western Americana, Princeton University Library, Princeton New Jersey, Box 1.

24 Letter from Tom Snapp to Dr. Henry Forbes, Aug. 27, 1962. Dr. Henry S. Forbes Papers, Special File on Alaska, Princeton Collections of Western Americana, Princeton University Library, Princeton, New Jersey, Box 3.

25 Interview with Howard Rock and Tom Snapp, Fairbanks, Alaska, 1972.

26 *Letters of Henry Stone Forbes,* edited by Hildegarde B. Forbes and Marjorie Forbes Elias, private printing, Milton, Massachusetts, 1981.

27 Interview with Hildegarde Forbes, Milton, Massachusetts, 1981.

28 Interview with Arthur Lazarus, Washington, D. C. 1981.

29 Interview with Hildegarde Forbes, Milton, Massachusetts, 1981.

30 Interview with Howard Rock and Tom Snapp, Fairbanks, Alaska, 1972.

CHAPTER 24

1 Interview with Howard Rock and Tom Snapp, Fairbanks, Alaska, 1972.

2 Interview with Rusty Heurlin, Fairbanks, Alaska, 1981.

3 Howard Rock, *History of the Tundra Times: A Prospectus,* Eskimo, Indian, Aleut Publishing Company, Inc., Fairbanks, Alaska, undated.

4 "Editorial: Why the *Tundra Times?*" Tundra Times, Oct. 1, 1962, p. 1.

5 Interview with Howard Rock, Fairbanks, Alaska, 1975.

6 "Humanitarian," *Tundra Times,* Oct. 1, 1962, p.2.

7 Howard Rock in a letter to Dr. Henry Forbes, Sept. 30, 1962. Dr. Henry S. Forbes Papers, Special File on Alaska, Princeton Collections of Western Americana, Princeton University Library, Princeton, New Jersey, Box 6.

8 Irene Reed in an interview, Fairbanks, Alaska, 1981.

9 Howard Rock in an interview, Fairbanks, Alaska, 1981.

CHAPTER 25

1 Oliver LaFarge to Howard Rock, Oct. 20, 1962. Dr. Henry S. Forbes Papers, Special File on Alaska, Princeton Collections of Western Americana, Princeton University Library, Princeton, New Jersey, Box 3.

2 *Harpers's Magazine*, Dec. 1962.

3 Henry Stone Forbes, "Personal Account of Alaska Trip with Arthur Lazarus, Jr.," Oct. 14-23, 1962. Dr. Henry S. Forbes Papers, Special File on Alaska, Princeton Collections of Western Americana, Princeton University Library, Princeton, New Jersey, Box 5.

4 Interview with Tom Snapp and Howard Rock, Fairbanks, Alaska. 1972.

5 Ibid.

6 "Officer Speaks to Indian Meet," Tundra Times, Oct. 15, 1962, p.1.

7 Henry Stone Forbes, "Personal Account of Alaska Trip with Arthur Lazarus, Jr.," Oct. 14-23, 1962. Dr. Henry S. Forbes Papers, Special File on Alaska, Princeton Collections of Western Americana, Princeton University Library, Princeton, New Jersey, Box 5.

8 Ibid.

9 Howard Rock, "Why Eskimos Opposed AEC Project Chariot," *Tundra Times*, Oct. 15, 1962.

10 La Verne Madigan in letter to Henry Forbes, Aug. 19, 1962. Dr. Henry S. Forbes Papers, Special File on Alaska, Princeton Collections of Western Americana, Princeton University Library, Princeton, New Jersey, Box 3.

11 Henry Stone Forbes, "Personal Account of Alaska Trip with Arthur Lazarus, Jr.," Oct. 14-23, 1962. Dr. Henry S. Forbes Papers, Special File on Alaska, Princeton Collections of Western Americana, Princeton University Library, Princeton, New Jersey, Box 5.

12 Interview with Terry Brady, Anchorage, Alaska, 1981.

13 Tom Snapp and Howard Rock in interview, Fairbanks, Alaska, 1972.

14 Interview with Richard Frank, Fairbanks, Alaska, 1981.

15 Mary Clay Berry, *The Alaska Pipeline: The Politics of Oil and Native Land Claims*, Indiana University, Bloomington, 1975, p. 36.

16 Interview with Richard Frank, Fairbanks, Alaska, 1981.

17 Robert D. Arnold, *Alaska Native Land Claims*, Alaska Native Foundation, Anchorage, Alaska, 1976, p. 98.

18 "Editorial: Things We Love," *Tundra Times*, March 18, 1963.

19 Tom Snapp and Howard Rock in interview, Fairbanks, Alaska, 1972.

20 Interview with Ted Stevens, Anchorage, Alaska, 1981.

21 Robert D. Arnold, *Alaska Native Land Claims*, Alaska Native Foundation, Anchorage, Alaska, 1976, p. 98.

22 Interview with Al Ketzler, Nenana, Alaska, 1981.

23 Tom Snapp and Howard Rock in interview, Fairbanks, Alaska, 1972.

24 Interview with Al Ketzler, Nenana, Alaska, 1981.

25 Ibid.

26 Robert D. Arnold, *Alaska Native Land Claims*, Alaska Native Foundation, Anchorage, Alaska, 1976, p. 98.

27 Al Ketzler in letters to Dr. Henry Forbes, March 15 and March 17, 1963. Dr. Henry S. Forbes Papers, Special File on Alaska, Princeton Collections of Western Americana, Princeton University Library, Princeton, New Jersey, Box 1.

28 "Alaska Task Force Makes Report, Recommendations," and "Policy Would Undermine Native Land Needs, Rights," *Tundra Times*, March 18, 1963.

29 "Editorial: Things We Love," *Tundra Times*, March 18, 1963.

30 Robert D. Arnold, *Alaska Native Land Claims*, Alaska Native Foundation, Anchorage, Alaska, 1976, p. 102-104.

31 *Alaska Natives and the Land*, Federal Field Committee for Development Planning in Alaska, Anchorage, 1968, p. 13.

32 Mary Clay Berry, *The Alaska Pipeline: The Politics of Oil and Native Land Claims*, Indiana University Press, Bloomington, p. 38.

33 "Pribilof Islanders Oppose Wage Plan," *Tundra Times*, Nov. 1, 1962.

34 Interview with Howard Rock and Tom Snapp, Fairbanks, Alaska, 1972.

35 Interview with Martha Teeluk, Anchorage, Alaska, 1981.

36 Interview with Mae Shroyer Jacobson, Kotzebue, Alaska, 1981.

37 *Tundra Times*, April 15, 1963, p.1.

38 Interview with Terry Brady, Anchorage, Alaska, 1981.

39 *Tundra Times*, April 4, 1963. p. 1.

40 *Tundra Times*, June 3, 1963, p. 1.

41 *Tundra Times*, April 20, 1964.

42 Interview with Howard Rock, Fairbanks, Alaska, 1971.

43 *Tundra Times*, Nov. 23, 1964, p.1.

44 *Tundra Times*, Sept. 7, 1965.

45 Mary Clay Berry, *The Alaska Pipeline: The Politics of Oil and Native Land Claims*, Indiana University Press, Bloomington, 1975, p. 43.

46 Ibid, p. 34.

47 Robert D. Arnold, *Alaska Native Land Claims*, Alaska Native Foundation, Anchorage, 1976.

CHAPTER 26

1 Lael Morgan, "The Tyonek Indian Tycoons," *Alicia Patterson Foundation Newsletter*, New York, Aug. 4, 1972, pp. 1-7.

2 Mary Clay Berry, *The Alaska Pipeline: The Politics of Oil and Native Land Claims*, Indiana University, Bloomington, 1975, p. 44.

3 Interview with Mike Gravel, Pebble Beach, California, 1988.

4 H. G. Gallagher, *Etok: A Story of Eskimo Power*, G. P. Putnam's Sons, New York, 1974, pp. 87-88.

5 Interview with Mike Gravel, Pebble Beach, California, 1988.

6 Interview with Howard Rock, Fairbanks, Alaska, 1971.

7 H. G. Gallagher, *Etok: A Story of Eskimo Power*, G. P. Putnam's Sons, New York, 1974, p. 13.

8 *Tundra Times*, April 10, 1966.

9 Formal Agreement between *Tundra Times* and Dr. Henry Forbes, June 13, 1965, Dr. Henry S. Forbes Papers, Special File on Alaska, Princeton Collections of Western Americana, Princeton University Library, Princeton, New Jersey, Box 6.

10 Howard Rock in letter to Dr. Henry Forbes, Jan. 4, 1966, Dr. Henry S. Forbes Papers, Special File on Alaska, Princeton Collections of Western Americana, Princeton University Library, Princeton, New Jersey, Box 6.

11 Formal Agreement between *Tundra Times* and Dr. Henry Forbes, June 13, 1965. Dr. Henry S. Forbes Papers, Special File on Alaska, Princeton Collections of Western Americana, Princeton University Library, Princeton, New Jersey, Box 6, and *Tundra Times*, Dec. 31, 1965.

12 Letters dating from Oct. 29, 1965 to Feb. 23, 1966, name withheld because subject could not be notified.

13 *Tundra Times*, April 29, 1966.

14 *Tundra Times*, May 6, 1966.

15 *Tundra Times*, April 10, 1966.

16. H. G. Gallagher, *Etok: A Story of Eskimo Power*, G. P. Putnam's Sons, New York, p. 131.

17 Robert D. Arnold, *Alaska Native Land Claims*, The Alaska Native Foundation, Anchorage, p. 112.

18 *Tundra Times*, March 4, 1966.

19 Interview with Charlie Suter, Fairbanks, Alaska, 1981.

20 *Tundra Times*, July 26, 1966.

21 Interview with Emil Notti, Anchorage, 1981.

22 Interview with Morris Thompson, Anchorage, 1978.

23 *Tundra Times*, Oct. 22, 1968.

24 Interview with Howard Rock, Fairbanks, 1971.

25 Letter from Jimmy Bedford to Seraphim Stephan, chief of the Tyoneks, Oct. 28, 1967. Dr. Henry S. Forbes Papers, Special File on Alaska, Princeton Collections of Western Americana, Princeton University Library, Princeton, New Jersey, Box 6.

26 Letter from Howard Rock to Dr. Henry Forbes, November 10, 1967. Dr. Henry S. Forbes Papers, Special File on Alaska, Princeton Collections of Western Americana, Princeton University Library, Princeton, New Jersey, Box 6.

27 Letter from Howard Rock to Dr. Henry Forbes, December 28, 1967. Dr. Henry S. Forbes Papers, Special File on Alaska, Princeton Collections of Western Americana, Princeton University Library, Princeton, New Jersey, Box 6.

28 *Tundra Times*, June 2, 1967.

29 Robert Arnold, *Alaska Native Land Claims*, Alaska Native Foundation, 1976, pp. 122-23.

EPILOGUE

1. *Tundra Times*, Dec. 17, 1971.

2 Interview with Jimmy Bedford, Fairbanks, 1981. When Rock died the *Tundra Times* savings account was $13,000 ahead.

3 *Tundra Times*, April 28, 1976.

4 The summer before his death Howard invited his close friend, Charlie Suter, and myself to attend the whaling festival with him in Point Hope. Rock was still fairly strong. It was a nice visit and not in the least morbid, but after pointing out Attungowruk's grave in tour-guide fashion, Howard voiced a wish to be buried next to the famous chief. I mentioned the request when his sister, Helen, was planning his burial and after a little thought, she honored it.

Index

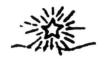

About the Author

Lael Morgan was raised in rural Maine, graduated from Boston University, and became an Alaska resident in 1959. She met Howard Rock in Skagway, Alaska, in 1965 while she was on assignment for the *Juneau Alaska Empire* and he was taking the only real vacation he ever had from the *Tundra Times*. Hoping to work for him, she moved to Fairbanks in 1966. He couldn't afford to hire her so she signed on at the *Fairbanks News Miner*, covering the Alaska Legislature and occasionally writing for *Tundra Times* on the side.

Morgan left Alaska from 1967 until 1971 to serve as a reporter photographer for the *Los Angeles Times*, then returned to the state to work for Rock under an Alicia Patterson Fellowship. Later she traveled the bush as roving editor for *Alaska Northest Publishing Company* and *National Geographic*, but she continued to fill in at the *Tundra Times* in emergencies.

Currently she is teaching photo-journalism at the University of Alaska, Fairbanks.

Other Books by the Author

Alaska's Native people

And the Land Provides: Transition of Alaska Natives from a Subsistance to a Money Economy

The Aleutians

Alaska Whales and Whaling

The Kotzebue Basin

Women's Guide to Boating and Cooking

Tatting: A New Look at the Old Art of Lacemaking